Cheerio
Tom, Dick and Harry

Cheerio

Tom, Dick and Harry

DESPATCHES FROM THE HOSPICE
OF FADING WORDS

Ruth Wajnryb

ALLEN&UNWIN

First published in 2007

Allen & Unwin
83 Alexander Street
Crows Nest NSW 2065
Australia
Phone: (61 2) 8425 0100
Fax: (61 2) 9906 2218
Email: info@allenandunwin.com
Web: www.allenandunwin.com

National Library of Australia
Cataloguing-in-Publication entry:

Wajnryb, Ruth, 1948- .
    Cheerio Tom, Dick and Harry : despatches from the hospice
    of fading words.

    Bibliography.
    ISBN 978 1 74114 993 7.

    1. Linguistic change - Social aspects. 2. English language.
    I. Title.

420

Internal design by Zoë Sadokierski
Set in 10.5/14 pt Minion by Midland Typesetters, Australia
Printed in Australia by McPhersons Printing Group

10 9 8 7 6 5 4 3 2 1

This book is dedicated to the memory of
Dr Nicole Burman

CONTENTS

» PART IV
VICTIMS OF MODERN CANDOUR

» PART V
A NEW CENTURY WITH ITS OWN SENSIBILITIES

» PART VI
THE PAST IS DEAD, LONG LIVE THE FUTURE

Acknowledgements

I WANT TO THANK THE TEAM at Allen & Unwin—Richard Walsh, Jo Paul, Catherine Milne, Catherine Taylor and Angela Handley—whose collective enthusiasm, optimism and support make writing such a pleasure.

It was Richard who came up with the notion of a hospice of fading words. This was an evolved creation, unfolding gently over time, not spontaneously in a moment of genius. And before the hospice was a hospice, it was a hospital. Before that, it was a cemetery, derived loosely from the 'Cemetery of Lost Books' in Carlos Ruiz Safon's novel of Barcelona, *The Shadow of the Wind*. But we realised that these disappearing words were in fact not sick, not at least in the sense in which people are when they go to hospital. But nor were they dead, or not yet. Certainly, they were cemetery-bound, but so are we all, ultimately. Out of these ruminations emerged the notion of 'hospice'—a penultimate resting place for words before they vanish into the ether of the archaic. The vignettes became 'despatches' and the title, *Cheerio Tom, Dick and Harry*, offered some seminal examples of what the book was about.

Fellow writer Mark Cherry believed in the project and supported me throughout. His skill at visualising a work as accomplished rather than disjointed, along with his ability to make me laugh, account for a happy process and, I trust, a successful outcome.

I also want to thank all the people who sent me 'their words'. Early in the project, I had feared that having come from a non-native-English-speaking home, my intuitions on fading words may not be trustworthy. I didn't know it then but I ended up calling happily on the intuitions of an army of willing informants from around Australia. Over a year ago, an article I wrote was published in *The Sun Herald*'s *Sunday Life* magazine. In it I drew attention to my impression that much of the traditional language that the baby boomer generation learned from their parents was not being passed on to their own children. At the end of the article, I invited readers to write to me with their experience of words they used to hear but don't hear very much any more. Subsequently, I was inundated with responses, and while I tried to respond individually to all of them, I sometimes fear a few escaped acknowledgement.

In an early conception of the book I had imagined including all the words that were sent to me in the text of the work, and again as an index at the back. That was when I expected to develop a database of, say, 500 words. However, when the yield from my readers' responses took the figure to over 5000, I knew I'd have to rethink the book, making it more of a social history, informed by linguistic insights, rather than simply a collection of fading words. In sum, I was elated at the shared interest in language and, specifically, in these endangered words, as well as in the recent social history of Australia.

Ruth Wajnryb
Sydney
April 2007

∾ 1 ∾

The hospice

IN OUR THROWAWAY SOCIETY, where even the style of one's fridge door or office decor goes out of fashion, the concept of recycling is a big ask. Mostly we just throw away. I tried composting once and all the rats in the neighbourhood celebrated. In any case, it isn't hard to appreciate—or even imagine a conspiracy theory if that's your thing—that there are strong vested interests in keeping consumerism vibrant, happening and growing by 10 per cent-plus annually. Material growth is, after all, a fetish that is premised on the throwaway habit. I recall as a teenager wondering why fashions, from skirt hems to jean colour, always seemed to overturn the previous season's must-haves. That was before I saw the link between fashion, consumerism and capitalism. Once that link was established I could never again look at fashion without thinking of manipulation.

While recycling, for many, is nothing short of cultural revolution, there are precedents to not-throwing-out. Take antiques, for instance. Surely here part of the beauty one admires is that quality of keeping on keeping on. Surely some like to imagine, as I do, who once might have used and loved this beautiful table before I stumbled onto it. I'm reminded of a book I once borrowed from the library for my daughter. It was the story of an old house, much like one you might find in the Rocks area of Sydney, told as a kind of biography from the house's perspective. The house remembers its former occupants, going back generation beyond generation to where it all started, with the penal settlement of Australia. The beauty of the story is akin to the beauty of antiques, mementos of the past that you're able to touch or hold in your hand. With today's faux-antiques, it's the same, except that more has to happen in the imagination.

Old cars have a charm similar to that of recycled antiques. I don't mean old car as in 'jalopy', but rather old car as in 'vintage'—restored and very expensive. Although driving a vintage car might seem a touch twee, some of the attraction, surely, lies in the fact that the car itself has been through a restorative process. When I see an old vintage car on the road, obviously headed towards some vintage car rally event, I'm reminded of the dress-up historical enactments you encounter in the southern states of America, where local history clubs assiduously relive the battles of the Civil War and then, once all the ammunition (faux, I assume) has been spent, well, then they have a picnic. It's got to be good for mental health—better an outdoor communal get-together than a foreign war or expensive time on the therapist's couch.

Recycling certainly comes into its own with old clothes. Since 'preloved' replaced 'old' in regard to second-hand wear, things have really taken off. There are markets every weekend in which one person's old trash becomes another's newfound treasure. I'm told, however, that markets are for the old yokies, that the cluey people are using eBay to seriously supplement their income.

Given these solid precedents of recycling, it shouldn't seem too off the rails, I hope, to ponder: Where do preloved words go when they begin to lose currency, when the love they once enjoyed starts to fray? Ultimately, of course, we know they'll end up in a dictionary, alongside an italicised *obs.* (for obsolete) or *arch.* (for archaic). It's sad, really. They have served us well; they've toiled tirelessly to meet our needs, from the transactional to the poetic; on occasion, they've brought us moments of pure joy. It does seem retrograde, then, to relegate them, and so very unceremoniously so, to their *obs./arch.* fate. Surely their passing deserves to be noted?

I'm proposing, therefore, that we consider the value of setting up a 'hospice of fading words'. This would be a special place for words that are past their prime, still being used in certain demographic pockets, but undeniably on the way out. A place of palliative care, quality of life and acceptance. Please don't write to me and say you just heard one of these allegedly fading words being used in a conversation between two people waiting in line at the butcher's, and therefore it is 'alive', and ergo I don't know what I'm talking about. I'm not saying these words are dead and buried, for in that case I'd be recommending a cemetery or a crematorium for dead words, rather as features in *The Shadow of the Wind* where it applied to 'lost books'. No, here I'm suggesting a sanctuary for fading words. After all, we already have a mechanism—the *obs./arch.* device —for flagging words that have gone out of use, lost their currency, fallen off the shelf. So it's not words that have left us that I'm concerned with here, but rather words that are fading.

Admittedly, 'fading' subsumes a wide spectrum. It includes words that are not heard so much these days to words that a generation Xer or Yer would respond to with a 'huh?' And they don't hang around in cohorts or all fade at the same rate. Fading is not a steady, predictable process. A word can be nearly gone and then suddenly be granted a new lease of life for some random quirky reason that has little to do with logic or merit. The word 'recalcitrant', for instance, may have been en route towards the state of being faded when Paul Keating, then prime minister, used it in a highly public way, and as a result catapulted the word back into a high-profile position, from which it may have once again begun to slide towards the fading corner. Calling any ex-prime ministers wishing to do the nation a service . . .

There's little that's even-handed, egalitarian or democratic about fading. A word can fade in one part of the country but be alive and well in others. And as for geography, so too for class and gender. The long and the short of it, the bottom line, is that fading happens slowly, unevenly and ambiguously. Mostly we can do no more than point to a trend rather than to a solid fact or event. Compared with fading, death is far more precise, definable, finite.

Why a hospice? Well, consider the options. A hospital would not be apt—it's for emergencies or surgery, or short-term intensive treatments. If they can't treat you (or infect you), they're very keen to have you discharged (otherwise you're liable to become a 'bed-blocker'). And not a sanatorium, as in Thomas Mann, and Swiss mountains, where people like Henry James' Ralph Touchett go, not so much for a cure as for some comfort from the ravages of symptoms. Not a rehab (or detox or dry-out centre), à la Betty Ford. And not a spa for the pampered, or a retreat for the spiritual.

A hospice offers not a remedy but a brief sojourn. It's palliative rather than remedial, and it's realistic about promises. *Hospes* in Latin is a guest or traveller, one who seeks shelter for a short time. There's also a clear link to the English 'hospitality', with the word 'host'—one who receives guests—dating from the 13th century.

Our fading words would come to the hospice for succour and solace. They'd be sojourners in the penultimate stage of the journey that will end at the designation *obs.* or *arch.* At the hospice they would not need to be confined to bed, unless they are feeling particularly weary, but would be encouraged to mix and mingle, use the library perhaps, sit outside in the shade, strike up conversations with like-minded souls, or take a beverage in the late afternoon while watching the sun go down.

There may be journaling facilities, where the words would be encouraged to reflect on their history, their semantic ups and downs; or for the less introspective, there may be Scrabble perhaps. There would be a chapel, too, for our words would be encouraged to see their demise not in terms of individual responsibility or blameworthiness, but rather in terms of trends and shifts, and zeitgeist. There may be a resident sociologist or anthropologist on call (à la grief therapists or bereavement specialists), to help place individual decline in wider social or cultural contexts. And, of course, a number of sympathetic linguists, who would comment non-judgementally on the process of lexical fading and any emergent patterns that appear in significant numbers.

A hospice of fading words might best be construed as a sanctuary. There our words may shelter from the ravages of modern life. And even if this means, ultimately, the end of a very long road, at least the event would be noted, if not eulogised.

PART I

AS THE PACE QUICKENS

∾ 2 ∾

Cheerio

....

THE DAUGHTER WAS WALKING TOWARDS the back gate when I called out, 'Cheerio.' I swear it just slipped out. Not sure where it was stored, as it's not my usual valediction. I'm more likely to say 'see ya' (with or without a 'later'), 'ciao' or, increasingly, simply 'later' all on its own. But cheerio bubbled up from somewhere, broke the surface and popped out. The same thing happens occasionally with 'fair dinkum' when I'm bowled over in a moment of incredulity, but that's another story. I'm starting to think we store these oddballs on dusty shelves in the filing cabinet of the mind and they pop out when our guard is lowered. I imagine a cognitive scientist or a neurolinguist would have a more technical explanation.

She was nearly out the back gate, the daughter, when the cheerio must've registered. She swung around, looked at me in disbelief—a look that any parent of a teenager will know and attest to; it's the kind of look that is an active ageing agent— and said, without expecting an answer, 'Cheery WHAT?'

So, this led me to wonder when exactly it was that we stopped saying cheerio. Around the same time we stopped saying toodle-loo, (h)oo-roo, see you later alligator/in a while crocodile, if you can't be good, be careful, toodle-pip. You still hear some of these expressions, but you're more likely to encounter them in Anglo-dominated regional Australia than in multicultural urban centres. And even while cheerio has faded, the word still has rather happy associations. That may be why it was given as a name to a breakfast cereal, or to those party cocktail frankfurts that children, and lurking parents, seem to love, especially when bathed in tomato sauce.

I'm inclined to wager that cheerio started to vanish around the time we stopped whistling. In fact, I'd warrant that cheerio and whistling form a natural coupling. Separately and together, they bespeak a different time—a more leisurely paced existence with fewer activities scheduled into less jam-packed days. Nowadays whistling is far more functional—it'll get your dog's attention, it might hail a taxi when you need one—but of course that kind of whistle is not the whistling that goes with cheerio, not by a long shot. Carpenters used to whistle on a construction site—and not only at a passing short skirt. It was the casual whistle that accompanied concentrated focus. I have a plumber who whistles, but he's in his sixties and when he retires I don't expect to hear much whistling again. I did notice that canary-yellow free postcard that you see about the place. It is printed in big block black letters, as befitting a noticeboard sign, and says: CHEERFUL WHISTLING PERMITTED HERE. The irony, of course, is that if a workplace requires a sign to grant licence to whistle, it's very unlikely to have employees in the mood for whistling.

The 'permitted here' is a dead giveaway. In the past, whistling, like being of good cheer, didn't require a permit. You just whistled whenever you wanted. Roofers were particularly adept at it—I once had the thought that they whistled so you'd know what part of the roof they were on at any particular time. Though why you would need to know that, I have no idea.

But it's not only tradesmen. Whistling was something you did while doing something else. Like some repetitive task (sweeping the floor, stamping envelopes) or while you walked idly along, taking maximum pleasure in your carpe diem kind of day. That time has passed: these days hardly anyone walks idly along. In fact it may even be something you could be arrested for. You only walk in a goal-targeted kind of way. And it's hard to whistle when you're so focused. They don't collocate.

The closest we come to 'whistling' these days is 'whistle-blowing', a term that has a wholly different hue and tone. In fact, that kind of whistle—the umpire's or referee's, sounded for the purpose of attracting attention or asserting authority, or both—is altogether different from the idle whistle à la Snow White's Seven Dwarves.

Words like 'cheerio' and the act of whistling provide a window on another time. 'Chew the fat' is another expression that has gone the direction of the hospice, partly because both chewing and fat, let alone doing one to the other, are not favoured thoughts in our post-Kentucky Fried Chicken zeit-geist. The other reason, of course, is that meal times, like other times, are hurried events (the Slow Food movement notwith-standing), and there's hardly time to chew your thin, lean Thai-style beef let alone engage in talk. Ask for the bill before you have cleaned your plate and there's a chance you'll be out of there and back at the office in record time.

Your old fat-chewing, nattering chinwag was a relaxed event, with topics undetermined though roughly predictable, apparently unstructured, with an equitable sharing of the available discourse space between speaker and listener. Long pauses, comfortable spaces where mull time could hover and nourish (akin, in a weird way, to those boxing managers who attend, in roped corners, to their bloodied investments in the brief, concussed interludes between rounds). Fewer time-constraints, less all-round Filofax pressure. Perhaps it was the presence of fat in the mouth—there for the ongoing chewing, in the bovine masticatory sense—which made the act of talking less important than the actual comforting fact of company shared. As for 'company', sociologists claim that with each passing year we are even less likely to know our neighbours' names, let alone wish to borrow a cup of sugar or share a natter on the verandah. Once, the entire street, if not the village, kept an eye out for whoever's kids might be playing outside. Today you keep away from other people's children, and you keep yours away from them. Overall, it's no big surprise that with the acceleration of time, the breakdown of community and the plethora of nutritional information, 'chewing the fat' has become an odd little phrase, eccentric in the way of bow ties and trouser braces.

And so it is that 'chew the fat' is now comfortably housed in the Hospice of Fading Words where, ironically, it can indulge reflexively in its own semantics and spend the best part of each day shooting the breeze, as it were, on the ward's verandah with other like-minded fading oddballs—indeed idiomatic siblings—like 'chinwag' and 'natter', who would all get on like a house on fire.

'Cheerio' belongs there, too, because it's the kind of valediction that would likely end a daily natter. In its expanded form, be of good cheer, it means to put on a happy face. It comes to us from the Greek *kara*, for face, via the Latin *cara* and Old French *chiere*. Being of good face, no doubt, implied that everything would be well in your life, or at least well enough for you to have a cheerful face. By Middle English, the meaning of 'cheer' had extended metaphorically to mean mood, demeanour or otherwise invisible mental condition as reflected in the face. Thus around 1500 it was no oxymoron to be in 'a dreerye cheere', whereas today, combining the two might win you a diagnosis of bipolar.

By the start of the 15th century, 'cheer' had a positive meaning only, so if you wanted to be dreary you'd have to make separate arrangements. Much later, under the influence of nautical slang, cheer took on a plural –s and morphed into an exclamatory 'cheers!', emerging as a shout of encouragement or a celebratory toast. In fact, today, depending which variety of English you speak, you can make 'cheers!' sing a whole lot harder for its supper—as a toast, a thank you, a goodbye or merely an acknowledgement of another's existence.

∼ 3 ∼

Peopled phrases

....

A FEATURE OF ENGLISH in the past has been the frequent colloquial use of (mainly) first-name people, sprinkled aphoristically across conversations.

I remember as a child hearing the phrase 'happy as Larry', and wondering who on earth Larry was, what he had to be so happy about, and exactly how he came to be the benchmark for joy and delight. Then one winter I went on a skiing holiday; my Austrian ski instructor's name was Larry, and because he was appropriately jolly this put an end to the Larry line of inquiry, hitherto so bothersome.

Larry was not alone. By adolescence, Tom, Dick and Harry (TDH) had moved in. I worked out quick smart that they didn't actually exist but stood for blokes who might. Handy really, especially when you didn't want your parents to know precisely with whom you were partying, though in my case it backfired since, being foreign-as-in-ethnic, my folks wanted surnames and then some. There was no way I could have gotten away with referring to a boy I might have liked as Tom, Dick or Harry.

Over the next decade I met a lot of blokes. There was Pete who went everywhere for his own sake; Blind Freddie who was equal parts thick and myopic; Dick who was especially clever; Alec who was too smart by half; and Jack Robinson who would finish what he was doing before you could even say his name. Punch was always pleased to see Larry whenever he popped around, as he did occasionally, his good cheer always a great antidote to Buckley and Murphy (two of the surname exceptions to the first-name rule), who were in a constant state of rivalry when it came to being pessimistic. It's my view today that they both should have been started on medication much earlier. There was Flynn, supposedly named after our rascal Errol who rarely went outdoors and developed a bad reputation as a sexual rogue, although very occasionally 'in like Flynn' meant something other than its crude reading. While on the topic of Flynn, there's also Roger and Willy, but best let's not go there.

One constant in this life of flux was Bob, who was my uncle but, strangely, everyone else's as well. Mostly what I remember about Bob was that he was irrelevant. He'd drop in, along with the statement of kinship ('and Bob's your uncle') which, as far as I could determine, had no relation to anything in sight. Though, of course, he did have a wife—the rejoinder to 'Bob's your uncle' was 'and Fanny's your aunt'. For comfort in moments of confusion I'd think back to how Larry had come good on the ski slopes, and I invested faith in the belief that one day, when he was good and ready, Bob's story, too, would be revealed.

There were multiple Johns. Apart from the dead body (John Doe, husband of Jane), one John was the bloke who got the letters calling the relationship off. Resilient, he'd always bounce back from those dumpings that seemed to develop a ground-hog-day style of repetition. Another John was the rather earnest fellow on mock Commonwealth Bank cheques. His surname was 'Citizen', there was an (assumed) wife, kiddies and a mortgage in the background, and one knew that John was pretty unswervingly noble. John Citizen had a cousin who was Joe Average, much beloved of statisticians and social scientists. He was also the middle-class counterpart to the much more layabout and often disreputable Joe Blow. Much more in Joe's league was Johnny, who had a reputation for showing up once the hard work had been done. Johnny-come-lately's nemesis was Johnny-on-the-spot, who was any TDH who happened to be where some action was needed.

There was also Joe Sixpack, a less blow-away version of Joe Blow, and as reliable as he was ordinary. And perhaps because John, in all his garbs and versions, was such a common name, it became a euphemism for the men's toilet. Adam was indistinguishable from himself so if you didn't recognise him, you'd know it was Adam. Otherwise, it was Arthur or Martha.

And mentioning Martha reminds me that it's not all about blokes. All-purpose Sheila tried to bolster plain Jane and dumb Dora who both had self-esteem issues, each secretly believing that a name change would fix everything. The quietly morbid Jane Doe was the antithesis of the very superior, if aspirational, Lady Muck, who shared a hot-potato-in-the-mouth accent with His Nibs. If the truth be known, they probably shared more than an accent, having remained thick as thieves long beyond the extra-curricular elocution class where rumour has it they met years earlier.

Surprises usually brought Betsy out while Nelly would crop up when you were being denied permission to do something. This defiant (not on your) Nelly was very different from her namesake, nervous Nelly, who had been on medication for her nerves for as long as anyone could remember. Mention of either Nelly would usually invoke in me thoughts of Larry—a curiousity I suppose that, though I didn't know it at the time, was the first restless stirrings of an etymological longing.

Anyway, I soon learned not to be confused by the Nelly overlap and came to take great comfort in the disambiguating function of context.

The thing is, as a child growing up in a non-native-English-speaking home, I had zero idea that anyone else was on first-name terms with all these peopled phrases that dropped in on a daily basis. And the knowledge, when it came, was less a penny-dropping experience than a slow, dawning realisation. So Mrs Kafoops was anyone (well, anyone female, married and getting on a bit) whose name you'd forgotten. Pat Malone (as in 'on your Pat Malone') didn't actually exist (he just rhymed with 'on your own'). Nor did Joe Bloggs or Blind Freddie, about whose disability I subsequently had serious doubts. Then there was that whole mob, the Callithumpians, a general term for any eclectic bunch of vaguely related boister-ous noisemakers who swept in, made themselves at home and then swept out again.

In hindsight, it was the kind of experience usually attrib-uted to children when they find out the truth about Santa, the Easter bunny and the tooth fairy. But it was bigger than that. The characters who up until then had peopled the phrases that I heard on a daily basis suddenly vanished, their names mere epitaphs fluttering in the breeze.

While back then I might've wondered who these people were and how they came to get their names, now I'm more likely to wonder where they went, why they faded out of use, why they seem to have lost their currency. Of course, they're not all completely disappeared—these things don't happen overnight. You'll still hear an irate father trying to pack the family into the car for a road trip, saying, 'For Pete's sake, get a move on, will you?!' However, because Pete might have some slight reverberations of Saint Peter, his currency has devalued greatly in a far more secular age. Indeed, I'd warrant that Pete's best hope for hanging on to his place would be to sever all connections with his ecclesiastical namesake. Certainly John of the 'dear John' letter has long faded, probably pushed out by technology. These days you're more likely to get dumped by email or SMS than by a long flowery letter that spells out the unpalatable truth in florid detail.

But the winds of change are larger than the new secularism or the Digital Age. In general we live now in a society that relies less than it once did on context for shaping and influencing our values and understandings. Once, when we were a more homogenous and uniform society, we were able to draw on context as a resource for meaning. These days we don't all share one single cultural context. As postwar Australia has become increasingly heterogenous and pluralistic, people have different backgrounds, call on different milieus. This makes an overarching context less available to all as a tacit, common, shared resource. With context now less available, we give increasingly more store to what is said that can stand alone.

Larry as the benchmark of happiness, or Joe Bloggs as the baseline indicator of ordinariness—they don't cut it anymore. Larry has lost his credibility. If you uttered the line 'as happy as Larry' today, most people under the age of forty-five would not know what you meant. I'd wager that if Larry is going to have more than Buckley's chance to get back his currency, the least he'll have to come equipped with is a full name, a CV, a website and his own personalised ring tone.

~ 4 ~

Darn

....

DOES ANYONE DARN ANY MORE? No, I don't mean 'darn' as in the rather mild curse ('Darn it! Has anyone seen my car keys?'). I mean, 'darn' as in sew, and sew as in repair. I'm thinking of holes in socks, worn elbows on jackets, rips in jeans, frayed seams, loose elastic, and that kind of thing. And when I say 'anyone', I mean anyone under fifty.

When I asked a few young people this question, they looked at me as if I'd just stepped out of a time capsule. Some asked me what I meant. One said his grandmother was always wandering around the house (he seemed thankful that at least it wasn't the neighbourhood) with some darning or else looking for some darning to do. He linked it to age, as in decrepitude, and treated it as a symptom of encroaching Alzheimer's.

Yes, it would seem darning has gone the way of billycarts and pinafores. Quaint cues to a quaint past. If you try to account for its demise, the explanation that most easily springs forth is economic. The pre-baby-boomer generations born around the world wars grew up having the first- or second-hand experience of deprivation inscribed indelibly onto their psyches. Going without, or living in the shadow of those who went without, is a powerful experience. (I sometimes think the second-hand experience is worse than the first-hand one, because living in the shadow gives you a refracted trauma outside of the context that would help you to make sense of it all.)

The first part of the 20th century had a lot of bleak moments. First the Great War, then the Depression, then the inter-war period and the nervous lead-up to the (next) war. As some little boy once asked his mother about the Depression era, 'Was everybody sad then?' Sad or not, the economic hardship was more than enough to put a patch on your knee, or worse.

Darning fits that era. Clothes were homemade. Even in the 1950s, 'store-bought' was for very special garb for very special events. Hand-me-downs were handed down, and then down again, and again. You couldn't do this without darning. With fourteen children and a husband out of work, a needle and thread were mandatory survival tools. It was darn or die.

So affluence is a very real explanation for the demise of the darner. We don't use 'darn' because we don't need to darn any more. We don't need to darn because we don't keep things long enough to wear holes into them. Children usually outgrow their clothing before they outwear it, and because of falling birth rates, a dozen siblings aren't waiting in line for a sorely needed item of clothing to replace something already threadbare.

Now there's another word you don't hear anymore. 'Threadbare' goes hand in glove with 'darning'. Seems these days if your threads are bare, it's a fashion statement, and looking around—everyone's doing it.

So it's not the case that darning just stopped. It was part and parcel of an entire paradigm shift that accompanied postwar economic boom times, the rising standard of living, the new quality of life, the flashy materialism of growing socio-economic status and the aspirational zeitgeist. The paradigm shift started gingerly, moved steadily and then accelerated with each passing decade, ultimately achieving a speed that only the young could enjoy.

The old paradigm valued utility, repair, maintenance and preservation. It went with words like 'thrift' and 'frugal', at a time when 'means' meant how much you had to go around, and 'making ends meet' was the weekly challenge. Your casserole was your way of making yesterday's leftovers stretch another day or two (I'll stop at two). It was replaced by a paradigm that demands the new, that involves chucking out, buying fresh, replacing old. I have a friend whose only dietary prohibition is 'casseroles', something I discovered when I invited him to dinner. Why, I asked him, naively. That's when I found out about his Depression-traumatised upbringing and the pretty ugly associations he has with one-dish stews. My promise of first-time freshness and a name other than 'casserole' fell on ears unwilling to hear. Clearly the scars run deep.

Frugal times called for frugal measures. We're talking about a period when you could fix anything. If you couldn't, the bloke down the road could. And if he couldn't, he had a mate who knew someone who'd do a foreign order in a factory during a dogwatch shift. Such blokes would improvise by fabricating, modifying or converting something into what was needed. It really wasn't so long ago that there were hundreds of electrical fix-it shops. A little man would be seated behind a dusty, cluttered glass cabinet, surrounded by old machine parts and other mostly metallic bits and bobs, and you'd take your old jug or blender or cassette recorder to him and he'd fix it, and it'd last you for another five years, which was a lifetime because time passed so slowly then, and overall you'd be well pleased. I loved those little shops. But one day, he stopped doing that. He'd shake his head, adjust his glasses and quietly say, 'It'll cost you less to buy a new one.' And then eventually came the day when he wasn't there anymore. He didn't make the leap to the new arcade where the weekly rent is more than a quarter's takings. He kind of faded away. Gone. Like darning.

I don't know what year, even what decade, it was, but obsolescence slowly got built into the manufacturing equation and then into our expectations. These days we don't expect things to last forever and are hardly even disappointed or angry when they break down. (I overheard a young person say to a companion that she resented buying expensive wedding presents for marrying couples—she'd feel better if she knew it was a union that would last. Her friend commiserated and together they came up with the idea of a five-year anniversary present in lieu of a wedding present. That at least would be evidence of achievement, of reward for effort.)

Yes, we've stopped fixing things or having them fixed. We throw stuff out with the council clean-up. And not just fridges and washing machines. If relationships aren't working, we think new rather than work on the old. If a computer's antivirus software finds a virus, it half-heartedly tries to repair it and if it can't, it might quarantine it (the sus file gets put in the 'vault', which always seems rather like the disposing of nuclear waste), but usually it recommends that you delete it. Of course you comply, if only to avert large-scale contamination. And so the vault is to the virus as the nursing home is to the aged. Let's say nothing more of delete at this stage . . .

The closest we come to darning these days is designer jeans that have 'worn' built into them at the point of production. It's a Disneyland aesthetic where you can visit Canada or Venice without leaving home. Distress (I mean the manufacturing process, not the state of mind), along with fade and rip are the new darn, and they can set you back a pretty penny.

~ 5 ~

Tinker

....

DICTIONARIES ARE WONDROUS BOOKS, but even the best have their limitations. If you look up 'tinker' in the *Macquarie* you'll find that it's an (often) itinerant mender of household tin pots and pans. Well, yes, that may have been true when tinkers got about by horse and cart, traipsing from village to village, announcing their presence and availability by the clip-clop of the horses' hooves and the accompanying tinkering sound as they lightly hammered on metal and called out, the way the paper boy still does (minus the tinker) on Sunday mornings. These days, we tend not to fix pots and pans; we throw them out and buy a bright shiny new set, or maybe an electric wok. So there goes your need for your travelling tinker.

'Tinker' now is in use less as a noun (the person doing the tinkering) or as an act (what the tinker does), and more as a verb, usually accompanied by 'with'. To 'tinker with' broadly means to take something mechanical apart in order to look at how it works and identify any malfunctioning, normally without any useful results. Little boys (it's still mostly boys) who sit on the floor tinkering for hours with anything mechanical are thought to be budding engineers, although these days they're probably more likely to go into computer hardware. In fact, the new tinker may well be the 'geek'. In any case, whatever their future, that type is handy to have about after you've been shopping at Ikea. All in all, there's a laid-back side to 'tinker with'—a sense of experimental hit and miss, of adventure in the spirit of trial and discovery. Not the kind of verb you would want to apply to the surgeon removing your gall bladder.

Today's verb 'to tinker' maintains its informal sense. You wouldn't use it of an employed engineer, for instance, in relation to the work he is paid to do. But you might use it of the same engineer who's unwinding from a hard week by tinkering about, out in his shed. It's lost its negative connotations of a clumsy, bungling, unskilled Jack-of-all-trades. It's acquired a better image of being techy or nifty. And the further the majority of us moves from the forms and processes of pro-duction of our lives' daily accoutrements (milk comes from supermarkets, not from cows), the act of tinkering with things mechanical takes on a quasi-romantic, even folksy charm. Think shamen.

To meander down a side path for a moment to explore the nifty side of tinkering . . . 'Nifty' itself has a rather mysterious lexical past. We generally use it as a positively connoted word to signify something good—from a nifty idea or a nifty profit to a nifty new outfit—always with a keen sense of smart, adroit, skilled and appropriately made or placed. It is widely attributed to Mark Twain's use in the mid-19th century, but there is also a British claim to the word as a slang noun, meaning fifty pounds, and given the rhyme (fifty/nifty) and the wealth of British slang associated with money, there seems to be some validity to the argument here. There's even a suggestion that it is theatre slang, a derivation of 'magnificent', offering praise and commendation. The jury remains out on 'nifty'.

To tinker successfully today, at the beginning of the 21st century, you need three factors to be in place. These are what we might call 'felicity conditions'. You need an aptitude or knack for the mechanical or technical. You need an enjoyment of the process of losing yourself for a few apparently aimless hours in a minor mechanical task. And you need time to burn or, if you lack time, you need a lax attitude to other competing commitments. And I'll say this, too, at the risk of being gender-slapped, that it also helps, at least statistically, when you're tinkering, to have a penis.

In any case, tinkering now, in the post-industrial knowledge society, probably has more to do with tossing some ideas over, think-tanking, rather than anything faintly meccano-esque. You tinker with ideas, mull them over, play with them creatively. If I say to a colleague, 'Leave it with me. I'll tinker with it', I mean 90 per cent thinking—yes, some activity, but mostly rumination. A lawyer might tinker with a case in the shower, that is, if lawyers were the kind of people who ever fessed up to tinkering, and if they did, it'd probably come down to billable hours.

Two generations ago, or further back, society seems to have been far less chronocratic, less ruled by the calendar, less tyrannised by the clock. One indicator of the change is that there is less calling today on the seasons as points of reference—'See you in the spring' or 'Let's get together after winter.' Of course, if Al Gore (in his *An Inconvenient Truth*) is to be believed, reference to the seasons will diminish even further, or take on different meanings, as climate change wreaks havoc on conventional understandings of the seasons.

One of the time expressions that is heard less frequently now is 'donkey's years', which used to mean a long time. First recorded in British English in the second decade of the 20th century, in the original form it was 'donkey's ears'. Different interpretations argue whether this was an allusion to their length (donkey ears being very long, certainly compared with horse ears); but in any case, within a decade or so, 'ears' had morphed into 'years', and the apparent allusion now was to the rather impressive longevity of the average donkey. 'Yonks' is another one, as in, haven't seen you for yonks. I used that on a young person once and they responded with 'Who's Yonks?'

Not far removed from the donkey and the yonk is another time-vague expression—'a month of Sundays', which dates further back, to the 1830s. Literally, the phrase means about thirty weeks, but has never been used in a precise way given that it's always been intended as an exaggeration. The connotation, too, was a slight sense of time being dreary, probably because Sundays in a more religious age were spent on structured, God-fearing pursuits. More importantly, the fun activities were specifically proscribed, and in any case, all the shops were closed.

Then there was the saying, '. . . since (or when) Adam was a boy', which expresses a period of time from a point in the long distant past. I don't recall ever having heard a feminist version (say, '. . . since Eve was a girl'), but then I never really knew that the Adam they were referring to was the alleged first man. Somehow, in the convoluted submerged, non-articulated logic of the child, I thought Adam was chosen because A was at the beginning of the alphabet, and somehow in a don't-ask-silly-questions kind of way, time was being measured along this handy 1–26 template. In any case, one could easily figure, if one were looking for patterns to hang one's hat on, that the Adam of 'Adam as a boy' was the same Adam as the one you didn't recognise. It seems logical to have supposed a link between the two.

I started having a better general feeling about Adam when I learned that the word derives from the Hebrew for earth or ground (*adamah*), with the Hebrew word for human being (*ben adam*), or 'son of the earth' having a nice primordial feel to it. Yes, 'son of the earth' is a bit sexist, given Eve's role in the proceedings, but maybe there's some comeback in the supposed origins of Adam's apple. It's said that the piece of forbidden fruit (apple or pomegranate, depending on which version you believe) got stuck in Adam's throat. The Hebrew for Adam's apple, *tappuach ha-adam*, is a reference to a swelling in the man. It's generally agreed that this is the lump in his throat, rather than the one in his trousers, though of course 'lump in the throat'—à la emotional response—has other connotations that we need not pursue at this point, for I have already strayed too far.

To continue with the pattern of time expressions, many with a quasi-religious sense and all denoting a loose calculation of time, the phrase 'a seven-day wonder' was applied to someone or something that caused interest or excitement for a short period but was then quickly forgotten. Her new boyfriend was a seven-day wonder. His interest in Portuguese was a seven-day wonder. However, the allusion to the creationist narrative of the start of the world gives one cause to pause: is the suggestion entailed within the expression that God tired of the task after seven days? That He bored easily, rather in the manner of a dilettante? Something like, ho-hum, did the world this week, what's scheduled for next week?

There appears to be no religious significance whatsoever in phrases like 'chew the fat' or 'shoot the breeze', both of which betray an indulgence of leisure that seems a thing of the past. 'Chew the cud' (a variation on the theme) alludes apparently to the fact that cows give the appearance of talking when chewing grass. 'Shooting the breeze' has always suggested two old codgers smoking while lounging on a verandah in the late afternoon of a hot summer's day. For me, this probably came from a scene in the film *To Kill a Mockingbird*, in which, if I'm right, a couple of old codgers do exactly that. It seemed connected in my mind with spinning yarns of the 'you should have seen the one that got away' variety. The contrast with the present is striking. These days, spending time in apparently idle chat or seeming leisurely conversation may likely be a matter of networking; in marketing-speak, 'prospecting'. If you wanted to find out about the dimensions of the one that got away, you'd look it up on the net.

Perhaps no expression better captures a past era than this increasingly rare term—'to while away the time'. In fact, dating back to 1635, 'while' was itself a verb, with the meaning of 'passing the time'. Today, 'while' is mostly used as a time conjunction, allowing us to do one thing with one hand, *while* doing another with the other, and so get twice as much done in the same unit of time. The pressure of getting things done, working twice as hard today to make tomorrow easier, is captured in these words of American journalist Ellen Goodman: 'Normal is getting dressed in clothes that you buy for work and driving through traffic in a car that you are still paying for, in order to get to the job you need to pay for the clothes and the car, and the house you leave vacant all day so you can afford to live in it.'

Mind you, back then, when 'while' was a verb, it was never just *any* verb. It was a verb that gave you permission to do nothing. Or, if you preferred, you could just tinker.

～ 6 ～

Hobby

....

HERE IS A TYPICAL CHUNK of language that a young non-native speaker of English might use as they become acquainted with someone in English:

> Hello. Yes. Nice to meet you. My name is (so-and-so). I
> from Japan. I am a student. My hobbies are (origami) and
> (shopping). I also like swim in beach.

Another such giveaway—and here I'm overlooking the stodgy grammar, accented pronunciation, or emPHARses on the wrong syllARBLES—is the use of the word 'hobby', as it's used here.

It's very hard to know why people are taught to speak like this. It could be that they're learning from old-fashioned text-books (*Run Spot Run* vintage, where they're drilled in utterances like, 'Excuse me, is this the right way to Tottenham Court Rd?'), and in books like that, people may still have hobbies. Or it could be that their teachers were taught, wayback when, that this is what you say, and nothing since has come their way to make them think otherwise. Or perhaps they don't meet enough native speakers to receive the negative feedback that may eventually trigger the recognition that people don't speak like this any more. (Did they ever?) Or it could be that while 'hobby' is no longer a word with much currency, people know what is meant by it, and therefore if confronted by an international student asking about hobbies, most could muster an answer that seems a reasonable fit, and then slip away quickly, and that's how the student never gets the negative feedback they need that might serve as an intervention to prompt them to self-correct. Or it could be that people are just too embarrassed by the word to advise a non-native to desist from using it. (I'm the only person I know who does this on a regular basis. Benevolent despot style. Listen to me. I have your best interests at heart. Stop using 'hobby'. Don't bother with why. Just stop using it.)

It might even be fair to say that if it were not for non-native speakers of English (now more numerous than native speakers of English), 'hobby' (as in spoon-displaying or bug-collecting) would have been dead and buried long ago. Instead it lives on, in a pseudo-quaint kind of way, in limbo land, artificially resuscitated by world-wide learners of English. I'm excluding here very specialised uses of 'hobby' such as 'hobby farm', which, at the price of a cutesy title, provides a nice little bit of tax relief for those who may think they already pay too much for the welfare of others.

That said, however, I'm of the view that it would be a generalised kindness to relocate 'hobby' from the hothouse English language textbook. Perhaps its new residence might be in some kind of stand-alone care facility, like the Hospice of Fading Words, with a sign over the bed saying 'No heroic measures', where at least it could live out its final days without causing embarrassment to itself or society.

How and why did 'hobby' go this way, and what if anything replaced it? I suspect 'hobby' comes from an era when work and play were clearly demarcated domains of action.

When you stopped work, that was it for the day. After that, it was non-work—family, friends, leisure, sport and . . . yes, hobbies. Making things, collecting things, assembling things. Something to keep the hands busy. After all, the devil makes work for idle hands. I wonder what this actually means—that said creature lurks about in search of idle hands and then, upon spying a set, opportunely provides some mischief with which to occupy them? This is a most one-eyed, un-ecological interpretation of bad or subversive behaviour.

Hobbies provided distraction value. Something to side-track and divert the mind, because in distraction is relaxation. That's the principle, I gather, behind diversional therapy in convalescent and rehabilitation centres for the elderly. Take your mind off your worries. They call it 'divert' instead of 'distract', probably euphemistically, but the principle is the same.

Hobbies once provided a creative outlet. Assuming that people have this need to express themselves in a unique way that bespeaks their individuality. Many hobbies were solitary past-times—collecting coins, making model aeroplanes, sewing doll's clothes. This is not to say that you couldn't talk about them with others, or do them with others (consider the communal quilt-making made famous by that American movie of vaguely the same name), but rather that they also lent themselves to non-social time. They certainly satisfied the introverted, contemplative personality, allowing them to be still, engrossed and engaged, and not obliged to deal with the stress and oh-so-exhausting demands of the social world.

In those days, too, your hobbies helped to define you, your special distinctiveness, the things that made you different from everyone else. Those were the days when there was less choice—in the clothes you wore, the food you ate, the books you read, the refrigerator you bought. There was a sameness about the material world, and in sameness you don't find individuality. Even the jobs you went into after school had this quality. Boys went into the bank, as tellers, or into the trades, as apprentices. Girls went into secretarial work or nursing or teaching. What defined you was what you did outside of work, and that's where hobbies came into their own.

At different times in the past, I was into horse-riding and stamp-collecting. I knew the latter was considered nerdy, so I gave it a low public profile. Horse-riding, however, scored me some brownie points—it was the great outdoors (the Australian cathedral), it involved a skill outside of the intellect, and speed was likely to be involved, so you could mention it to boys without losing face. At the very minimum, it gave you something to talk about with people you didn't know very well, and for a shy kid, that was a tremendous boon. Believe me, long after I stopped horse-riding I continued to proclaim it as a hobby.

However, those clearly demarcated days are gone. The entire nature of work has changed. First, the time spent there is no longer governed by the hands of the clock. It leaks beyond and intertwines with what might have been considered hobby time a generation ago. Mobile phones, text messaging, email and fax mean you're always available, always on call. This may be good for the ego (you're needed, you're indispensable, everyone is trying to reach you), but it's hard on the soul.

Second, we're more affluent now, even if we're paying for it with less home time. Certainly, we're far more consumerist. In the homes of baby boomers when they were growing up, there may not have been a telephone or a TV set. Now each of the offspring has a mobile phone, so do the parents, even the nanny. Scrabble and Monopoly have been replaced with surround-sound entertainment systems. Shopping is the new hobby. Board games have gone the way of the jalopy.

Third, what you do is all about identity. It provides information about you that signals who you are. To mark the change from 'hobby' to 'lifestyle', we'd no longer say of someone that he surfs as a hobby, but rather 'he's a surfer'. In other words, he probably has a job, but whatever it is he does, surfing is his thing, his passion. Likewise, in the past golf might have been a hobby, whereas now one might be called 'a keen golfer'. You won't be asked what your hobby is, but what you're 'into'. And when you're asked what you do, the 'do' may reflect your particular, idiosyncratic blend of work and play—for example, 'I'm a surfer, and when I'm not surfing, I'm a merchant banker.' I know of a bunch of ex-merchant bankers who are keen surfers—their work is to play the stock market, and they operate out of a kind of office (they call it a 'pod') close to the beach and slip out to surf whenever they feel like it, whenever the waves call them or whenever the market loosens its grip.

Whatever you choose to lay claim to, you know that the questions you're really being asked are: What do you value? Who do you want to be seen as? What are the plot-points that you use to locate yourself in the universe? The questions are now about your 'down time' or your 'me time'. Certainly, 'hobby' is altogether too narrow and confining. It doesn't live up to the task of describing something that's big enough to permeate your life. It's got to embrace as congruent the poles of say, surfing and merchant banking . . . or whatever. One word that's occasionally used about generation Y is 'occupassion'. It refers to their alleged need to be working at something that's personally meaningful, or to have something outside of work that is personally meaningful.

There's a man I briefly met who's a doctor. He's also a singer, with a beautiful voice that's entirely wasted in the surgery. On evenings off, he would sing with a band whenever he could. As time went on he loved the singing more and more, and the doctoring less and less, yet the doctoring paid the bills and it was not something he was willing to let go of entirely. I suppose five years ago he'd have said he was a doctor who liked singing with a band on his nights off. Now he might say he's a singer who works as a doctor on the weekends. So even though he doesn't earn his keep through singing, he foregrounds it because it's central to his sense of self. It's as a singer that he wants to be identified. It's his little place in the cosmos. He'd never call it his 'hobby', though fifty years ago someone like him might have.

On the internet dating website, RSVP, there's no 'hobbies' category for your profile. There are headings like 'music', 'sport', 'movies', 'reading', and that's where you say what you're into, or what it is you want others to think you're into. I doubt anyone says they read Mills & Boon, play solitaire or go trainspotting. Then there's the rather loose-ish category, 'other interests'—and this is where you'd cite your stamp-collecting if you really wanted to shoot yourself in the foot. If I've offended any avid stamp-collectors, allow me to make a pre-emptive apology. A male correspondent of mine once responded to this remark with: 'Stamp-collecting was a hobby of mine years ago. The wound in my foot is now completely healed.'

$\sim$ **7** $\sim$

Steady

....

DOES ANYONE REMEMBER 'STEADY'? Who would have thought that such a beguilingly simple word would become a victim of fashion?

'Steady' was a mainstay in the world into which the baby boomer generation was born and raised. It was one of those pillars that held everything in place. It was the sort of thing no one ever thought would change. In fact, no one ever thought about it. You don't, when it's a fact of your life. Fish don't see the water they swim in. 'Steady' was assumed, taken as given. Like a southerly buster after an impossibly hot day.

Track races at school sports days began with 'Ready! Steady! Go!' You didn't go straight from 'ready' to 'go'. You went through a 'steady' phase—where your readiness was suspended in mid-air for a few precious moments. 'Steady' really meant an extended 'ready'. In fact, the function of 'steady' was to stop you from being too eager, rushing pre-emptively and impetuously from 'ready' to 'go'. You might say, if you can forgive this metaphor, that it was 'steady' that prevented too many premature ejaculations on the field.

In the qualifying trials for his favourite event, the 400 metres, before the Athens Olympics, Ian Thorpe famously fell in the water before the 'Go!' signal, and one pithy commiserating communication he received afterwards was a text message that said 'Oops'. So if we extrapolate from this one incident, then we might say that 'steady' is the fail-safe by which means 'ready' won't be undone by an oops. Or perhaps that's overly-convoluted. 'Steady' comes after 'Ready' and before 'Go'. Hang onto that. Or maybe not. I have the suspicion that in some competitive events, they've dispensed with the 'steady' and you move from 'ready' to 'go'. Irrespective of the particular conventions, it's a precarious time, those nano-whatevers between 'ready' and 'go', as was so beautifully captured in the relationship between the Denzel Washington character and the Dakota Fanning character in the film *Man of Fire*. The Washington character takes it upon himself to cure the girl, played by Fanning, of her fear of the gunshot that is used to start the swimming races in which she competes. The gun as a race starter assumes metaphorical meaning later in the film.

No doubt, all this is a metaphor for an age that was generally hooked on the Protestant ethic and made an art form of delayed gratification. Save now for rewards later. Work hard now, reap the harvest in the future. There are plenty of axioms and proverbs that admonish haste and laud caution. Look before you leap. A stitch in time saves nine. Don't count your chickens before they hatch. Don't cross your bridges until you come to them. Without delayed gratification as a shared value, who would have put up with the demeaning conditions of an apprenticeship?

Back then, you 'went steady' with a boyfriend or girl-friend, and oftentimes you ended up engaged and then married. 'Going steady' was a precursor to commitment. It was a lead-up to a larger step. It was part of the process of ratification. It showed that you had been socialised into the formal institutions that defined your society. A social anthropologist would have a field day.

'Steady on!', the imperative verb, was the admonishment by which (usually) an elder chided a younger person over whom they had some authority. It was a counsel to 'pull yourself together', and implied that there was a need for control to be exerted so that one wouldn't 'fall apart'.

Falling apart wasn't just a metaphor—it was an all-round no-no. Poise and steadiness were the glue by which one's organs and one's limbs stayed intact and in place when emotion threatened to ruffle things up. In fact, 'ruffling' in general, and especially someone else's feathers, was equally likely to elicit a 'Steady on!'

It would seem the times in which we now live are so volatile that the old quality of steadiness is quite out of sync. When things change so quickly, 'steady' seems to move over to the corner of the room where 'stolid' sits. There in that corner we find stolid's siblings, none of whom are particularly attractive—'impassive', 'unresponsive', 'dull', 'emotionless', 'insensitive', 'indifferent', 'slow-witted'.

Would you want to be in their corner? No, I didn't think so.

Where once 'a steady hand on the till' was valued, now it's more likely to be seen as overly cautious, even controlling. It's an irony, of course, because a steady hand on the till doesn't mean a tight or firm grip, but rather a lightness of touch that perhaps lends even more control. Certainly, the steady hand on the till bespeaks an expertise.

But 'steady' is now out of sync with the zeitgeist. We might say it's unzeitgeistian. I'm thinking of other out-of-sync customs, like writing with a quill pen and using real wet ink in an inkwell; or wearing a smoking jacket and expecting to join the other men in a separate room for a smoke after dinner. While the women, if they weren't cleaning up or minding children, would retire (as in withdraw) to the drawing room, which for years I ignorantly believed had something to do with art.

Yet 'steady' hasn't completely gone the way of the quill pen or the smoking jacket. Perhaps as a verb it's seen its last days, but as an adjective it still appears, albeit in more confined circumstances. Where once it was an admired quality of mind, now it seems to come into its own in financial contexts. We talk of 'a steady income', 'a steady cash flow', 'a steady flow of customers', 'a steady expansion of business'. Any financial adviser will tell you to diversify your portfolio, invest in the long term rather than play the market, and your reward will be 'steady growth'.

'Steady', in fact, is far from obsolete. A net search reaps more than 59 million hits. One of them, perhaps one that can speak for the zeitgeist, is intended as a support and training place for young people with bipolar symptoms, and you can see why in such a context 'steady' might be a good name, indeed a beacon of light and hope. If we're searching for a new metaphor—and let's, because a metaphor always helps—then perhaps the new 'steady' is something akin to cooking's 'simmer'—it's certainly not the sexy part of the process, but it has its place and is worth maintaining.

So maybe 'steady' doesn't belong over there in that corner with grumpy old 'stolid'. I'm starting to think that there's a more conducive and comfortable place in the hospice for 'steady'. Possibly on the patio in the shade, sharing memories with 'fortitude' and 'stoic', as they, all three, reminisce about fond and shared values of yore. There's no smoking room, of course, at the hospice, but in winter there's a glass of port on the patio and, together with convivial company of mixed genders, a good glass of port is not to be sneezed at.

PART II

OLD WAYS, OLD LANGUAGE

∽ 8 ∽

Jalopy

....

THE FIRST BOY TO TAKE ME out drove a jalopy. Had my parents laid eyes on it, we would have been over before we started. That car bespoke risk, and not just the mechanical kind.

Today, parents can't leapfrog so easily from cars to the prospects they evoke. These days cars sporting provisional driving plates are often relatively new models, and they're usually in pretty good nick. Typically, the family's second car is shared, often acrimoniously, by mother and adolescent(s). What saddens me somewhat is that there's rarely a jalopy among them.

It would seem that the jalopy is becoming a thing of the past. While you can still spot the odd rusty bomb cruising the highway, as a species it is surely endangered. And included in its demise is the word itself. Gone the same direction are other words for battered old wrecks of cars—'rust bucket', 'rattletrap', 'old bomb', 'old banger'—though none of these comes anywhere near to matching the quality of affection contained in 'jalopy'.

Around 'jalopy' there accrued a whole culture. For instance, there was the sensitive issue of what to do when your car started costing you an arm and a leg. The dilemma—when to bite the bullet and trade it in?—used to carry the same emotion as the decision to put down the loyal but frail and ailing family pet. Those who train budding auto mechanics sometimes caution the need for 'bedside mechanics'. They want their charges to appreciate that jalopy ownership may go beyond mere economics. One such teacher said it can be a 'deep personal philosophy'. He tells his charges that, 'to some people, the jalopy is an old friend. They'll hang on long after it belongs in the junkyard.' So he tells his students, 'it's as if a doctor told you your brother was going to die. That's similar to what happens when you tell a customer their car's not worth fixing.' This may throw light on a Valentine's Day notice I once saw in the newspaper. It said: 'Debbie, I love you more than my car.'

Sometimes, stories about reuniting after a jalopy has been stolen have all the poignancy of finding a lost pet or having a kidnapped child returned safe and sound. Here's an excerpt from a newspaper report of a jalopy being found after an absence of twenty-four years:

> David Helms [of Charlotte, North Carolina] never thought he'd see his old jalopy again. The 1955 Chevy Bel-Air was stolen . . . while he was at work back in 1974. It was his pride and joy. He had rebuilt it and took his future wife out in it on dates. The Washington State Patrol called last week and told him they had found the blue, two-door Chevy in Seattle. 'It's always kind of a thrill when you get one of these real old ones—and you can contact the victim,' said Inspector Lance Fry . . . who had the honor of calling Helms with the good news. 'He's one happy camper.'
>
> Helms [had] bought the two-door car as just a body with no engine and rebuilt it. 'David loved that car.

He was brokenhearted when it was stolen,' said his wife, Robin. 'We rode around Charlotte and all the surrounding areas every weekend—that was our dates. We spent over a year driving around looking for that car.' Weeks went by, then years, and Helms . . . never heard a word about the car.

After receiving the good news, a forty-seven-year-old Helms immediately flew to Seattle where he collected his jalopy from the police impound yard, and set out on the long drive home. No doubt all the way home he was reliving memories of his youth, and by the time he reached North Carolina he'd have been positively boyish.

But 'jalopy' is fading and you have to wonder why. Increasing affluence no doubt provides better choices for new-generation drivers. And presumably the age of programmed obsolescence is contributing. We upgrade fridges and TVs when age interferes with smooth running, or when we imagine it does. No longer does the handmade, the customised or the 'creatively repaired' carry much weight. What's new carries status, and status of course is at the very heart of capitalism. 'In a consumer society everything revolves around the art of consuming. Consuming what others consume (or don't consume!), consuming the best, the most, the rarest.'

And maybe we have more rules and regulations now. For example, P-plate drivers are no longer just 'P-plate' drivers. There are different categories of P-ness, each one colour-coded and attached to different stipulations, especially about speed. So, perhaps the threshold for 'roadworthiness' has shifted. It's likely that back when a jalopy was your first car there were less stringent registration checks. These days, if it's too much of an old bomb it simply won't pass the inspection. Then, tinkering with an old rattler that's unroadworthy becomes an expensive leisure pursuit.

The jalopy's passing took other things with it. Boys used to spend whole weekends drinking, bullshitting and dreaming while tinkering with their old bombs. They learned a lot about cars, and other things, from their mates, older siblings or dads. These days, with the exception of budding mechanics, the closest to 'tinker' you get is attending a Regional Evening College course on car maintenance, and even these promise more than they deliver. I'm told it all happens through a textbook. You can get through the course, earn a certificate and not have tinkered with a single make-do gasket or muffler, let alone a battered one repaired with beer cans. The word 'tinker' would probably never even crop up. And half the class is female.

Now 'jalopy' is an interesting word. It doesn't just mean a beaten-up old bomb of a car. Built into the word is the relationship between youth and first wheels. There's affection there and pride of ownership, and gratitude for the freedoms that having wheels entails. These days, anyone who partook of that culture will remember and bleed nostalgia.

That the word's origins are mysterious only invests 'jalopy' with greater charm. The earliest recorded use of the word is in the United States in the 1920s. It meant a battered old motor vehicle, and the variations in the spelling signal that it started out very much as spoken slang—*jaloppi* (from a 1929 book about racketeering), *gillopy* (from Steinbeck, 1936, *In Dubious Battle*).

As is often the way with etymological mysteries, versions of possible connections sprout like urban myths. One contender is the Yiddish word *shlappe* (an old horse), derived from a Polish word. Another is French, with the word *chalope* (a kind of skiff), though the boating connection remains obscure. A third is a derivation of the Italian-American mispronunciation of 'jelly apple'. The *jell 'oppy* was a kind of decrepit old cart from which Italian immigrants sold this delicacy in the early 1900s. There's also a Spanish link, with the word tied to the Mexican town of *Jalapa*, where many old vehicles ended their lives as scrap. (The globalised world's equivalent is Bulgaria, where the import-a-wreck economy is facilitated by lax regulations that at the same time cater for tinkering on a massive scale.) Another suggested Spanish link is *galapago* (a tortoise), evocative of the jalopy's notable lack of horsepower.

So what we have in 'jalopy' is a unique blend of affection, nostalgia and grim realism. This was captured in a recent remark of Jane Fonda's—when being interviewed around the launch of her autobiography, the still stunning actress said: 'I'm sort of like a jalopy. I'm losing hubcaps and fenders.' It was a moment to remember, and you might have felt the reverberations across an entire generation of similarly ageing men and women.

～ 9 ～

Handkerchief

....

THE JAPANESE MAKE THE MOST beautiful handkerchiefs. They're a good, generous sensible size, too. And they're oh-so versatile. You can mop your brow in the humid weather. You can take care of the odd spill in a restaurant. You can wipe a child's mouth after a meal (your own child, I mean—I'm not suggesting you look around and see where you can help out). You can dry your hands after a visit to the loo if there's no paper or towels available. You can polish your eye glasses. I could go on and on, but it's sometimes best to leave a little to the imagination.

If you're into irony, it's a lovely example that the Japanese handkerchief, beautiful as it is, is not actually designed for nose-blowing. The Japanese use paper tissues for this purpose, little packets of which are often handed out at railway stations, presumably as some kind of promotion. In any case, nose-blowing is a very private activity for the Japanese, who are rendered uncomfortable by the thought—or sight—of Westerners emptying the contents of their nasal cavities into a piece of cloth which is then stuffed into a pocket to be re-used through the day. (Although, from reading the blogs of young travellers to Japan, it would seem globalisation has brought young Japanese attitudes to nose-blowing into close alignment with the West.) For the older generation of Japanese, at least, it remains preferable—indeed it's totally okay—to sniff loudly all day than to dispose of the offending phlegm in the Western way.

In Japan handkerchiefs are sold everywhere, from train stations and the equivalent of our $2 shops to very fancy department stores. In the latter, handkerchiefs of every conceivable design and colour cater to an immense range of tastes. In one of those ground-floor hanky departments you can easily spend hundreds of dollars—rivalled only by what you might go on to spend in stationery. Handkerchiefs are ideal gifts, too—small, light, attractive.

It used to be my custom, after my many trips to Japan, to bring back some of these delicate cloths for my young daughter-in-law, who'd always smile and beam graciously. I took her response at face value and was delighted that she shared my love of these small, square Japanese cloths.

It turns out all that smiling and beaming were politeness in action. One day my son, putting on his uncomfortable look—the one he uses when he wants to tell me something that he thinks I might not want to hear—said, 'Mum, about those hankies you always bring home from Japan . . . well it's nice of you . . . (pause) and they're very pretty and all that . . . but young people today . . . um . . . don't use hankies.'

'Why on earth not?' I shot back, amazed.

He said, 'Well I could beat around the bush, but . . . to be honest, to cut to the chase . . . who wants to blow snot into a bit of material and then carry it around all day?'

So there you have it—the generation X perspective on the boomer handkerchief. As cross-culturally distinct as anything an anthropologist could come up with. Indeed, ironically, it's quite an old-fashioned Japanese reaction!

There's comfort, perhaps, to be taken in the fact that the

handkerchief is not alone in having nearly had its day. Items like the cravat, the cufflink and the armband seem all to have had their day, too.

The last of these, armbands, were worn above the elbow, and their purpose was to keep the shirt cuffs at an appropriate height. There was a Depression-era version of the metal armband created from the cut-off ends of old rubber gloves. These did the trick, though for aesthetic reasons they were worn under a suit coat rather than displayed proudly like their upmarket cousins.

Armbands were especially loved by left-handers in the messy old days of ink. That was the time of the nib, the inkwell, blotting paper and the old-fashioned refillable fountain pen with its bladder that sucked up ink from the bottle. Such circumstantial niceties meant that you simply could not have your cuffs trailing onto the paper as you wrote. Enter armbands, to great applause.

Now, I know the world of vogue recycles these sorts of items when a decade suddenly becomes fashionably nostalgic or the in-thing for fancy dress. Hey, Mum, do you have any of those big shoulder pads they used to wear in the eighties? It's not the mainstay item that, say, the hanky was in the past. I'm sure I'm not alone, however, in hoping that current fashion items like low-cut, crack-exposing pants will not come back in a hurry, even for a short re-run.

Still, when these items do come back, it's only for a season and it's as expensive little frivolous accoutrement. Like these armbands, available online as per this advertisement: 'Men's Armbands: Available in gold or silver colour, these armbands will easily stretch comfortably over most arms, to hold your shirt cuffs safely away from your plate. Both functional and stylish, they make a perfect gift for the man about town.'

While our handkerchief sections in department stores and so on are nothing like the Japanese ones, they still exist, though I imagine there will come a day when they won't. They'll go the way of haberdashery and mercery.

The word 'handkerchief' dates from the early 16th century. It comes from 'kerchief', first recorded in 1223, and derived from the Old French *couvrechief*, where *couvrir* is to cover and *chief* is the head. By the time handkerchief came along, people were presumably familiar enough with the idea of a cloth on the head to manage the contradiction of a name that combines two references to separate parts of the body (hand, head), and maintains the French sense of cover yet means something rather different—namely a piece of cloth that you hold in your hand, when you don't have it in a pocket, and that you use to mop up various body wastes.

When my daughter was recently packing for a gap-year trip, at the last minute she said, 'Can I take one of your hankies?' Sure, I said, delighted that she'd come to see their value. I must've made one of those smug told-you-so kind of sounds, because she continued by saying, 'I'm not going to *use* it—it's just to remind me of you.'

I'm not one for lamenting (though I like the word, so much better than 'bemoan'), but if I was, I'd no doubt lament that if hankies completely go, how will little children ever play 'Drop the hanky'? For those who don't know, this old children's game goes like this: All the players stand in a circle facing each other. One specially chosen child walks slowly around the outside of the circle, eventually dropping the handkerchief at the feet of one of the players. That player then spins around, picks it up and chases the hanky-dropper, who races around the circle and tries to capture the other person's space without getting tagged. I suppose that when mobile phones go rubbery they can drop them instead of hankies.

Another function of the handkerchief, as featured in sexist legends, Jane Austen–era literature and on the Shakespearean stage, is its use as a dramatic device, or more broadly as a social broker. The woman drops the handkerchief and the gentleman picks it up, graciously returning it to its owner. This may then lead on to small talk that may then flow on seamlessly to a fully-fledged conversation, which may then lead to some, well, hanky-panky. Or you could go straight to the hanky-panky, forgoing the conversation in your rush.

The handkerchief found in a suspicious place does powerful things to an already jealous lover (ask Othello). Those given to making obtuse links between social events might suggest a connection between the demise of the hanky-mediated panky and the rise of internet dating. One story ends, another begins. A fading word, a lost practice, a new technology.

~ 10 ~

Hats

....

MY IMPRESSION OF CANBERRA, whenever I drive through, is that I have invariably arrived a few hours after an evacuation order. There just don't seem to be many people around, certainly not in relation to the width of the roads.

Last time I was there, I again noticed the dearth of people in the streets. Back at my hotel, which was a bit dark and dingy because the walls were painted a deep burgundy colour, I noticed some strange pictures on the rather off-putting walls—all oldish photos of public occasions in Canberra, like the first opening of a public building or some such. They were quite boring photos, really, except for two things. One was the crowds of people in the streets—they're never there when I drive through—and the second was what they were wearing. It certainly was a time before jeans, with the women dressed in skirts and dresses, and the men in dark suits. And on everyone's head—absolutely everyone's, without exception—there was a hat.

Of course, you needn't go to Canberra to see pictures of be-hatted people in former times. In fact, you needn't go anywhere. Just open a Max Dupain collection of photographs and you're there. Like *Dupain's Sydney*. The photograph titled *Meat Queue—1946* captures wartime austerity in a line of people queuing to buy meat with government-issued coupons.

In the foreground are five sombre women, all be-hatted. And in Dupain's *Draughts in Belmore Park—1938*, the scene is of two men playing draughts outdoors, with five rather keen male onlookers. Only one of the seven male characters has a head bereft of hat.

Any history of millinery will tell you that hats have been around for centuries, performing head-protection functions, but also, at times, having a fashion-accessory quality, and always a symbolic meaning—a way of announcing one's identity. Think of the Puritan's peaked black hat, the cardinal's red cap, the artist's beret, even the hangman's hood.

Hats went out in the 1960s—at the time there was a pretty widespread reshuffle of values and mores—and while there are still seasonal moments when a hat is de rigueur (some horse races, some weddings), or not (in church, inside a building), the hat has never really made a momentous return to the fashion scene—even despite its need as protection against the sun and its recently conferred status as a compulsory element of school uniforms.

I doubt it helps the cause of hats when Prime Minister John Howard appears on television, as he does every now and again, in his tell-tale akubra. (There are ups and downs in everything: in Howard's case, the hat covers the bald patch but compromises the perception of stature.)

A good poke around in dictionaries under 'hat' reveals a wealth of expressions that incorporate the word, many of them still in currency, even though the very literal sense of a hat as a head covering may not necessarily apply. When you go to someone hat (or cap) in hand, desperation is likely to have reduced you to the most abject humility: think feudal serf approaching the landed gentry to beg a deferment in taxes. This use of the humble hat-in-hand sits comfortably alongside the notion of tipping one's hat (as gentlemen did to a lady to say 'good day'), and taking one's hat off to someone to express admiration, respect or deference. When you're asked to keep something under your hat, you're being included in, and sworn to, a confidence that is constructed as a material thing to be safeguarded under your hat. To pick someone out of a hat is to choose a person at random—it's possible the names of contenders may still actually be written on folded bits of paper, to be drawn from a hat (if one can be found) or some other container. Likewise, passing around the hat is when a collection is taken up for a cause, such as a colleague's retirement present or a fund for the survivors of a bushfire. In a pub it may still be the hat that is physically passed around; in other venues, the hat is metaphoric, although the money raised is literal enough. Even in an era of low demand for milliners, people still speak of wanting a peg to hang their hat on, which implies the need to be grounded or centred, or to have a reliable framework. It's not so long since magicians on stage would pull a rabbit out of a hat (or rather, would seem to do so) that the phrase still has currency as performing a miracle or doing the impossible.

Hats have always done double duty as both shelter from the elements and as symbolic indicators of rank or function, or more broadly, of identity. Comedians on stage who shift rapidly from one identity (such as street cleaner) to another (such as magistrate) can do so with a simple swap of a hat. It's not hard to speculate that even back in the days of cavemen, individuals wore different styles of headdress to indicate their relative status. This would not have made much difference to the wildlife they clubbed for dinner, but it may have determined who got to eat first or who got the best bits from the day's killings. I'm also speculating that women were all of one status and did not need hats to differentiate themselves, other than perhaps Wife #1 from Wife #2.

The notion of hats bearing symbolic meaning has many realisations in language. 'Which hat are you wearing now?' requires an answer if people are to interpret the context of an action or statement correctly. Edward de Bono utilised this metaphor very aptly in his book *Six Thinking Hats*. Here, instead of different hats carrying different symbolic status, each hat represents a way of thinking, or a particular perspective, such as objectivity, negativity, creativity and so on. By separating the thinking into discrete domains and assigning them to different team members in the form of different coloured hats, the idea is to allow the various issues involved in any decision-making event to be identified and unscrambled.

As hats have drifted out of fashion, so too have many phrases in the language that involve the hat in either a literal or a more symbolic sense. For example, the phrase, I'll eat my hat if such and such happens, is an expression of high improbability—which no one would say if they thought there'd be any chance of being pressed into such an unpleasant lunch. If we call something 'old hat' we're suggesting that it's either out of fashion or not new and smart enough for the occasion. It can be applied to anything from an actual hat or item of apparel to a notion or concept. For instance, 'Fortunately, the whalebone corset is now old hat.' To knock something into a 'cocked hat' means to twist something so that its original form is hardly recognisable, an act that can incite admiration or disdain, depending on the context. And as hats have their seasons, 'to buy a straw hat in winter' suggests you are buying in a depressed market when most other people are sellers. 'At the drop of a hat' is a very small unit of time, the exclamation 'Oh my hat!' for surprise or dismay, is much more likely to be replaced by something a little more foul these days. It probably, though, came from the surprise factor of a gust of wind coming up suddenly and threatening to blow one's hat off—you grab it in time and say, 'Oh my hat!' To put the tin hat on something is to finish it off or bring it to an end, an expression some believe dates back to trench warfare in World War I, when putting the tin hat on was the last thing many soldiers did prior to being killed while charging the enemy lines.

Various folk etymologies exist to explain the expression, to talk through one's hat, which was apparently a widespread (uncomplimentary) idiom by the late 1880s, meaning to talk nonsense, although it initially seems to have carried the added connotation of to lie. One proposition maintains that the phrase refers to men in church who hold their hats over their faces while feigning prayer. Another possibility is that it refers to the emptiness of the hat atop one's head, suggesting a match between the empty hat and the empty head. It's possible, too, that to talk through one's hat is an oblique reference to another phrase, to talk off the top of one's head, meaning to speak speculatively, without thorough consideration.

Various hat phrases go hand in hand with throwing. To throw one's hat in the ring still stands for making a public announcement as a contender for a race or competition, or a political election. For example, 'Hillary Clinton is expected to throw her hat in the ring for the 2008 elections.' On the other hand, to throw your hat in the air is a spontaneous act of joyfulness, as if your positive emotion has pushed right up through your body to your head and forced you to throw your hat off. And to throw your hat at something is to express anger. On the other hand, to throw one's hat in the door means to test the warmth of one's reception, as if, were the hat to be welcomed, its owner/wearer would be, too—though given the verisimilitude of hats, especially men's hats, it might be hard to pick the owner/wearer from the hat.

Looking ahead from the present moment, it seems unlikely that hats will have a Max Dupain-style come-back. Still, I may have spoken too soon. ('Keep your hat on!' you might counter, urging me to get a grip or steady on.) In the fashion world, of course, you should never say 'never', as couture is well known for its dramatic 360-degree volte-faces. So with caution in my heart, let me suggest that expressions with 'hat' are likely to continue finding their respite in the Hospice of Fading Words. If I'm wrong, and millinery is indeed headed for its own renaissance, then please excuse me for talking through my hat.

~ 11 ~

Mercers

....

WHERE HAVE ALL THE MERCERS GONE? Good question! Gone the way of haberdashery, confectionary, millinery, iron-mongery and all the rest.

The –ery ending was once a common suffix for denoting a specialised area of trade. Not exclusive ('Manchester' is a prime exception), but generalised enough to bring to mind dusty, country-town Australia of the 1950s. Specialty shops, faded signs, like 'B.J. Fox, Mercer'. When department stores first came into being, many of the words remained, morphing into single departments of a larger store.

It's only a few years now since Myer closed down its haberdashery department. No point looking for it. I did, before I'd heard or noticed that it'd closed down, and the young lad just looked at me. In case you're about his age, haberdashery was the place you used to go to buy buttons, thread, needles, ribbons and any other goods associated with sewing. In a sense, the word stopped being when the department went. And in case you're wondering, the space now sports a range of gym gear. The big question now is where do you go for a reel of cotton. Try a 7-Eleven. As for needles—that now means some-thing altogether different.

The –ery suffix corresponds to the French *charcuterie* or *patisserie*, or to the Italian *rosticceria* or *trattoria*. The

Macquarie says they are designations according to occupation or office (*boulangerie*/bakery), while their derivatives refer to the office-holder (*boulanger*/baker). The collective noun may denote the class of goods ('crockery', 'machinery', 'finery', 'cutlery'). There's a sense, too, of the place or setting or workplace—hence, 'bakery', 'brewery', 'ironmongery', and even 'piggery', 'fishery' and 'vinery'. Included, too, should be 'cemetery', 'nursery' and 'grocery'. The suffix also graces words that depict certain behaviours, often in a deprecatory sense ('knavery', 'tomfoolery', 'treachery', 'devilry', 'rivalry'). And of course, there are the exceptions (like, 'slavery') that all good rules need.

For risqué topics, we used to lean conveniently on the French (*lingerie*), borrowing such words (like the brothel's *Madame*) to mask with apparent delicacy that which we'd rather not speak of directly. Now we're as often happy to be somewhat more direct. 'Intimate apparel' is everywhere, but then 'intimate' as a label has a wide spread, from condoms to perfume. We used to have *corsetry* with its compressed ending (pun intended), but not since the women's movement.

Accounting for the demise of millinery is easy. Compared with Dupain's Sydney, our streets are peopled by the bareheaded. But what happened to napery? The proliferation of lifestyle shows on television dictates a need both for the social markers furnished by the accoutrements of tablecloths and their collective noun. There are still shops selling sweets, but confectionery is replaced by 'Darrell Lea'. Confectioners of old were lolly shops, with big glass jars and a bell that rang as you entered and left. Now we have self-serve plastic at K-Mart.

Hosiery is a rare thing today. You can understand people getting it mixed up with garden equipment. I once knew a businessman who sold women's stockings. With the winds of change in the 1970s, when stockings largely stopped being worn as a daily matter of course, he did a radical shift to ladies' swimwear.

But cutlery is doing okay. It's an ideal wedding gift, most likely loved by department stores: minimum floor space, maximum returns, no fitting rooms. Grocery is quietly under-going an upper-middle class renaissance—vastly overpriced oils, previously unheard-of spices, which themselves were fading before they became reappropriated. I mean, I clearly remember a time when 'spice' meant a very dry bay leaf or two that you had to remember to remove before serving the cas-serole. Crockery—a cheerful word bringing to mind the rattle of breakfast dishes and the waft of fresh baked bread—is giving way to tableware. This is a case of shifting category boundaries. Tableware now embraces glass, metal and wood as well as china. Pottery survives and connotes, now less rigidly than before, earnest, smock-clad ladies, wobbly bowls and spidery backyard sheds. Of them all, jewellery shows no signs of decline. Witness the recent spending surge triggered by the bling vogue—unbeatable perhaps for its convenience as a displayer of conspicuous consumption.

'Mercery' is now a complete dinosaur. The *Macquarie* says it is the stock of a 'mercer' or one dealing in textiles, espec-ially silk. We have shops dedicated to sewing materials, including if not limited to silk, so why have we lost mercery? Could it be that it rubs phonic shoulders with that very un-PC word 'mercenary', as in a hired soldier of war? If such words are casualties of modern life, why then did I recently pass a shop devoted entirely to men's ties (plus the odd cravat and scarf)? And on the same day, a shop entirely given over to knives? Given these instances of specialisation, we cannot attribute our losses to modernism or even PoMo aftershock.

Marketing's to blame. B.J. Fox, Mercer gave way to The Linen Press. Today for things sweet, there's Forbidden Delights and Death by Chocolate. For other things—Right Angles (framing), The Urgent Image (photo development) and Good in Bed (lingerie). My local fruit-&-vegie man renamed as Fruitgasm; the sign is three-dimensional (swelling with promise?), the 's' was replaced by a strawberry, and the stock has gone organic and upmarket. Clearly, frivolous, self-conscious plays on words cannot abide the sober, collective nouns of a Victorian or Edwardian yesterday.

It's hard not to mourn the passing of the old stalwarts with their associations of tradition, stability and certainty, if not dust. They connote a time when work was a surety, climate a constant, the boiled lolly a reward at the end of the day. These days it's hard to imagine a shop's ownership passing from one generation to the next. My plumber bequeathed me his son, also a plumber, on retirement. But that's unusual these days.

The sands are shifting. A word like grocery creeps back in. Unsettled, we can't easily distinguish the genuine-old from the authentic-like new. But when we encounter this neat parody in clean aprons, bulk in barrels and exotica-filled bags, there is some certainty—dignity, too, comes at a price.

~ 12 ~

Nongs and yobbos

AN ARTICLE ABOUT CRICKETER Shane Warne appeared while news of his messy divorce was in the headlines and while he was playing brilliant cricket for Australia. In the article, Andrew Stevenson wrote: 'He may be a nong and a yobbo off the field, but Shane Warne is poetry in motion when he takes the ball in hand.'

Well, there's a contrast for you—'poetry in motion' versus 'nong' and 'yobbo'. Later in the same article, Stevenson heightened the contrast when quoting poet Dorothy Porter, who said of Warne: 'His bowling is absolutely cerebral —it's almost as if there's witchcraft in the ball.'

'Nong' and 'yobbo' and even 'drongo' are a long way from the poetic and the cerebral, and even witchcraft. Yet they are classic Australian words for a classic Australian phenomenon. Perhaps, given our convict origins, none of this is surprising. Writer Luke Slattery reminds us that this is 'a land whose first architect, Francis Greenway, was a convicted forger; whose first poet, Michael Massey Robinson, was transported for black-mail; whose first publisher was a shoplifter; whose first citizens were human ordure, banished to the globe's unknown under-side by a people of great culture.'

Of course, when Shane Warne was described as a nong and a yobbo, we all knew what was meant. Such terms are still part of a collective, national lexicon, but I suspect it's one that is now largely passive—that is, they're words no longer widely used. I suspect that after 200-plus years of white settlement, things are finally starting to shift, if almost imperceptibly.

Many of the ockerisms that were once commonly heard are today headed for the Hospice of Faded Words. They no longer fit in. They aren't in the spellchecks or online dictionaries, they aren't a part of anyone's curriculum. They aren't clever or smart or even cool. In an upwardly mobile, aspirational world, they flag working class, uneducated and unsophisticated. There's a whiff of the convict about them. And if they are used in any voice other than the ironic or quotative, they say more about the person who uses them than about those being described.

'Nong' and 'yobbo' were always meant to be insulting, but just how insulting is a matter of conjecture, and certainly a matter of context and circumstance. I suspect that calling someone a nong or a yobbo was mostly in the order of a mild rebuke and, depending on who was speaking to whom, could also be a friendly term of address. They are loose terms, often used interchangeably, though nong had more of the stupid in it while yobbo had more of the uncouth.

Of course Australia doesn't have a monopoly on nongery or yobboism. Most cultural/lingual groups have a word (or two hundred) for a category of people who make a career out of being foolish. French has *bete* and *con*; Spanish has *idiota*; German has *dummkopf*; Italian has *cretino* and *imbecile*; the Japanese say *baka* and *manuke*; Yiddish has a ton—*schlemiel, schlepper, schmuck, schmendrick*—any one of which may be usefully borrowed into English.

Still, while such traits are not uniquely antipodean, they have a long and comfortable history here. As Sidney Baker wrote: 'Fools of one kind and another have carved a considerable niche for themselves in Australian speech.'

Let's have a closer look at 'nong'. The *Macquarie* lists it as 'a fool; an idiot' and offers cousins 'noong', 'ning-nong' and 'nig-nog'. The *Oxford* cites it as Austral/NZ informal, 'a foolish or stupid person'. In the *Collins Australian Dictionary*, it's 'a stupid or incompetent person', a 19th-century word hailing, possibly, as an alteration of the obsolete English dialect word 'nigmenog', meaning a silly fellow. All told, 'nong' seems to come in two forms, sometimes at the same time. One has elements of congenital foolishness (born like that, not one's fault) that are contained in the now rather archaic word 'simpleton'. The other suggests a certain sloth-linked ineptitude (lazy, should try harder). Here we're talking useless, bungling, lacking ability, unskilled, ineffectual, not up to it, hopeless, a dead loss, a no-hoper. There's one in every extended family. Schoolteachers used to use this word a lot—there was one in every class. Sometimes out the front.

There were other words like nong in the stable. Certainly enough companions for nong never to get lonely. I'm thinking of 'thickhead', 'turkey', 'dope' and 'dopey', 'scatterbrain', 'dimwit', 'clodhopper', 'pinhead', 'nit' and 'nitwit'. Others are: 'boofhead', 'clunk', 'gloik', 'hoon', 'prawnhead' and 'tonk'. Such terms are often used in the third person, about someone rather than to their face. Some might be deemed roughly affectionate, deployed when the problem at hand is less a matter of retardation and more one of attitude or willingness to make an effort—like 'don't be a bozo' (or a 'dodo', 'egghead', 'bonehead', 'lolly', 'bunny', 'dill' or 'galah'). In other words, sloth, not birth defect. There's a quality of pull-your-socks-up-mate in 'nong' that entails forgiveness and the offer of a second chance. In any case, having the mickey taken out of you in bantering name-calling is a sign that you've been accepted. It's a quality of Australian camaraderie.

Today, there's a refreshing quality about hearing someone being called a 'nong' or a 'yobbo', or any of the other terms in the stable. We're more guarded today about denigrating or demeaning or putting down, partly because of political correctness and partly because of antidiscrimination legislation.

Despite being lumped together with nong, yobbo has an altogether different lexical DNA. Probably derived from British back slang for 'boy', it suggests a person who is unrefined, uncultured and generally slobbish. In the words of Sue Hart-Byers, alternative names for the yobbo are 'ocker', 'rough diamond', 'salt of the earth', 'pleb', or 'real Aussie'. These traits can manifest in references to apparel such as the following example from the *Macquarie*: 'I gotta change out of these stubbies, I don't want to look like a yobbo.' They can also manifest in behaviour, especially loutishness or hooliganism, such as in 'football yobbos'. Other word combinations are: western suburbs yobbos (in Sydney), working class yobbos, rich yobbos, jet ski yobbos. Like 'nong', it's a word less used than it once was, and I suspect when it is used it's with less affectionate camaraderie than in the past.

Perhaps both nong and yobbo should be grouped under the superordinate 'ocker', which is defined by the *Macquarie Dictionary of Australian Colloquialisms* as 'the archetypal uncultivated Australian working man'. The female counterpart is 'ockerina', and the society of such boorish, uncouth, chauvinistic types is collectively, if jokingly, called 'ockerdom'.

I'm not suggesting that ockerdom itself has vanished from Australia. It is still sufficiently substantial to make a politician wary of displaying aesthetic, cultural or intellectual tastes. As Luke Slattery puts it: 'By tradition, Australians have been suspicious of intellectuality—any intellectual who aimed to walk the corridors of power was advised to leave his learning at home.' In his heyday, Paul Keating's penchant for fine suits and antique clocks didn't win him many votes, unlike his penchant for 'nong' abuse in parliamentary diatribes.

Of course we've still got nongs and yobbos, so what do we call them? Today, many of these negative designates would be subsumed under the general label of 'loser'. Even less common/more faded now than nong is 'drongo'. Like nong, it combines the two senses of slow-witted and incompetent, a good example of which is the raw recruit who has not yet learned the ropes. In the Melbourne of the early 1920s, a horse named Drongo won the dubious fame of always coming last or nearly last in every race it entered. Subsequently, a cartoonist on the Melbourne *Herald*, Sam Wells, adopted the no-hoper Drongo as one of his signature cartoon characters. Over time, idioms break away from the original uterine wall so that if today we hear or use the term 'drongo', it is without a moment's thought about the slow-moving Melbourne horse.

In a lexical sense, nong and yobbo are located within close proximity to those words for a person so lacking in social attractiveness as to have no friends. A 'neville' used to be short for 'scott neville', which itself is short for ''s got no mates, never will'. A related term was 'nigel', short for 'nigel no-friends' or 'nigel no-mates'. This class of social outcasts might be summed up with the acronym 'nof'—not one friend. Being labelled as such is the very worst that can happen to you at school, and if it does, it can take years and years, as well as thousands of psychotherapy dollars, to mollify the damage.

There's one thing we can be sure of. Even if nong and yobbo are headed for the hospice, new words for the same phenomena will pop up to replace them. Take 'bogan' for instance, the new-ish word for anyone that the cool crowd designates as uncool, someone perceived as a charmless try-hard. While bogan started out as a regional term (Melbourne's equivalent of Sydney's 'westie'), it has spread, and was recently nominated for inclusion in Microsoft's Australian English spellcheck. A bogan is a bogan, apparently, mostly because of his desire not to be. Postcode is a factor, as is socio-economic class, as well as the clothes you wear (black, plaid flannelette, ugg boots), the mullet you sport, the music you play (heavy metal) and the wheels you drive (loud, modified). According to the *Macquarie Word Map*, bogans earn their place by meeting three distinct criteria: dress sense, with it-ness and postcode. Hence the definition given—'an untrendy fashion tragic, out of touch and from the outer suburbs.'

What does it say about us that we have no lack of vocabulary to cast the world into inviolable categories of 'them' and 'us'? Perhaps it is an index of the fact that the pace of change, technological and otherwise, has vastly outstripped our primordially tribal natures. Perhaps we're hardwired into attraction to likeness, deriving emotional comfort by flying with our own flock and looking down on any other.

Yet the tribal divisions, such as they are, are often shallow and insubstantial. Frequently, the perceived charmlessness of 'the other' is a function merely of the fact that the bogan or dropkick or yobbo or geek or whatever is into things not shared by the so-called cool crowd. This might be computers or electronics or certain kinds of music or forms of communication, and then a label is applied—'dork', 'nerd', 'dingbat', 'weirdo'—which allows all members of category 'us' to make easy reference to any of 'them'.

Remember the room full of nerdy geeks in *The X-Files?*

They're friends of the hero, and we recognise that he's *like* them, if not perhaps quite as far gone down that track of geek-hoodery.

PART III

QUAINTERIES ESCHEWED

~ 13 ~

Waxing lyrical

TODAY IF WE WANT TO COMMENT on the size of something, we're likely to use a prefix like 'mega' or 'hyper', or sometimes if you're really out there—especially if you like the sound of the Germanic over the Classical Latin or Greek—then you might throw in an 'uber'. I heard a young woman the other day describe something—hard to know what—a music band? a price tag? a dance party? a diamond?—as 'meganormous'. The word slipped out as a superlative of 'big', and no doubt she was clearly understood by the people she was addressing.

When was it we started to say words like 'meganormous' or 'ginormous' or 'humungous' to denote, or connote, a sense of immensity? At the risk of provoking a mirthful scoff, let me remind ourselves that one rhetorical means by which size used to be calibrated, in a literary sense, was the Bible. Yes, the Bible. Mostly, but not exclusively, the Old Testament.

For instance, there was the expression 'of biblical proportions'. That meant really big. Initially, or at least back in the latter 14th century, the comparison to the Bible was to the size of the book, but over time, it became a standard benchmark for denoting hugeness. The phrase 'of biblical proportions' conveyed a sense of epic scale, part of which was implied because of the embedded sense of disaster. After all, where better to go if you were looking for a range of catastrophes.

The Bible is full of plagues, droughts, famines and pestilence. There are mass exoduses, razing of cities, genocides, burning bushes. There is feeding of thousands, along with starving of thousands, and the odd parting of seas. If it's of biblical proportions, you can be sure that it's big, very big. Think of all those Hollywood blockbusters of the 1950s and 1960s such as *The Ten Commandments* and *The Greatest Story Ever Told*. In fact, *Ben-Hur* was the end point of bigness; after that, size was all lumped into a gross category called 'bigger than Ben-Hur'.

However, size wasn't everything. The influence of the Bible is notable, too, for its impact on the language. Working hard by the sweat of your brow; being your brother's keeper, escaping by the skin of your teeth; living not by bread alone; bringing someone's head on a platter; the blind leading the blind; practising what you preach; living and dying by the sword; washing your hands of a problem; keeping your head in a crisis; hearing the news directly from the horse's mouth. All biblical in origin.

Then there are the direct allusions. Some of these call on major biblical protagonists whose names have come to be linked with certain abstract-noun qualities. We have the patience of Job, the wisdom of Solomon, the loyalty of Ruth (I threw that one in because it's often neglected). Sometimes the allusion is more locational—Paul on the road to Damascus, Lot's wife looking back at the destruction of Sodom, Jesus with the fish on the Sea of Galilee.

But things are changing. Not only do we live in a more secular world, but in a world of mass migration, globalisation and cheap international phonecards. We're less able to embed our communications in shared cultural and educational backgrounds. We have many more myths in the ether. The past, on the other hand, was more monocultural, more sheltered, less exposed, more ignorant. It was a different country and they did things differently there.

Just as our values have changed, so too has our language. We do different things with language now; we posit our emphases in different places. In other words; the linguistic culture of today is different from the linguistic culture of yesteryear, and comparing the two is akin to comparing the rhetorical conventions of synchronic cultures—for example, comparing the way contemporary speakers of English or French or Greek or Croatian or Urdu might achieve comparable speech events.

Say, for instance, you're the owner of a parked car and you return to your vehicle just in time to see a parking officer place an infringement notice on your car's front windscreen. You think it's not too late to plead your case. Of course, it is, it's always too late, certainly once the ticket's been written. But never mind that for the moment; this is simply a theoretical exercise.

You rush up and begin your argument, which naturally will be devoid of physical or verbal assault for, after all, such avenues are contemptible and unlikely to have positive effects, and in any case, the parking officer is merely the messenger, the vulnerable face of an inviolable bureaucracy. You will use 'appropriate' language to make your last-ditch stand against council revenue collection, and in doing so, you will be calling on your own linguistic and cultural traditions and conventions. You will express yourself in a manner that, as a fully-fledged linguistic-cultural being, you deem to be most likely to bring about a favourable outcome. In terms of the shape and choice of language, depending on whether you're a speaker of English, French, Greek, Croatian or Urdu, and depending on how much you know about the dominant or host culture's rituals, the pleading of your case will be different.

There's nothing surprising about this. Different languages and cultures do things differently. My point is that we can employ the same cultural metaphor to compare current and past practices in the *same* language. Given the rapidity of social change in the last half-century, there's little doubt that the way in which back then the same parking-ticket case would have been made in English is likely to be very different from the way it would be made these days. Different rhetorical conventions will shape the form and content of the language event, just as if we had a case of two different but co-temporaneous languages/cultures. In other words, culture shapes rhetoric and culture is not set in concrete. The English in use on a Sydney street in 2006 is not the same English that was in use in the same street in 1946.

Yet with a stamina that could be called primordial, some expressions associated with the old culture, for want of a better label, continue. Like idiom and metaphor, generally, these have naturalised to the point that we don't notice them. We've come to know them by their conventionalised meanings rather than their literal meanings. We say 'drop me a line' when we want to remind a person to stay in touch, giving not a moment's thought to either the 'drop' or the 'line'. The 'drop' may have originally been the action of posting a letter, and the 'line' presumably stood metonymically for a line of writing.

'Line' has leapt into the electronic world and the leap has been relatively easy, for it applies equally well to a line in a handwritten note or a computer-mediated one. So too the 'line' in 'reading between the lines'. Once again, the line here visualises a line of writing yet is used even in spoken circumstances, where of course it is preposterous to suggest we speak in lined utterances. 'Reading between the lines' refers to the ability to appreciate a text's real-world, pragmatic significance, rather than perhaps its formal or textual representation. Reading between the lines can also be called reading the subtext—what is figuratively below the line—not said, but implied. This is not a past-time of the deviant mind. Indeed a good case could be made to claim that being a fully-fledged member of a speech community assumes the ability to read pragmatic meaning—correctly and adroitly, for the most part, not even knowing that that's what you're doing.

The 'bottom line' also uses the line metaphor. We imagine the last line of a page, containing a set of calculations, possibly but not necessarily mathematical, to reveal the broader meaning, the net effect of a series of developments. 'Give me the bottom line' can mean skip to the end point, to the projected outcomes; even focus on the absolutely essential and don't beat about the bush.

And 'swallow the line' rather dramatically conceptualises gullibility as the process of ingestion. There's the sense of bait and trap, and a possible overlap with 'hook, line and sinker'. Related, too, may be 'the line' used conversationally, something you say to another, so as to con or tempt or bring them into your sphere of availability. Such lines are often old and tired, but for that one-off chance in ten that they will work, they keep being patiently trotted out, anywhere from shoe shops to nightclubs.

And so it would seem that our example, 'line', is comfortable with one leg in the pre-digital age while the other leg has become firmly electronic. Many words develop the flexibility to straddle two worlds. 'Pen' is another. While most current writing is as removed from the pen as your office biro is from the quill, we still say 'put pen to paper' for sorting out our ideas in written form; or 'with the stroke of a pen' to indicate the power of a written edict. Considering the power of the signature to a document, it might be the case that the pen still rules the day. Nonetheless, most writing is keyed in rather than produced by hand, in turn making the issue of handedness, which used to be almost exclusively determined by which hand you wrote with, increasingly a thing of the past. Giving new meaning to egalitarianism, the act of keying in doesn't favour one set of fingers over the other. The skill of ambidexterity is no longer a matter of note, perhaps because it's no longer noted.

When we say 'nothing to write home about', we're imagining a handwritten letter, even while we know the phrase is a metaphor for nothing impressive. Similarly, to 'write one's own ticket' has the sense of getting down in handwritten form one's preferred terms and conditions. The 'writing on the wall', as a sign of impending disaster, alludes to the Old Testament's *Book of Daniel* 5:5–6, but if your bible is more along the lines of popular culture, you might take your cue from Monty Python's *The Life of Brian*, where the writing on the wall (in this case Latin graffiti) was subject to random grammar checks by the odd, passing conjugating Roman foot soldier, and where the threat of punishment was far greater than anything meted out at a contemporary school, with two slabs of wood and a couple of nails more likely serving the function of capital punishment.

However, not all linguistic referents from previous times exhibit the same stamina and portability as 'line', 'pen' and 'writing'. Some have remained entrenched in the context and circumstances of a previous time so that today they're increasingly liable to sound, well, odd. 'To pull up your socks' or 'sharpen your pencil' used to amount to a warning that the quality of your work was below acceptable standard. You'd be aware then that note had been taken of your sock height and/or your blunt pencil by those with the power to do things to you that you'd rather they didn't.

Perhaps as workplace relations become more tenuous, workers won't have the luxury of a warning before being laid off. Nevertheless, it is a source of wonderment that the height of your socks and the sharpness of your pencil's point would be taken as something other than a mark of individual (even obsessive) eccentricity, and certainly not as evidence of time-on-task or creative thinking, let alone of personal worth. Perhaps, like justice, some things just need to be seen—pulled-up socks and pointy pencils are, if nothing else, very visible. Over time, such items come to be seen to stand for substance, not veneer.

The colourful language of the past endures to varying degrees into the present. Overall its common flavour, however, is vanishing. Standing back from the phenomenon and looking for patterns, it would seem that colourful language is less valued for its own sake than it once was. The advent of mass public education, less than a century old, has given literacy a functional bent, the stamp of utility, and in the process it has lost a good deal of its aesthetic sensibility. People read newspapers, magazines, TV programs and train time-tables rather than Austen, Dickens or Faulkner. We now speak of multiple literacies, where literacy means the ability to navigate a particular discourse. Numeracy, for instance, is not only about notions like addition, multiplication and division, it is also about the language in which mathematic texts are clothed and mathematical concepts mediated. Even contemporary fiction is closer to a common colloquial vernacular than it once was. And given the educative role of modelling, it is no surprise that less exposure to traditionally literary texts means 'less literary' writing is being produced. Production is preceded by reception: you have to be steeped in it before you can produce it.

It is of parallel interest that the term 'flowery' is pejorative when used to describe a kind of elaborate, ornate prose that is self-consciously constructed with a close attention to form, at least from the 13th century. 'Flower' once meant the finest part or product of anything, but 'flowery' in its pejorative sense, seems particularly recent. When it's used in regard to your writing, it's an unambiguous put-down. Creative writing classes encourage spare and minimal text, eschewing adjectives and adverbs as superfluous wadding. In the arts at university, the favoured rhetorical conventions have a focus on factual texts that feature a critical stance with cogent argument and pristine structure. I recall a history essay of long ago, probably first-year university, in which I referred to Napoleon's troops marching through Europe 'with appalling savagery'. The essay came back marked up for my stylistic deficiencies, including, inter alia, a comment on my 'appalling savagery'. The 'appalling' was crossed out and a margin note said 'savagery' was arguably (love that word—it takes anyone off the hook) more appalling without the adjective. With the hindsight of many years of writing, I now see that that tiny piece of feedback encapsulated a whole cultural attitude towards preferred language. It ranks up there with the best pieces of strategic advice available to the undergraduate novice. I've never ever again knowingly been appallingly savage.

Perhaps flowery language came from an era that was still heavily influenced by oral traditions of story-telling, when the telling style was massively important as an instrument of cultural continuity. The emergence of image—in photography, film, television, magazines, the internet—perhaps has satisfied much of the need for visual illustration, for colourful parallel support to written text. This has taken the pressure off text, removed its aesthetic responsibility perhaps, allowing it to concentrate more thoroughly on content or message.

Further, text is now produced and packaged for mass distribution and consumption. From here it's not a big leap to see how factual texts, minimalist prose, a clean and spare style, would come to be valued. 'Flowery' now lines up, thesaurially speaking, with 'high-sounding', 'lofty', 'Johnsonian', 'polemical', 'purple', 'sonorous' and other (mostly unpleasant-sounding) words. What matters is the message—just the facts, ma'am. So enter email and SMS, and watch them become the favoured offspring and move to the head of the queue. Yeah, right, get to the point. I'm taking too long. Even 'whatever', catapulted to fame by *Little Britain*, has become abbreviated to a hand gesture, so much ruder than the old two-finger rebuke.

Our attention span has contracted. Our tolerance threshold has shifted. We don't expect words to be floral, and when they are, we're impatient because they're not doing the job we value them for. If we want pictures, we'll ask for them, thanks very much. If we need more, we'll fill in the blanks ourselves.

Knowledge is no longer the preserve of the elite. In theory at least, it's available to anyone. We no longer need to reference the old in any mention of the new. We don't need to use the old, the given, to scaffold the entry of the new. The washing powder that has 'NEW!!!' or 'IMPROVED!!' stamped on it is inherently, intrinsically superior to last week's product.

Further, if the education cake has been enlarged to feed more people, it has also become thinner in the process. The elements of cultural literacy that once valued written texts, giving them their textured quality (such as those used by the Romantic poets), are just as likely these days not to be understood. Autumn, as Keats described it, as the 'season of mists and mellow fruitfulness', is not only grounded in a very English landscape and climate but relies for its full appreciation on a recognition of the allusion. So too the description of a person—'a countenance more in sorrow than in anger'—from Horatio's description of Hamlet's father's ghost, arguably (there's that word again) only makes full sense when one can call on knowledge of the original play. Shakespeare, the Romantic poets, the Bible, Aesop, and Gilbert and Sullivan are less known as texts, and therefore less recognised when they appear, intertextually, in different shapes and forms in modern texts. Not known means not noted. Not noted means well on the way to being lost. 'The flowers that bloom in the spring' may well seem a mere encyclopedic entry, and yet the Gilbert and Sullivan operetta can be downloaded within minutes as a ringtone for your mobile phone. What an odd world.

The role of English in the world and on the world stage has changed. English was once the language of the English and the outposts of Empire, and with it came a long and rich literary tradition. English today is influenced more by the English speakers of America who are less steeped in the glories of English literature—they have their own—and anyway they bring cultural attachments that are more likely to be popular than high culture.

Furthermore, English is no longer the advance guard of the Empire. It's now the world's lingua franca, having changed within half a human lifetime from flowery to functional. More people now speak English as a second, foreign or international language than speak it as an ancestral tongue. Complicated obtuse prose with embedded allusions obstructs communication. It's not the language in which to get poetic. It's the language with which to sell merchandise on eBay. It's not English; it's Globish.

It was a haughty German who said to me, some forty years ago, when I met him in a shared squat accommodation in East London, that it was no wonder the world of the great unwashed would gravitate towards English as a lingua franca. After all, he said, English was merely the barbaric early beginnings of what would develop into German. He'd come to England on a working visa (this was pre-Euro) to do community work as an alternative to otherwise compulsory military service. And he made these pronouncements about English after I'd complimented him on his fluency. It's a single sample and not much should be read into it, but why then has it stuck in my memory so obdurately?

Let's face it. The subjunctive is dead. 'Who' has dumped 'whom'. The passive is in retreat. 'Brought' and 'bought' have blurred into one. Plain English is on the march. Space is at a premium. Streamlined is the new black. Speed is of the essence. Competition for airplay is fierce and expensive. Time is money. Direct and straight-talking is good. Oblique is bad. Waxing lyrical and colourful language is, if you'll excuse me, a bit of a wank.

～ 14 ～

Fixed rejoinders

IF YOU GO TO INSPECT AN ultra-modern apartment today, you'll likely find minimal furnishings, neutral colours, clean streamlined forms, recessed or hidden handles, with little on display, a minimum of clutter and fuss, and a maximum of functionality. You'd be forgiven for wondering where you might find a coffee cup or a teaspoon, let alone the salt. Minimal is an –ism. The Tate Modern has a whole section devoted to it. It's austere, bordering on sterile, seemingly committed to the suppression of nuance. Minimal is as far removed from your chunky, cluttered country kitchen look as the imagination will take you.

As with the kitchen decor, so too with language. We once adorned our language as we might've adorned our homes. An almost baroque, self-conscious ornateness, ostentatiously colourful, complicated and metaphoric.

This valuing of language almost for its own sake is illustrated in a common habit of language that is faded now, or at least, fast fading. I refer to the custom of fixed rejoinders to (often) unwanted questions. Now I don't mean rhetorical questions, which are questions you ask when you're not actually requesting information but merely setting up the mechanical framework to allow you to say and/or do what you want to do. Not unlike putting your indicator on as you line up next to a parking spot, ready to execute the perfect reverse park. It might be that you want to pronounce the very opinion that you would pronounce were someone else to be good enough to furnish you with the right question. If such a question emerges, well and good; if it doesn't, that's when the rhetorical question steps in and saves the day. Politicians seem to favour this device. This is partly because they mostly come to the conversation with a preset agenda. It's also because they may be unprepared for an actual question and so seek to maintain their hold over the direction of the conversation by asking the question for which they do have the answer. It's not very subtle. Mostly we see the mechanics of the manipulation, but it happens, and we all move on.

The question/answer couplet I'm referring to is different, largely because the question itself is genuine, asked by one party, while the answer, given by another party, is not a real answer to the actual question but a means of deflecting the curiosity contained in the question to another direction.

A classic of this genus that I remember well from the mouths of righteous teachers takes the form of an exclamatory rhetorical question followed by a pretence of an answer. The teacher would say, in response to a question deemed outlandish, 'What do you think this is—bush week?!'. While it never occurred to me to ask when I was a child, I later learned that 'bush week' was a fictitious festival (yes, it's in the *Macquarie Dictionary*) when folks from the country went to the city, an occasion that was so special, so different or so far outside the ordinary that allowance might be made for unusual behaviour. After all, it was bush week, wasn't it?

The remark was made with a tone of ironic indignation, a kind of 'what kind of fool do you take me for?' or 'I didn't come down in the last shower, you know.' It's the long-winded, bush-beating (there's that word again) way around saying something as simple and unambiguous as 'No!' And it was always used in this way, never in the authentically information-seeking way of, 'Is next week bush week or the week after?' You'd never, for instance, seriously reply with 'Yes, it's bush week!'

The fixed question itself is a useful device, without doubt, and there are others of this ilk, such as those that mean 'yes', or 'absolutely yes' or 'bleeding obviously yes'. 'Is the Pope Catholic?' (Well, yes, that's a precondition of the job, isn't it?) 'Do bears shit in the woods?' (Well, one imagines so; where else would they go?) 'Are the Kennedys gun-shy?' (Poor taste but vivid.) I still use all of these on occasion, although, increasingly, I get that 'poor thing, she's a bit eccentric' look. My younger child's facial expression says, 'Who the hell are the Kennedys?'

The rhetorical question has a first cousin that is also part of a question/answer couplet, but more focused on the rejoinder than the trigger. Let me illustrate.

To the question 'What are you doing?' the straight answer is the provision of information that fills the gap that caused the question in the first place. But say the person doing the doing doesn't want to answer or can't be bothered doing so. They might reply with, 'Wouldn't you like to know?' Which, classically, answers a question with a question and so informs the questioner that they're not going to find out. Another retort, which had an all-purpose feel to it, was 'That's for me to know and you to find out.' There are also standard avoidance returns like the blue-collar retort of 'Whatdyareckon?'

The classic context for such an exchange is adult-to-child, probably at a point in the day when the adult has had it with inquisitive questions. It's a 'never you mind' shutdown kind of rejoinder which children become pretty adept at reading. Even nonsensical ones like the retort to 'What are you making?'—'A wigwam for a goose's bridle'—was adopted by parents when, for whatever reason, they didn't want to reply.

That blasted wigwam! The child, first time round, would make the inferential steps—What's a wigwam? Why does a goose need a bridle? Why are you making one?—and through this laborious literalising, arrive at the end-point understanding that the information was not up for grabs. With a little exposure, the child would interpret the wigwam rejoinder as code for mind your own business, or rack off, stickybeak. This is what is meant by 'pragmatic knowledge'. It's an acquired skill.

You can see the benefits of the code. Primary carers, mostly mothers, have to deal with endless questions from their brood about everything and nothing. And they don't get penalty rates after the one-hundredth question. A coded response can be the pathway of least effort and, perhaps, least resistance. This is also how rhetorical traditions are passed on. Mothers or carers model discourse markers for their progeny and these tend to be anything but literal. But they're understood pragmatically, and their meanings become both grounded and passed on.

Take the 'I wish . . .' remark of yore to which a mother might retort, aiming to sidestep the issue and thereby deflect the wish (which the family budget would more than likely not be able to accommodate): 'If wishes were fishes, they'd fill the whole sea.' Another one like this was: 'If wishes were horses, beggars would fly.' A child may well not grasp the niceties of conditional entailment here (if X, then Y), nor function effectively with the twin hypothetical notions (if wishes were horses, if beggars were birds), but that is not to say that they would not grasp that the response was as negative as 'No, you can't . . .' It was likely followed by the turned-down childish lower lip, the standard accompaniment, generationally transmitted through the ages, to wish non-fulfillment. As too was this rejoinder to an expressed wish: 'Wish in one hand, pee in the other and see which is filled the first.'

There are other such couplets that operate in a similar way. 'Where are you going?' might elicit 'To see a man about a dog', or 'Where is so-and-so?', 'Up in Annie's room behind the clock'—irrespective of whether there was a dog, an Annie in the house, a room upstairs or a clock in it. In fact, the absence of an Annie, an upstairs or a clock, or any combination of these components, would simply reinforce the primary meaning— that there's no joy likely to be forthcoming from this source.

Likewise, there are phrases that have in common their attempt to distract children. For example, telling a young child that there's a horse in the bathroom, or an elephant in the living room was a very common way of distracting attention. Often commercial advertisements were deployed for this purpose. For example, in the advertisement for Tosca chocolate bars ('Where's George? Gone for a Tosca'). 'Gone for a Tosca' for a while became the standard non-answer to a 'where?' question.

This is not unlike the more recent 'Not happy, Jan', which also emerged from an advertisement, in which an employer or supervisor reprimands an employee, using the shorthand 'Not happy, Jan' to signal the dissatisfaction. This subsequently morphed into a bumper sticker during a federal election, 'Not happy, John', referring to the record of John Howard, the then prime minister. Clearly, the majority were happy, John, because he was returned to office that year.

To a child's complaint of hurt or pain, the rejoinder 'A dead man would be pleased to feel it.' To someone asking too many questions like, What's that? What do you use that for?, the rejoinder was, 'Fly paper for a nosy stickybeak.' To a question requiring a numerate answer (like, how long something was going to be and how many of something could they have) the answer was 'eleventy-seven', a blatantly non-numerical numeral. To the question: 'What time is it?' there was 'Half-past a freckle' or (the more risqué version) 'Half-past a monkey's arse.' In a circumstance where the one asking is dragging the chain, the rejoinder might have an added tag, '. . . and the freckle (or monkey) is catching up.'

Some retorts operated in formulaic couplets. For example, when two people seem to have had the same idea at exactly the same time, one might say, 'Great minds think alike', to which the other would retort, 'Fools seldom differ'. Platitudinous though these moments are, the shared code induces intimacy among the participants, who realise they're playing by the same rules, adhering to the same code.

There were others. A common one had to do with protocol at doorways. A young person would allow an older person to go first, as was the polite custom of the day, and may say, cheekily, 'Age before beauty', an immodest claim to being both young and beautiful. The older person, in accepting this gesture, would then say, 'Dust before the broom' in apparent droll self-deprecation with a hint of a put-down.

As regards the linguistic accompaniments to doorway etiquette, there grew up a range of options, some mock-serious, some ironic. A man allowing a woman to go first might say, 'Beauty before the beast.' A younger woman allowing an older one to go first might say, 'Age before beauty', which is nominally respectful but, in the context of bitchy female competitiveness, a tart reminder of who really holds the cards. Or an older woman may allow a younger through, with

the *sub voce* words, 'Pearls before swine', a circumstance attributed, via urban legend, to a range of female celebrities, from
Bette Davis to Dorothy Parker.

As I was growing up, my non-native-English-speaking
father would very often have fun with these phrases, mixing
them all up, always semi-ironical, always with a twinkling eye.
Out would come, 'Dust before beauty' or 'Broom after age.' For
some time I'd urge him, embarrassed child of migrants that
I was, to either get it right or desist, but he heeded me not,
having far too much fun the way things were.

To the ubiquitous 'What's for lunch/dinner?'—'A snake's
bum on a biscuit.' The rear end also featured in the retort to the
complaint, 'It's not fair'—'Neither is Jack Johnson's bum.' (Jack
Johnson being a black boxer.) And also in the rejoinder:
'Everyone to their own taste, as the woman said when she
kissed the cow's bum.' According to writer Nancy Keesing,
women who put great store in keeping up appearances could
relax and be themselves with other women folk and young
children. So 'bum' could be said with impunity in such
company.

All these rejoinders are sliding away. When we hear them
they ring as echoes of a time when communities were tighter,
the nation-state was stronger and when people stood up in
cinemas to sing the national anthem. Community was more
bonded and tighter networks connected people. For many, the
same connections are missing today. People of non-English-
speaking backgrounds and their first-generation offspring
don't recognise or connect to a past tradition of the cultural
assumptions that may be entailed in the language.

When English is used as a lingua franca, it often deletes
the colourful expressions that give it a strong and keen sense
of itself but get in the way of intelligibility. Ultimately, it's a

trade-off: clarity comes at a price. Stripped of its colour and character, its idiom and ornateness, English becomes plain and bland, available to more, treasured by fewer.

≈ 15 ≈

Doubling up

COMFORT. SOME FIND IT IN WARM MILK or soft slippers by an open fire. Others in the fragrances of a spring garden. Children find it in repetition. Returning again and again to the same sentiment or phrase in a storybook. And not only in narrative. Children love routine, and what is routine if not another term for repetition? Some might say that as human beings we are genetically coded for repetition. Perhaps it is change that is deviant.

And it's not only children who find solace in refrain. Think of the conventions of prayer and mantra. In fact, most text-types are just that—form, shape and texture convention-alised by repetition, naturalised over time, to the point of unawareness. It's also the familiarity, the absolutely recognised nature of things when they are pitch perfect for their social purpose. There's comfort in the fit, in the alignment.

Repetition is an inherent feature of conversation. A linguist who studied this in depth managed to identify a wide range of functions that are served by repetition of words or phrases. An important one has to do with the relationship between the speaker and the hearer, where repetition may signal as well as ratify participation. We are social beings. We need to engage with others and we mostly do this through talk. Repeating elements of our conversant's language can be a bonding device. It's not only children who take comfort in the routines.

This applies to jokes, too. Consider this old one, reconstituted for the current circumstance:

> One sunny day in 2007 an old man approached the White House from a park bench on Pennsylvania Avenue. He spoke to the US Marine standing guard and said, 'I'd like to meet with President Bush.' The Marine stiffly answered, 'Sir, Mr Bush is no longer president, and no longer resides here.' The old man said, 'Okay' and walked away. The following day he reappeared and the scenario repeated. 'I'd like to meet with President Bush.' Again the Marine said, 'Sir, as I said yesterday, Mr Bush is no longer president and no longer resides here.' The man thanked him, and again walked away. The third day, the same man approached the White House and spoke to the same Marine, saying, 'I'd like to meet with President Bush.' The Marine, understandably agitated at this point, said, 'Sir, this is the third consecutive day you've asked to meet with President Bush. I've already told you that Mr Bush is no longer the president, and no longer resides here. Don't you understand?' The old man replied, 'Oh, I understand. I just love hearing it.'

If repetition can happen at the whole-text level, as in the joke above, it can also occur at the micro-level of a single word. Think of 'heebie-jeebies', 'airy-fairy', 'higgeldy-piggeldy'. The technical term for this is reduplicative (from the Latin *reduplicare*, to double up)—ironically, somewhat of a misnomer, for duplicative per se suggests duplication. Anyway, apart from that anomaly, a reduplicative is very simply a word that has duplicated itself in some degree into a compound.

Now reduplicative compounds are still very much with us (think of 'pooper-scooper', 'fifty-fifty', 'big-wig'), but as we'll see, increasingly they seem to be characteristic of the language of yore more than contemporary talk patterns. Quite simply, they are fading away. This applies to the three types of reduplicatives.

In the first kind, there's an exact duplication ('hush-hush', 'never-never', 'tut-tut', 'goody-goody'). In the second, we have two similar words, the only difference between them being a change of consonant in the second word ('hanky-panky', 'helter-skelter'). In the third, which often loses the hyphen, for no explicable reason, the difference is a vowel change ('chitchat', 'mishmash', 'zigzag').

Semantically, the patterning is even more interesting. Sometimes, you take a base word, which is meaningful unto itself, and repeat it with a slight change, creating a new word ('super-duper'). Sometimes, you take a base word, change the ending, then add a rhyming version ('lovey-dovey'). Mostly, the compound is meaningful, but neither of the bits is ('hocus-pocus', 'riff-raff', 'fuddy-duddy', 'namby-pamby'). And sometimes, each part of the compound is meaningful, but they don't appear without each other ('walkie-talkie'). 'Walkie-talkie' in particular, because of its dated technology, indicates how old hat these reduplicatives have become.

Reduplicatives were a common feature of relaxed spoken language where precision and correctness are less important. We don't need to know exactly where Woop-Woop is to know that we don't need to know. Au contraire, that's precisely the point. Sometimes, there's a deliberately laid-back quality ('hunky-dory', 'okey-dokey'). Sometimes, especially with children, there's an infantilising element ('silly-billy', 'itsy-bitsy', 'roly-poly', 'pitter-patter', 'topsy-turvy'). Sometimes, it's deliberately disrespectful ('arty-farty', 'hoity-toity', 'mumbo-jumbo'). And sometimes, borrowing a pattern from Yiddish, it's a downright put-down ('fancy-shmancy'), where the second word is deliberately constructed to take the wind out of the first.

And they are disappearing differently. Sometimes, the first word might remain, as in 'super' where the 'duper' is lost. And 'lovey' is quite happy now without its former 'dovey'. And 'hush' doesn't need itself repeated; it can stand alone. These, however, are the exceptions. Most of the reduplicatives can't work as singles. For instance, we can 'dilly-dally', but we can neither 'dilly' nor 'dally' on their own. Same with 'hunky' vis a vis 'dorey' and 'helter' vis a vis 'skelter'.

One notable exception is the way 'yadda yadda' spiked a few years ago as a flow-on from the *Seinfeld* phenomenon. Even so, despite its popularity and spread, it didn't last. Maybe it's inherent in the DNA of a reduplicate that it have a relatively short shelf-life.

∾ 16 ∾

As easy as

IN A RECENT SYDNEY WEEKEND newspaper supplement, some delicious-looking pie recipes were featured in the food section. They came highly recommended not only because of their taste but also because, allegedly, they were 'as easy as . . .' There was no 'pie' there; I mean, there were plenty of pies in the picture, but not a one in the text. Just 'as easy as'.

The 'pie' is gone I thought; gone, possibly never to return. Now I'm not lamenting the loss of the pie. Truth is, I never understood why pies used to be singled out as the benchmark for what is easy. This is possibly because being majorly challenged in the baking-skills department, it's not something I would ever say, really, if I were thinking literally about what I was saying (although the truth is, none of us much thinks about what we say literally in the ordinary cut and thrust of daily conversation, and, ironically, when we say 'literally', we usually don't mean it). As it turns out, I have a colleague for whom pies were an important part of childhood, and he assures me that the 'easy as pie' had to do with ease of eating, not ease of making or baking.

Whatever. I happen not to believe in 'ease' and 'difficulty' as absolute qualities, but rather as a function of a range of variables in any one context. You could say 'as easy as breathing', but even breathing is not a given (think distressed asthmatic).

And so it is for me with 'as easy as pie'. So maybe it's a good thing, all things considered, that they've let the pie go.

Now apropos the actual pie recipe, there's no question that in our time-hungry society, the ease factor is no less important than the delish one. Who in their right mind is going to approach a recipe that requires the best part of a long weekend to achieve? In my book, there simply has to be a reasonable balance between preparation and ingestion times.

But I stray from the 'as-easy-as'. This was the first time I'd seen 'as + (...) + as' in print. Being the parent of a teenager, I had, of course heard it said, on many occasions. In fact, I'd already come to the conclusion that there's a law around that says if you want to qualify as adolescent, you need to be using 'as + adjective or adverb + as' at least twelve times in any one twenty-four hour time period.

This feature of teenspeak is something I think of as 'the circumcision factor'. Adolescents simply like to chop the ends off phrases. And it's not only with comparisons. When they want to agree with a remark one of their own just made, they say 'Same'. When that remark is negative, in the grammatical sense, they'll say 'Neither':

A: I so wanna go to that concert.
B: Same. I wasn't allowed to see their last one.
A: Neither.

In this conversation, if that's what it should be called, the listener quietly fills in the blanks left by the speaker. It's rather like a dance step. And I'm convinced that all the tacit-but-shared inferencing makes each of them feel more intimately engaged. They feel good about the connection without any clue as to why. Perhaps this isn't surprising. After all, ritualised customs like circumcision have kept whole religions intact and on task for centuries.

Now I suspect that this quality—I'll call it inferencing-brings-you-closer—is a universal principle of language. I was having a conversation just this morning with a woman my age and we were talking about an incident where miscommunications had led to a bit of a hiccup in a relationship. She shook her head knowingly and said: 'Well, omelettes, you know . . .' In my head, I silently filled in the gaps ('you can't make an omelette without breaking eggs'), and felt warm and fuzzy through the shared inference, as no doubt did she when I signalled my understanding and agreement non-verbally, or at least, didn't look confused. Likewise, I recently congratulated a colleague for submitting her PhD thesis, and she responded that she'd hold off on embracing the congratulations for the time being, pending her results, because 'there's many a slip'. It took a nano-moment, but I knew what she meant.

As a linguist, I try not to make value judgements about the language of one group of people such as generation X or Y in comparison with say, that of their parents. Certainly I can see qualities in circumcised language—at the very minimum, it's a winner for economy and cultural solidarity. And sufficient evidence exists that some expressions start out in a fringe subculture like teenspeak, and end up in the mainstream, much like tattoos and body piercing. We need go no further than consider how 'so' has migrated into new places in sentences produced by all kinds of people.

In any case, probably no generation gave its elders more of a headache than Homo sapiens' first batch of teenagers, the beat generation of the 1950s. Prior to that, you went straight from being a kid (a small-sized person) to being an adult (a big-sized person). Kids used to emulate the way their parents spoke, as is very evident when watching old re-runs of *Leave it to Beaver*.

That said, however, there's a stark contrast between 'as easy as' and the kinds of phrases used in the past, when comparisons were far more graphic and visual.

There's no question we now invest less energy into our similes and analogies and, as a result, some of the old colour is being bleached out. The kind of effort that used to be invested in the graphic is not as valued, with form and colour now subservient to meaning and message. Modern tastes are far too streamlined for the wordiness of an earlier generation's speaking style. No reason to bother with saying, 'You look like you've got ants in your pants', when you might simply say, 'You're antsy.' Young people know what being 'up shit creek' means without needing to mention, or even know about, the paddle that's been left off. And you can see their point—it's bad enough being up shit creek *with* a paddle without contemplating the hypothetical of how to self-extricate minus the paddle.

Of course, there is a special subgroup of quirky, rather cerebral young folk who seem to get a self-indulgent little kick out of using the old-and-colourful in an air-quoty kind of way. And even minus the air quotes, a slight pause or change in tone is sufficient to cue anyone in earshot that they've shifted gear, that they want you to know they've shifted gear and that, in fact, they're taking the mickey out of you and maybe themselves, too. It's precisely this tone that my adult son uses when he calls me cobber—it lets me know that he thinks 'cobber' is the kind of word my generation would have used 'back then before the war'. He knows that, despite the guide books, not many urban types say cobber, but I think he thinks people used to. It's a long while since I heard anyone honestly and authentically calling anyone else cobber. I suspect the word has moved—or is moving—into some kind of folk history: the history we make up and pretend is history.

He has another phrase that he likes to use with me—and that's 'before the war'. It neutralises all protest in one single sweeping verbal gesture by which he classifies everything in the before-now zone as subsumed under ancient-and-irrelevant. Meanwhile, the time zone of now is differentiated to within an inch, or centimetre, of its life. I'm not even sure which war he's referring to. When I ask, he mockingly mentions the Boers.

Who among the young, or even the not-so-young, has time for elaborate, complete similes? I'm thinking of expressions like 'as bold as brass', 'as mean as a cut snake', 'as right as rain', 'as hungry as a horse'. It's hard to imagine anyone commenting on 'shooting through like a Bondi tram', especially as the tram service is long gone and most people who remember it are on their last legs, like the expression itself— not to mention the fact that you kind of have to know how slow a Bondi tram used to be to appreciate the irony of shooting through in that manner.

Some fixed expressions were even longer. You might moan on about something which has got your nose out of joint, to which a mate would have you count your blessings by reminding you that 'it's better than a poke in the eye with a burnt stick.' There are ruder versions, but we'll stay with the eye for the moment. Many such expressions—for example, 'off like a bride's nightie'—were notable for their deliberately titil-lating quality. If nothing else, they drew the line at the bottom of the page.

Many of these old ways of talking are memorable for their homely, everyday quality of grounded ordinariness. Like describing someone as 'mad as a dog trying to bury a bone in a concrete floor'; or as 'going at something like a bull at a gate'; or as having 'more front than a government bus'. Others mix earthiness and incongruity—like putting down ostentation with 'as flash as a rat with a gold tooth'; or describing loquaciousness as the ability to 'talk the hind leg off a donkey'.

They all have a quality of realism (without the magical), a telling it like it is. Having 'grit on the liver' or 'muck on the pluck' describes a mood of irritation or bad temper, while ants in one's pants, as already mentioned, capture that fidgety, restless feeling. Someone with a bee in their bonnet is overly focused on one particular matter, and if it's deemed trifling they might be described as 'carrying on like a pork chop in a heat wave', an analogy that has visual as well as olfactory associations. While no one wears bonnets any more (aside from the occasional baby or female character in a film set among the Amish), and while your pork chop today would be well-and-truly refrigerated during a heat wave, these expressions might still work, so long as they're used idiosyncratically, in a self-conscious, iconoclastic way where the speaker overtly distances themself from the demographic which, rather ironically, is being echoed/quasi-mocked. When my son calls me 'cobber', he has a smart-alec smile on his face that says, 'hey, this is one of your words, isn't it?' It's not a question so I don't reply.

So the long-winded similes and graphic expressions are mostly deemed tiresome these days, unless they can be deployed cynically. One ingredient in the tiresome factor is that the young are often deaf to the cultural references embedded in time-worn idioms. These can be thought quaint or old-worldy, or frankly, just inscrutable or weird-as. For example, I was trying to get away from an idle-chat kind of conversation with a sweet young thing in a book store, but she wasn't taking my cues. When she said something about wanting to find a new apartment but not having had much luck. I responded, as a pre-exit, 'Well, we live in hope, don't we?', with a downward intonational curve to discourage an answer, to which she replied, 'No, I don't live with Hope, I live with this Spanish guy who rages all night and is never there and always leaves a mess in the kitchen.' She probably went away and reported the conversation along the lines of: 'I was talking to this old biddy about wanting to move out and she just random like suggested I live with Hope, but I haven't seen Hope for years and, in any case, I'd already said I was sick of sharing, so it was all a bit what-the.'

～ 17 ～

Useful tits

....

In the past, we didn't always say what we meant, or mean what we said.

Being able to blur the boundaries, fudge the edges, and employ the odd white lie, fib or obfuscation helped us through many a hairy moment. Certainly, without such pragmatic space, politics as we knew it, and as we continue to know it, would have ceased to exist and martial law would have been invoked to keep the peace.

Fortunately, language obliged us by providing resources that were as subtle and complex as our needs required. We could say and mean when and how we wished, with relative impunity most of the time. 'As camp as a row of tents' allowed a speaker to speak their mind without exactly doing so.

Things are different now. Young people today dispense with convoluted comparative constructions or ironic reversals. They prefer the absolute and eschew the relative. If something's good, then it's the best. If it's bad, it's the worst. It reminds me somewhat of the extremes of adolescence, but I'm trying hard to be open-minded. It would seem that minimal is in, and in a big way, if that's not a contradiction in itself. Comparisons are clunky and cumbersome. Superlatives slip in comfortably. The relaxed style makes exaggeration acceptable, renders precision uncomfortable. The net effect may be monochrome, but no one seems to mind.

Language choices in the past seem to have had greater texture. They allowed for more than a simple gap between intention and utterance. Sometimes we would fall back on an expression and use it rather as we do the pragmatic cliché—a set piece that helps us say what we say without fully engaging or committing the self.

Set phrases and clichés, after all, are what they are because they're owned by everyone. No one who uses one claims originality. And maybe that's part of the point. We don't have the time or energy to commit to individuality all the time. I do find very tiresome the schoolteacher's unilateral condemnation of the cliché. There's an irony in the perennial put-down ('hackneyed')—I wish I'd had the courage at school to write next to the teacher's neat inked 'hackneyed' my own scrawly 'cliché!' But I didn't.

Language affords us some very convoluted ways of not saying what we mean, probably because the words are too stark or volatile. Yet, as the words unfold, we end up with something so graphic it's probably more shocking than it would have been had we said it simply and directly. The fact that many such utterances have hardened through use into conventionalised, even formulaic phrases, testifies to their one-time utility.

Take, for instance, the phrase 'about as useful as tits on a bull.' The image projected is so graphic that the irony of speaking of 'usefulness' is immediately apparent. It's the co-positioning of two unlikely elements that makes the concept absurd. So we have 'as useful as an arse on an elbow', 'as a bucket under a bull', 'as an ashtray on a motorbike'. They're all totally and undeniably useless, and rarely if ever used any more. Probably a good thing, too.

In these constructions, the comparison focuses on a practical tool, aid or implement that in any regular circumstance would be quite handy. However, at least one crucial component in the mix is changed, and it is this fact that reverses the putative utility value from high to zero. Consider 'as useful as a road map in the desert', 'as scooping water with a fishnet', 'as a chocolate teapot', 'as a screen door in a submarine', 'as a suede umbrella'. Again, all totally and undeniably useless—in fact, as useless as tits on a bull.

Oddly, one-leggedness seems to come in as the favourite for that single unsuitable ingredient. For example, 'as useful as a one-armed juggler', 'as a one-legged man at an arse-kicking contest', or 'a one-legged cat trying to bury a turd in a frozen lake'. Like the earlier examples, the graphic element is often heightened by an injection of taboo terms. Unsurprisingly, body parts associated with sexual and elimination processes are a favourite.

Part of the convoluted processing contained in these comparative statements hails from the fact that, prima facie, the comparison does seem to be a genuine comparison, at least when it starts off. Even the fact that it's constructed affirmatively—'as useful as', rather than negatively 'as useless as' —contributes to the initial innocuousness which is about to be overturned. That said, most if not all of the 'as useful as' phrases have been replaced with the more explicit 'as useless as'—for example, 'as useless as a dry thunderstorm'.

Whether it's a useful-as or useless-as construction, such language has slid out of popular use. Occasionally you'll meet an individual who has held onto a favourite one, making it part of their idiolect, with varying degrees of self-consciousness. In general, however, the colour and shared cultural knowledge that go into phrases like 'as friendly as a black snake' are absent.

Such phrases, while condemnatory in a convoluted kind of way, nonetheless maintained a quality of the affectionate, the good natured and the forgiving. The exact meaning depended, of course, on the context and the way the words were uttered. So, the tone counted. It allowed you to say in a jocular way what you may not have said more seriously. And where there was humour, its cut-and-dried nature granted its own kind of licence. Linguists who analyse workplace humour, especially that which characterises social banter with the boss, have shown that jocularity can sometimes allow you to get across messages that would otherwise be impossible to convey.

All told, the new style of communication is closer to what-you-see-is-what-you-get. The pragmatic space between thought/intention and expression has lessened. Inference is less convoluted, more straightforward. Less energy is required for the interpretation of meaning. 'Poor as a church mouse' is now 'poor as'. And perhaps with church attendance down and improved pest management, who can say anything has been lost?

～ 18 ～

Cockney code

IF FADING WORDS ARE EACH DESERVING of a bed in the hospice, then a whole slang, or subdialect, probably deserves its own ward, or even a wing, come to think of it. It'll depend on the building and the state of the finances at the time, of course. Sympathetic and enterprising Friends of the Hospice might have to stage a cake stall.

The dialect I'm alluding to is that quirky, coded insider-speech known as Cockney Rhyming Slang (CRS), whereby a common word can be replaced by the whole or abbreviated form of a well-known phrase which rhymes with that word. Some say CRS originated as long ago as the 16th century, flourishing among the seamen, soldiers, gypsies, Irish, Jews and other ethnic groups, who used to work on or live near London's East End docks.

From the 1850s, it developed as a secret language among the London underworld and crime culture that was closely associated with the East End. Like other secret coded languages, its purpose was to enable insiders to communicate with each other with impunity, a large part of which meant keeping sticky-beak outsiders out. As a spoken language without written records, it is difficult to research the origins of CRS, a fact compounded by the secrecy that surrounded its development.

For a long time, CRS has taken a kind of reverse-snob pride in its working- or under-class status. It was no doubt most vibrant when it was most functional—that is, when it was firmly embedded in its regional and socio-economic context where it served its primary social purposes. The villains of London's underworld used the code to confuse police and give snitches and other untrustworthy eavesdroppers the slip. You could not be too careful.

In structural terms, the slang can be explained through a two-step process, the first step being lost to view beneath the final or top layer. In the first place, a substitute phrase takes the place of the real or base word that is being replaced. In this way the base word is masked or hidden, and remains secret to all but those initiated in the code. The substituting phrase is chosen for its final sound which rhymes with the word being replaced. For example, the CRS for a 'look' is a 'butcher's hook', as in 'Take a butcher's hook at that!' There's no semantic echo whatever of the original; the only link or clue is in the rhyme (hook/look). If you know the code, you know the word being masked. If you don't, you don't. You have to know that 'whistle and flute' means 'suit'.

In the second phase, the final part (the rhyme) of the substituting phrase is dropped off and all that's left is the first part of the substitution. So CRS for 'look' is 'butcher's' ('Take a butcher's at that!'). This is the top layer, the one you hear and understand or not, depending on whether you are privy to the code. Some examples: 'Let's go for a Ruby' (= Let's go for a curry [Ruby Murray]); 'Hello me old china' (= Hello me old mate [china and plate]).

Once, you might have heard snippets of rhyming slang anywhere working class Britons had migrated. In Australia this demographic was once a high proportion of its people intake, especially of sponsored migration. It was once common, for instance, to hear about people being on their Pat (Pat Malone = own) or in the company of the cheese and kisses (the missus), or on the dog and bone (telephone) or the frog and toad (road). These days it's very unusual, and when it does occur it has a weird, idiosyncratic feel to it. I used to know a man who slipped CRS into his language knowing full well that it compromised people's understanding. He wanted them to ask what he meant, and when they did he'd tease a bit and withhold the information, and finally give it up. He'd constructed CRS as an integral part of his public persona, and you either accepted this and played along or found it irritating and kept your distance.

While there's no longer a functional basis to the secret code, the slang has migrated to wherever East Enders have gone. This emigration or dispersal has altered the conditions that were in place before, removing the need for secrecy. The old practical purpose has been replaced by identity issues and clearly now, in the diasporan varieties of CRS, clannishness and solidarity continue to nourish its speakers. Plenty of evidence exists that new vocabulary is being added all the time—for example, Schindler's List (= pissed); Becks and Posh (= nosh); Bristol and West (= chest); Trevor Sinclair (= nightmare); Uncle Ted (= bed); no 'ope (= soap). No doubt, too, rather like the dialectal variations among Sign, the language of the hearing-impaired, CRS displays dialectal differences—for instance, 'to have a Captain Cook' is to have a look, with Cook replacing the butcher's hook as the rhyme of choice among Australian CRS speakers. Other local variants have crept in, too, like, 'Don't forget your Reg Grundies' (undies).

Once the associations were working class, British, smart-arse, cockney with just a hint at a shabby disrespect for the law.

But with Australia's present ethnic diversity, these associations are increasingly odd. It's become a historically laminated cultural cameo, a little like aspects of Victorian or Edwardian England. It gets rolled out in the occasional film (*Lock, Stock and Two Smoking Barrels* had a bit; so too did the theme song for *The Italian Job*). You hear it a bit on television (*Minder, EastEnders*) where it's meant to lend some authenticity to a character or setting. In their different ways, mass popular culture, globalisation and shifting migration patterns have each contributed to the gradual mothballing of the once-vibrant rhyming slang.

Some words from CRS have entered the language ('on your Pat' may be one) and are increasingly used by people who are unaware of the origin, treating the phrase as an idiom. Another one its former functions was to act rather as a euphemism on topics considered best not talked about in certain company. But as the taboo on swearing has lessened, so too has the need to avoid words formerly considered offensive—'not for polite company' or *pas devant les enfants*. It's now rare to hear someone use and others understand 'horse's hoof' (poof) for homosexual, or 'snake's hiss' (piss) as in 'I'm busting for a snake's.'

Of course, nowadays, the code is not needed in the way that it once was. Having lost its functional base, CRS has become a quirky vestige of itself. With secrecy no longer its raison d'être, and with the passage of time, there's no diminution in the odd-and-quirky factor. There's even a somewhat incongruent, show-off flamboyance about using CRS among people you know don't get it, like the man I mentioned earlier. Websites now exist that are devoted to CRS: you can translate from CRS to English, or the reverse, or you can have whole texts, like emails, translated into CRS for free! Here's a sampling: 'airs and graces' (= braces); 'all afloat' (= coat); 'apples and pairs' (= stairs); 'pig's ear' (= beer); 'pitch and toss' (= boss); 'queen mum' (= bum); 'sausage and mash' (= cash); 'Vera Lynn' (= gin); 'weeping willow' (= pillow). Today it's ironic, to say the least, that the code that was developed for concealment purposes is now translated online and used to attract attention.

~ 19 ~

Odds and sods

....

Do we ever wonder what we used to say before the f-word took over?

Granted, it's no surprise to anyone that 'fuck' has become the general stand-in, all-purpose adjectival and adverbial intensifier, capable of deployment on all manner of topics, from one's impression of a newly released film to the ubiquity of dog droppings on the suburban footpath and the dire lack of transparency in government decision-making. The process has been aided by the amazing morphological flexibility of 'fuck', which is able to be stretched this way and that to serve any speaker, at any time, for any purpose. To this end we have, just for sampler's sake, 'fuckwit' (noun), 'fucking great' (adverb), 'a fucking mess' (adjective), 'fuck off' (verb), 'a fuck-of-a' (noun phrase).

But do we ever wonder what it was like before? Before this all-purpose, one-size-fits-all, four-wheel-drive kind of word spread so ubiquitously. One answer may be found in a ward of the Hospice of Fading Words. It's a specially reserved ward for two-element compounds that have been slowly making their way towards the hospice, knowing that on arrival they would receive a warm welcome.

Before the f-word took over as an intensifier of both good things and bad, we had, among other rhetorical devices, a rather simple mechanism—a compound noun phrase. This phrase was constituted of noun #1 + noun #2, like 'odds and sods', 'trouble and strife', 'ways and means', 'bits and pieces', 'fear and loathing', 'cock and bull'. The compounds are mostly nouns, but occasionally a set of verbs ('rant and rave') or adjectives ('thick and thin') moves in. While structurally simple (in fact, the words tend to be monosyllabic), the apparatus was so efficient that it slipped below the level of conscious awareness and, bottom line, it served us well.

While from a semantic perspective, these compounds all serve roughly a similar function—intensifying meaning—structurally they exhibit some slight variations. They fall into three categories. The first is an X + X structure where the two words are synonyms, so the effect of the duplication is simple intensity. Consider the cases of 'rant and rave', 'hue and cry', 'airs and graces', 'pride and joy', 'bells and whistles', for instance, where the mere bald fact of quantity (two instead of one) achieves the desired intensification.

The second category is for phrases that contain two words, let's say X + Y (in the sense of not only X but also Y), which are not synonymous, but through their use they suggest a larger scope than one by itself would have; and it is in the scope that the intensification is achieved. For example, 'born and bred' (not only born but also bred), 'hill and dale', (not only hills but also dales), 'thick and thin' (not only thick but also thin), 'flesh and blood' (not only flesh but also blood), 'piss and wind' (not only piss but also . . . well you follow the pattern, I'm sure).

The third category is a compound of two elements that may or may not exist alone, but when they do occur in combination, and in a certain set order, they have an intensity of meaning that is greater than a single word rough-synonym.

For example 'bibs and bobs' is larger than 'bits', 'odds and sods' is more random than 'oddments', 'nook and cranny' is more thorough than 'everywhere', 'flotsam and jetsam' is more descriptive than 'wreckage', 'kit and caboodle' is more complete than 'whole', 'spick and span' is more spotlessly gleaming than 'clean' or 'new', 'cut and dried' is more seamlessly complete than 'finished'.

More and more we are using fewer and fewer of these little two-element compounds. As they head towards the hospice, we lose both linguistic colour and imagination. Another instance of form losing out to function. Now you could argue that this is the way of the world. We don't live in a cook-your-own-stock kind of society any more. We buy stock in little packets at the supermarket. We struggle to do more in less time. We live in a world where everything is urgent. Time is money and money is everything. It seems absurd, but think on this: a two-element compound phrase takes longer to say and longer to write than a simple one-word synonym. Multiply this many times over, and why would anyone in a to-do-list-dominated world opt for a vivid ornate compound over a sleek little single-word equivalent?

Further, there is the transforming role of technology. A chasm yawns between a former, less technologically complex era (characterised by bibs and bobs, and odds and sods) and today's brave new world. Consider warfare for instance. We fight our wars from a distance today, action is taken through the press of a key. We call these actions 'clean' or 'smart' and any casualties are 'collateral', so it's not surprising that old expressions—like, to fight or resist 'tooth and nail', which suggests the ferocity and intensity of a wild animal—are, well, almost quaint. All that biting and scratching and ripping somehow doesn't gel with the post-mechanistic, uber-digital world of contemporary warfare. While we don't necessarily consciously think of animals fighting when we use 'tooth and nail' (e.g., 'she fought tooth and nail to get to university'), there is some residual association that makes the phrase feel old fashioned.

There are others, too, of this ilk that have an 'old technology' feel to them, such as 'home and hosed', meaning finished for the day in that the horses have been brought home and hosed down. People still bring their horses home at the end of the day and hose them down but, per capita of the population, less homing and hosing goes on that it once did. So a space has grown up between the original literal circumstance and the idiom.

The expression 'touch and go' is another that has been overtaken by technology. We can use it today without any conscious awareness that it comes from the days of horse-drawn carriages (there's those horses again) where, in the circumstance in which two vehicles approach each other from opposite directions and pass very close, even touching their wheels, no damage is done to either and both proceed safely ahead. Definitely old technology. 'Touch and go' used to mean a close call or a near-perilous situation, averted at the last moment. A definite case of the 'phew!' circumstance. But 'touch and go' has evolved slightly. Today it means unstable and unpredictable, such as a patient in hospital in critical condition. Perhaps this evolved meaning—where an expression over time, detaches itself from the original semantic uterine wall, and starts to grow legs—will keep 'touch and go' out of the hospice longer than 'tooth and nail'?

Then again, perhaps not. For the moment it's hard to know for certain. Only time will tell which of the two will be the first home and hosed.

PART IV

VICTIMS OF MODERN CANDOUR

∾ 20 ∾

Nudge nudge

I'VE HEARD IT SAID THAT THE generations that came after get fed up with the alleged solipsism of baby boomers. There are plenty of put-downs. Like, if you can remember the sixties, you weren't really there—meaning, I think, that if you dabbled in the drug scenes of the sixties then your memory would have been fried. An exaggeration of course. There was more than one way to participate in the sixties.

Indeed, it is perfectly possible to have gone through the postwar period as an adolescent and still have fairly accurate memories. One such person is Don Aitkin, who has written a book about his generation. His descriptions of how things used to be back then give us an inkling of how things were back then.

One domain that stands out is sexual mores. Referring to how they were introduced to sex education, both formally and informally, he writes:

There was no formal sex education for that generation. Their parents, products themselves of a strict and repressed generation, were quite unequal to the task. One of the girls remembers being presented with an orange-coloured book by her mother with the injunction 'Read this!' Another was given a diagram of the female reproductive system. One mother discreetly left a book nearby for her son . . . During their final year at school, the local cinema showed a film about sexual reproduction to which entry was permitted if parents had given their approval. Some were refused approval; others were too embarrassed to seek it.

Aitkin paints a picture of a tight-lipped, behind-closed-doors, head-in-the-sand culture. It's no wonder that expressions relating to sexuality were indirect and evasive. It stands to reason really. If people are uncomfortable with a topic, they look for ways of getting around it, rather than tackling it head on. If attitudes towards sexuality had been less convoluted, the result would have been neutral language.

One of the stories Aitkin tells is of a twelve-year-old boy sailing to Australia, presumably as a new immigrant, who one day up on deck was asked by his mother, 'Do you know about sex?' He thought the best thing to say was, 'Yes,' to which she responded, 'Thank God! I'll go down and have another drink.'

C.S. Lewis once commented that, 'we lack a language to comfortably talk about sex.' And he's right, of course, though the way he put it rather implies this was all an unfortunate accident. But it's far from being an accident. Rather, it's a giant conspiracy born of the taboo itself. Because the point of the original taboo was to make it difficult to raise such topics in public. There's no better way to enforce a taboo than to remove any polite options. Nothing in the cornucopia of sexual slang and vulgar expressions, or the clinical terms reserved for clinical contexts, serves to resource the polite, public venue. In fact, any explicit reference to sexuality reduces one to select from three bounded sources—the gutter, the nursery or the anatomy class—and each of these is unsatisfactory outside and beyond its own context. It's for this reason that English has such a healthy supply of evasive terms. Euphemisms come in very handy when nothing else will do but, almost by definition, they're all beating around the bush.

As a result, if you wanted to avoid the language of the gutter, nursery or anatomy class, you needed to draw on a term from the bank of euphemisms, a ready and rich supply of alternative ways of saying things that weren't supposed to be said. The language was often coy. It sent its message more by what wasn't said than by what was. Terms for sexual organs, functions, processes and products proliferated, but the coy reference to 'down there' was often sufficient. Anything outside of coy was likely to be over the top.

Maybe it was to mask embarrassment or perhaps to create a diversion through bravado. Whatever the reason, much of the language called on metaphor, making it indirect, if also graphic. But whether coy or graphic, the subtext was always, nudge nudge, wink wink, know what I mean? Know what I mean? The 'nudge nudge' line grew legs when an advertising campaign for a peanut chocolate bar, tried to inject a bit of sex into their marketing by rather randomly using 'Nudge nudge, wink wink' as their product tag line.

Much of the language was sexist and male-centric—like 'dip the wick' and 'dunk the love muscle'—and remains an enduring testimony to male one-track-mindedness. The female perspective was ignored completely. Just consider the agenda of those who came up with 'spunk', 'fox', 'goer', as much as with 'slag', 'slut', 'mole', 'thing'. None of this is surprising, of course, because whoever's in charge of the metaphors is usually in possession of the power.

Many of the old expressions for the act of sexual intercourse owe their origins to British slang. Like 'how's your father', used as a noun phrase, as in, 'I wouldn't go in the front room at the moment, I suspect your brother's having a bit of how's your father with his new girlfriend.' It roughly means casual sex, or rough and tumble, or a roll in the hay, or slap and tickle. The origins are murky. There seems to be some agreement about its associations with the British music-hall comedian Harry Tate (1872–1940), who was known to exclaim the phrase as a way of changing from an awkward subject. Subsequently, the phrase took on a life of its own, a stand-in like 'thingummy' or anything the speaker did not wish to name. Soon after, it became a euphemism for sexual activity.

There's another version of the 'how's your father?' story which dates from World War II, with English soldiers in France joking about expecting to be asked the question by an old French lady with fond memories of gallant young English soldiers over in the Great War.

Then again, the role of the father is sometimes seen differently—as the protector of his daughter's honour rather than the agent in the actual tawdry action. In this version, dating back to the Victorian era, any man with a daughter's virtue to safeguard was expected to go to extraordinary measures to protect her. Daughters were watched vigilantly and rarely let out of the house unchaperoned. On the rare occasions when a young girl might meet a suitor alone, the question 'How's your father?' served as a code to confirm that the coast was clear for a little, um, hanky-panky.

Not surprisingly, there was no shortage of synonyms for 'how's your father?' Consider 'get your leg over' as in 'Did you get your leg over with that girl last night?' Or 'giving the dog a bone'. They're the kind that enjoyed popularity with English comedians of *Carry On Gang* vintage. And for in-your-face-while-stepping-sideways, I'll never forget the two beefy blue-T-shirted removalists who carried the double bed up the front stairs of our new house, puffing when they got to the stairs, one of them stopping to ask my then husband, 'So, mate, where do you want the work bench?'

Descriptions of potential partners, objects of sexual desire, might be called 'hot to trot', 'hot for it', 'dishy', 'a looker'. You might go up to the pub to 'check out the talent', or see if there was anyone who 'caught your fancy'. Teenage boys carved up the world of the opposite sex into 'good girls' and 'nice girls'. Nice girls had the same thing on their mind as the boys— they didn't 'tease' or leave you 'high and dry'; if you were lucky, they'd 'put out' and you'd 'score'. There was no doubt which girls—the good or the nice—the boys preferred. There was plenty of time to find and marry a good girl. Meanwhile, it was all about being nice.

Teenagers going out were often told by brow-furrowed parents as a parting line—'Be good. If you can't be good, be careful.' But what did 'being careful' mean? The phrase was so broad, so blunt, that who knew what it entailed? Perhaps it was, choose a boy who's carrying a condom. Or make sure the creased-up condom that's been in his wallet since who-knows-when is good to go. Ironically, with close to zero sex education in terms of hard-core information, formal or informal, 'being careful' was a hit-and-miss affair that had in it more fingers-crossed prayer than common (or uncommon) sense.

As ultimately it was all about scoring (the girls might've said 'going all the way' or 'having a naughty'), the boys had their own system of measuring success in the fumbling encounters that were variously called 'necking', 'making out', 'pashing', 'carrying on', 'canoodling', 'fooling around', 'getting some hanky-panky'. Aitkin elaborates on how the count was made 'with the boy as the scorer, the girl the scoree': 'Two for a kiss, four for a feel of the breasts outside clothing, six ditto inside, eight for a feel lower down and outside, ten ditto inside; twelve was "Bingo!" '

Apparently such coded language enabled boys to boast the day after the night before by raising the number of fingers to indicate the score, to the chortling envy or hooting denial of their peers. Of course, exaggeration was the order of the day; a girl's reputation could be sullied in a second and the news would spread like a fire across dry leaves on a hot summer's day.

These days, it's different. What once was private is now public. The careful language is fast fading. Magazines sport nudity, give advice on oral sex and have totally removed the wink-and-nudge from sexuality. Take the brand of clothes called FCUK (French Connection United Kingdom) which always looks like 'fuck' till you realise it's 'fcuk'. Of course the dyslexic double take is no accident; it's programmed in, hot-wired into the take-home message which at the very least is a thumb-nosing to the old literacies.

There's a fashion label for a line of T-shirts called 'How's Ya Father?' This is an instance of the old language being imported into a contemporary brand, a postmodern appropriation that is typically tongue-in-cheek, a sure-stroked, knowledged, ironic, winking use of language that is confidently, cheekily intertextual. They have titillating slogans designed to forge a nexus between the personal and the political, and, supposedly, to make people think—that is, after they've parted with their money (they wouldn't want them thinking before then).

One line of undies in the same brand has on the back the words 'crack of dawn'. Say no more.

～ 21 ～

The fall

WHEN I WAS YOUNG AND ROMANTIC, I thought that the 'fall' of 'fall in love' and the 'fall' of 'fall pregnant' were the same kind of fall. An accidental-cum-spontaneous, head-over-heels, swept-off-your-feet kind of phenomenon over which one had little control and for which one could not be held responsible.

Think about those images for a moment—being head over heels, being swept along, fall down. What they share is an absence—an absence of agency. They suggest a power greater than oneself. One is smitten, one is afflicted. The action comes from outside, envelopes you and takes you along with it. It's as if the universe intervenes, Cupid sends his arrows, mere mortals have to go with the flow, powerless to dodge or affect the direction of fate. Sigh.

Of course, there's an age when you might think such things, just as there's an age when you read *Alice in Wonderland* or enjoy ferris wheels, or sliding down sand dunes. Once the age for such past-times has passed, they become the past, able to be relived or revisited only through the imagination. Nonetheless, what is not yet lost for me is a vestige of fascination for this verb 'fall'.

'Falling', as in 'falling pregnant'—a term apparently more prevalent in the English of the United Kingdom and Australia than other varieties—bespeaks an era predating reliable contraception. And contraception, as has often been said, is arguably the most important scientific development of the 20th century, at least from a sociological point of view. It changed everything. Back then, pregnancy, or rather avoiding it, would have brought to mind words like 'roulette'—in fact the term 'Vatican roulette' was prevalent because of the papal position on birth control and abortion. Back then, many women would have rued, rather than celebrated, the day when the bun in the oven was verifiably undeniable.

In other words, this use of 'fall' seems a logical sibling of 'befall' and a first cousin of 'bemoan'. The clinical term 'gravid', meaning pregnant, is a direct borrowing from Latin. Obstetricians refer to a woman having a first-time pregnancy as a 'primagravid', which when I first heard it, at the obstetrician's, applied to me, sounded very serious indeed. Italian has *la gravidenza*, 'the pregnant woman'. The original Latin is '*gravis*', meaning burdened or heavy, and while few of us are light on our feet by the third trimester, I would venture here to suggest that the stated burden is as much metaphorical (the burden of uncontrolled fertility) as literal (the weight of the bundle-of-joy *in utero*). Perhaps, 'falling pregnant' is not such a weird phrase after all, when you recall that less than fifty years ago it was not uncommon for people to refer to being 'under the doctor'.

Perhaps the falling of 'fall pregnant' alludes to Eve's alleged tempting of Adam. I say 'alleged' because what we have is his-story—a very one-sided version of goings-on in Eden for which women have been paying heavy dues ever since. In fact, 'falling pregnant' and becoming 'a fallen woman' seem congenitally linked. One has to hope that, at the very least, the apple at the centre of the scandal was juicy, though even so, for those few moments of sensuality the price tag seems ludicrous.

Certainly falling, especially when firmed up into a noun and given a capital, the Fall, sparks the imagination and triggers allusions to various archetypal events. There's the Christian fall from grace, as represented by the events in the Garden of Eden and perpetuated through the notion of Original Sin. Albert Camus' *The Fall* and Arthur Miller's *After the Fall* refer to different kinds of falls, but they're both, in their own way, metaphorical. We talk of the fall of Troy or of Paris or of Berlin, as if the moment of capitulation to an invading enemy is itself a fall, and perhaps it is as literal as it is metaphorical. We think of empires and dynasties and Alan Bond as having a rise and a fall.

When the Berlin Wall came down in 1989, and along with it the communist world, it was referred to as 'a fall'. This suggestion of a spontaneous collapse is fallacious not only because the wall was actively dismantled, but also because the political processes that contributed to the so-called fall had been ongoing for more than half a century. In any case, the issues of agency and responsibility are once again notable for their absence. Somehow we're attracted to the romantic notion of the spontaneous combustion of 'fall'.

Certainly in the days before women could manage their fertility, falling into 'the family way' connoted passivity and powerlessness. It has to be significant that, more recently, 'fall pregnant' is making the shift to 'become pregnant'—a trend supported by a web search which yields 23,600 for 'fall' and 781,000 hits for 'become' when each is attached to 'pregnant'. It's a reflection of the increasing agency that a woman has over her body that a major event like 'pregnancy' is less associated with 'falling'.

But notwithstanding these figures, 'fall' is not entirely lost. Its semantic scope has shifted somewhat so that it would appear that women today do not only use 'fall' when the condition of pregnancy is unwanted. Those women struggling with infertility—an increasing number due apparently to older primagravids—also use the 'fall' verb. Perhaps the roulette is still at work, making the transition to motherhood easy for some, difficult for others, with luck being the consistent ingredient in the mix. Those women who are want-to-be mothers are as frustrated by the hit-and-miss factor in conception as were their sisters—barefoot, pregnant and in the kitchen—of previous generations.

A theory exists that the origin of 'falling pregnant' is bedded (sorry) in the Victorian century. Specifically, a pregnant woman's body, firmly constrained as it would have been within the suffocatingly tight undergarments of the day, contributed dramatically to the likelihood of her fainting—which is, after all, a kind of falling.

Then again, since about 1300, English has exhibited a metaphoric pattern of 'fall' + (some kind of) condition. Consider 'fall ill', 'fall foul of', 'fall on hard times', 'fall out of favour', 'fall prey to', 'fall out with', 'fall from grace', 'fall asleep', 'fall on your sword'.

And lest we fall for the misconception that 'fall' is always in the context of something unpleasant or unwanted, consider 'fall into place', 'fall in line', 'fall on your feet' and, of course, 'windfall'. Perhaps a more thoroughly consistent explanation would point to the sense underpinning falling as an unexpected turn of events—from an accidental pregnancy to a lucky Lotto number.

But because of the intimate link between pregnancy and sexuality, it's not unexpected that a host of euphemisms would have grown up as ways of expressing 'being with child'. The Victorians were in their element here: 'in the family way', 'expecting', 'a lady in waiting', 'in an interesting condition'.

Gestation was (and still is) perceived as a journey with terms like 'six months gone', 'two months along', 'three weeks left to go'. For those unhappy accidents, 'knocked up' or 'in a fix' said it all, with the former now available, as is so much else, on a T-shirt. In the southern states of the United States, a water well sometimes represents pregnancy—'drink out of the well'—and a baby almost full-term is 'on the road'.

You no longer hear of the 'bun in the oven'—that old, earthy expression for being pregnant, usually though not necessarily for an unplanned pregnancy. The metaphor of the oven as uterus, cooking something that with time will emerge in a different form, is easy to grasp. Related, but slightly more colloquial, is the much older 'up the duff', which has an interesting history. It starts with the word 'pudding' as a friendly euphemism for 'penis'. 'Dough' is an alternative word for pudding and 'duff' is a variant of 'dough', both in written form and pronunciation. 'Up the duff', as well as 'in the pudding club' were the evolved outcomes of this lexical development, in use in England by 1840.

Of course, if we're looking for a prime example of a text that euphemises sexuality, we might turn to the Bible, that classic textbook resource of avoidances. We have 'thigh' and/or 'loins' for genitals, both male and female (Genesis 24:2, Numbers 5:22) which, you might say, identifies by general vicinity, as does 'marriage bed' (Hebrews 13:4) for the sexual act, and 'lie with' (Leviticus 18:22). I remember being very confused about the sleeping arrangements that obtained between Ruth and Boaz. She started out sleeping, slave-like, at the end of his bed, but ended up, as you do perhaps, in the 'lie with' position, which, given his power over her, he wouldn't get away with in today's workforce. But things were different then—they didn't have posters on the wall defining the diverse subtle trajectories of sexual harassment. Boaz would have been less constrained.

The tradition of euphemising pregnancy continues, more for humour than for camouflage, even when the taboo of speaking of such matters has long been lifted. Some euphemisms for being pregnant are: 'renting out the guest room'; 'having a three-month pass for the morning porcelain express'; a nice military image—'secured a beachhead on the shores of the Uterine Sea'; and one that alludes both to the unplanned nature of the event and our current litigious bent, 'Suing Trojan'.

All this pussyfooting around sex and pregnancy. It's been savaged to the point of obliteration by the new conventions of modern candour. Now that the affluent West has been liberated from the tyranny of fertility, falling is no longer a matter of, well, falling. There's no excuse for it to be accidental. Now we might hear of couples who are 'trying'—and this means they're focusing on getting a bun in the oven or are enrolled in a fertility-support program. One man I spoke to about how pregnancy is perceived now, at least in middle-class circles, spoke rapturously of pregnancy as of some exotic condition that was prized and much sought after. Like an imported foreign car. 'I don't know any woman who doesn't want to have a baby,' he said. We have the term 'yummy mummy' for a young woman, ostentatiously pregnant or with a child or young children, and the more cynical 'slummy mummy'. An even more contemporary term, especially among young men talking among themselves, is the designation MILF for 'mother I'd like to fuck', arguably a kind of aberrant, albeit much nicer, spin-off from 'motherfucker'.

Pregnant women today don't hide behind modest smocks. They display their protruding belly with pride. They welcome the public's gaze, and when it's in-your-face, well, they get what they're asking for. Recognition that they're pregnant. It seems even to be a status symbol, a marker of affluence—'Hey! Look at me. I have a partner. I'm rich enough to take time out to do the family thing. I don't have child-care issues. Check this out, it's so happening.' No doubt this view is skewed by class considerations; no doubt there are plenty of occasions where accidents are still feared and fretted over. Nonetheless, in that tiny demographic of first-world, middle-class women, the sisters have come a long way. An informant tells me that 'motherhood is the new "it"'. An obviously pregnant woman says: 'Hey, I've got a man (maybe). I've got enough money. I am fertile. I'm pregnant. Guess what?—you're not! You might have cash, a guy, you may even be fertile, but you are not pregnant—I am.' Does it also say, 'Look, I've decided what direction my life is going to take, I'm not just aimlessly wandering, spending, working, marking time.' It's a pity, I think, that so many different significances are being invited. You're pregnant. Great. Get on with it.

The way young women talk so openly about pregnancy is a dramatic shift in itself. Here's one young woman, 'Beth', opening her heart, blog-style, talking about being pregnant:

> I like 'expecting' as a euphemism for pregnant . . . it
> sounds gentle, delicate, hopeful. I like the way that when
> you say it out loud the combination of the second and
> third syllables force your lips into a smile. 'Pregnant'
> seems to include so many things—how you happened to
> wind up pregnant, the sickness and cramps and swelling,
> the pain and struggle of labor. 'Expecting' seems to
> exclude those things and leave only the idea of the baby,
> as if you would simply sit quietly in your newly painted
> nursery and the baby would appear in your arms, new and

fresh and unspoiled. I like the focus on the waiting, the anticipation . . . how wrapped up in the waiting and yourself you become, how your whole life seems to focus on this one thing, how no matter what else you are doing you are always, always expecting.

And here are some responses to this reverie:

'It does have a nice ring.'

'That's rather poetic.'

'I feel like I'm "expecting" a pizza when I hear that.'

'It's a very genteel way of saying it.'

'Awww.'

'My grandmother STILL calls it "with child". I think I'll mess with her and wear the shirt that says "knocked up".'

'It's like being "next". Didn't some comedian do a routine on that? Being next is better than being first. The first guy in line is already at the window and getting his movie tickets or talking to the bank teller, so he's already out of the picture. But the guy who is next, he's the guy everyone wants to be. Next.'

'I know what you mean. Somehow "pregnant" screams out, "Look! We 'did' it!" Even to your mom and dad . . .'

'I just said the word expecting five times and my lips DID form the little smile. If I'm in an uncomfortable social situation, I'll just say "expecting" and make the little smile.'

'It reminds me of that weird man in downtown Dallas who always walked around mumbling "Well, what do you EXPECT, anyway?" '

'Expecting is kind of like being engaged. One of those beautiful, in between times where you don't really know what's coming but you know it's something good.'

'More poetic than "knocked up".'

'"Expecting" makes it sound like you know what you're in for. I kid . . . it was lovely and mushy and warm and fuzzy. You rock pregnant lady.'

'You know when *I Love Lucy* had a baby? They couldn't even use the word pregnant . . . The episode was called 'Lucy is enciente'. Sounds sexy, huh?'

'Delicate, feminine, and pleasing to the ear as "expecting" may sound, I plan to refer to myself as "preggies" [preggers?].'

'Ha! When you said "you would simply sit quietly in your newly painted nursery and the baby would appear in your arms" I thought to myself, yea, this is a "first born" cause there is nothing, no nothing at all that is going to even resemble THAT remark . . . Where did you get those lovely rose-shaded glasses?'

This casual, enjoyable way in which young women discuss pregnancy, in the intimate-cum-public venue of an internet diary, betrays none of the angst, shame, fear or trepidation that unwanted pregnancies typically triggered a few generations ago. Then, the 'fall' of 'falling pregnant' was the same 'fall' as of 'downfall'.

If 'fall' has largely fallen by the wayside, it's because it bears so little relationship anymore to social practice. In our compressed, commodified, packaged, outsourced, controlled and controlling world, fertility is firmly in the realm of the manageable, rather than the magical. Falling is now not at all the right term or action. Getting pregnant is often the end result of a lot of diverse kinds of planning: refinancing the mortgage, determining the desired gap between siblings; balancing demands of family and career; deciding when the carpets should go in, or how long to delay the much-needed upholstering. And at the extreme end of planning, there's all the energy expended in fertility treatments, minimally thermometers, maximally IVF.

Perhaps it's been left to 'falling in love' to maintain the mystique of the fall. This is not to say, either, that meeting the right person is purely a matter of chance. After all, there's a lot that can be done in the way of massaging Cupid's arrows—with dating agencies, internet introductions, blind date set-ups by mutual friends, speed dating and all the rest. Nonetheless, the role of serendipity is not entirely bypassed, and for this reason alone, 'fall' as in falling in love may last a little longer than 'falling pregnant'.

～ 22 ～

Oblique

AND SO, FROM SEX AND THE makings of new life, to dying and death.

Like much of the old lexicon of pregnancy and fertility, many of the old words associated with death and dying are finding a comfortable sojourn in our Hospice of Fading Words. They would not even have to dress euphemistically, or come disguised as something else, because they're likely to be accepted at face value. After all, at a hospice there's little pretence. It's palliative and honest, with that quality of transparency that an old advertisement for glass used to claim for its product: what you see is what you get. A kind of unconditional love in the tradition of earthmothering. Well, that may be an idealised picture, but I'm sticking to it as a model of best practice.

Our death-and-dying words may even share a ward, or perhaps an adjoining ward, with the sexually associated words. I'd wager that they'd feel rather at home there, in close proximity. You see, were I to posit that, in some regards, death has much in common with sex, I'd be on well-established ground.

Certainly, back in the Renaissance, the link between sexuality and death was widely accepted. People believed that sexual activity drained essential vitality away from the life forces and brought one closer to death's door. For a taste of this, flip open a John Donne anthology, or that of one of his metaphysical brethren. We're likely to find that the fly, along with the flickering candle and a host of other devices, symbolised life's brevity, fragility, and the price paid for unbridled sexuality. Generally speaking, lust was one's undoing. After all, orgasm was 'the little death'.

This mindset is not locked away behind castle turrets. Even four centuries after the Renaissance, hints of such meanings intertextualise their way into other art forms, including popular culture. Take the film, *The Fly*, in which an insect and a man fuse transgenically. Here the twin Renaissance motifs of sexuality and mortality are never far from conscious awareness. Probably a case of *plus ca change, plus ca change pas.*

But it is not only for these reasons that death words and sex words may find compatibility in the hospice. It is also because, historically, both these topics have developed their own taboos, at least in public talk. Until the last half-century, for both, it's all behind-closed-doors and *pas devant les enfants.* Indeed, death and sex words might find a lot to chat about at the hospice.

The power of a taboo can be measured by the number of euphemisms it inspires. According to one authoritative source there are more than two and a half thousand alternative terms in English for the male and female genitalia, all of them ways of referring, without explicitly naming, the said phenomenon/a. From our ho-hum liberated standpoint, six years into the third millennium, such expended energy does seem like a lot of fuss about very little.

In the 1950s and '60s death was not talked about openly and frankly. In fact, it wasn't talked about at all. If you didn't belong to a medical or undertaking family, you could go through childhood without ever hearing about it. Children often did not attend funerals or, if they did, their presence was fleeting and marginal. 'Grandma's with God now' was more often than not the length and breadth of it. Especially when a child died, a not uncommon occurrence given the then childhood diseases and infant mortality rates, the hush-hush approach was de rigueur, particularly for siblings, who were supposed simply to forget that there was once a little brother and there no longer is.

My parents were country GPs and I often went on rides with them when they did house calls in outlying districts. Mostly, I'd wait in the car outside or come in and be given a biscuit and some lemonade and be told I was cute or a chip off the old block, about which I had no idea but linked it to chips on shoulders, which were equally obtuse.

One time I recall quite a long trip to a place I'd never seen before. It was a biggish building, hidden by a long drive of overgrown bush. I imagine now it was some kind of convalescent home or perhaps a hospice, though that word was not used back then. Why are we here, I asked. 'I've come to say goodbye to a very brave young woman.' I knew enough about coded language to know no more questions were askable, but over some considerable years I worked it out. A young woman patient, who'd become very dear to my parents, died of breast cancer after a heroic battle.

There was a limited repertoire for talking about sickness, dying and death. An elderly person might be referred to as 'feeling poorly', or 'taken to bed', or 'bed-ridden', or 'doesn't get about much any more'. Sometimes she's had 'a turn' and she's 'under the doctor'. I heard a lot about 'turns' as a child and couldn't figure out what they meant, apart from being not-good. If you were dizzy and felt you were turning around, giddy, was that a turn? Or did you have a turn when it was your turn, so who was it that was keeping score? These things worried me. All I could work out was that if a 'turn' was mentioned, some elderly person had taken to their bed for a while and you'd likely not see them till they 'got over' their turn, if they did. Then it'd be someone else's turn.

We know more now, and we know it explicitly. We're far more likely to hear a response like this: 'Thank you for asking, yes, it was a stroke, he's partially paralysed down the left side, they're moving him to a rehabilitation hospital next week, and we're hopeful he'll recover most of the movement he's presently lost. We've set up a roster of family and friends to visit him around the clock. Would you like to be included?'

And if sickness and dying were euphemised, death took the cake. One of the Hallmark-style condolence cards I received when my mother died said, in big flowery pink letters, and with non-sensical capitals, 'She is Just Away'. The equally flowery writing on the inside suggested I take consolation in the thought of the reunion awaiting me when I too would also be 'away' and so Mum and I could 'be away' together, reunited, as it were, in 'another place'. My first thought, when I worked out what the card was not saying was, wait! 'Away' is not very precise. Mum and I can't read maps. What if I can't find her?

Being 'just away' is one of many such expressions. Others are 'passing on', 'passing away', 'passing over', 'crossing over', 'meeting your maker', 'joining Grandma', 'shuffling off this mortal coil', 'departing this life', 'returning to dust', going to the 'great beyond' or the 'big happy hunting ground' in the sky. Medical staff had their own set of euphemisms: 'We lost him'; 'He slipped away peacefully'; or even more elliptically, 'We did everything we could.' No one, it seems, dies in writhing pain. And if they do, it gets subsumed into the 'peaceful release'.

Metaphors abound. You could: 'cash in your chips' (gambling), 'check out' (hotel), 'have a good innings' (cricket), 'have your three score and ten' (biblical). You could also 'bite the dust', 'buy the farm', 'go out feet first' (or 'toes up'), 'push up daisies', 'go out in a blaze of glory', 'die in the harness'. If more-or-less natural death was hush-hushed into sideways whispers, imagine suicide. The phrase 'to kick the bucket', according to one theory, refers to suicide by hanging, although another theory relates the term more to the practice of animal slaughter. Either way, it means to die and to do so noisily.

We were, and still are to some extent, so fearful of death that we use euphemism to help us talk about it. Another quite antithetical device for managing talk about death is to use dysphemism—where we use crude, irreverent slang. Here, instead of masking our discomfort in euphemism, we do so in humour—so we have 'to croak', 'cark it', 'give up the ghost', 'drop dead', 'snuff it', 'pop off', 'conk'. This is typical of the in-house slang of people who confront death uncomfortably and frequently, like firemen or rescue workers, the culture of dysphemism in effect becoming an accepted coping strategy.

Death, and everything in terms of the demise of health that leads up to death, ain't what it used to be. And the major change is that we know more now. Death is less shrouded in mystery; and if the mystery is gone, so is the mystique. And all because we know more. When I say 'we', I refer in the first place to the profession of doctors, and all the related branches and services that call themselves in some ways medical—like the medical research community, nurses and the pharmaceutical professions, too. They know more; they're taught more; they're exposed to more; they're engaged (or are expected to be engaged) in life-long professional development. They're less reluctant to refer a patient on to a specialist now because they're more willing to admit to the fact that the scope of medical knowledge is presently too wide for one practitioner to know it all, to have it all in their head. 'Referring on' is no longer an indictment of the referring doctor, but an acknowledgement of that doctor's awareness of the parameters and (justifiable) limitations of their expertise. It's a great thing to know that you don't know; it's the first step towards finding out *what* you don't know.

Yes, we know more. My second 'we' refers to we the patients. We know more. And it's not old wives' tales (though some of these have turned out to be quite on the money). There's more on the topic on TV, radio, magazines and, of course, the internet. Whatever affliction you have the misfortune to acquire, there'll be a bunch of self-help books to coach you through to a cure; and if a cure proves elusive, then to give you a quality-of-life solution and help you manage the inevitable. Second only to cookbooks, self-help as a publishing category is a world-wide success. (The pièce de résistance is a self-helpy kind of book that also contains recipes, like *French Women Don't Get Fat*). Clearly, people want to know and they want the means to find out.

We expect to be told more. We expect to be treated as though we have the right to know more. We expect to participate in the decision-making about treatment options. We're all into 'informed consent'. We can't agree to anything if we don't have the information; informed consent is the doctor's best insurance against the dreaded L-word—and I don't mean 'lesbian'.

It wasn't always like this. Generally we used to ask no questions and trust the doctor. Seeking a second opinion was not the done thing, and if you did so, you did it secretly. My old GP father used to tell an anecdote that captures this don't-ask-questions-doctor-knows-best beautifully. A patient of his had gone into hospital for an operation—something small and elective. Everything went well. However, as she was being wheeled out of theatre, one of the heavy swinging theatre doors swung back and hit her in the chest. While she was in recovery a nurse examined her to see the extent of the bruising that may have occurred because of the collision with the door. And that was how they came to find a sizeable lump in one breast As soon as the woman gained consciousness from the anaesthetic, her doctor told her what had happened and how worried he was about what the lump might signify. He recommended an operation. She only said one word. 'When?'

The Grim Reaper is so passé now. It's just not an image of death we can relate to anymore—the hooded skeleton, the scythe, the picking off of people apparently at random. The mystery and mystique of death—the less you know the more random and unexplained it seems. The desperate human need to explain horrific events. Solution? Personification! And let's face it, personifying death has had a good innings, but it's all over now.

The Grim Reaper today is as ludicrous as Santa is jolly. He made an ugly one-off appearance at the outbreak of the AIDS epidemic in Australia in 1987. In that year, a nationwide TV advertisement had him, hooded as ever, wielding a bowling ball in a bowling alley, indiscriminately felling husbands, wives, children, picking them off, without fear or favour. The ad announced that 50,000 Australians might already be infected and this figure would continue to rise. While the campaign was said to be the most successful ever launched in Australia, my memory of it is different. It certainly aroused fear, and not surprisingly so, for the message was unambiguous: AIDS can get anyone, look out! Death does not discriminate.

This was misleading because, at that time, gay men were the single most affected group, and this may have contributed to the equivalence the public drew between the Reaper and homosexual acts. Many people were less fearful than they were outraged by the manipulation. After all, the Grim Reaper may have been appropriate in the past in times of plague when little was understood about the spread of infection, but the icon was certainly at odds with a modern, pluralist, secular, rationalist, science-respecting society that reacted fiercely to scare tactics. In any case, did anyone younger than a baby boomer know the verb 'to reap', or where (outside the regional farm supplies depot) you'd most likely find a scythe?

We know how to find out more now, too. These days you're likely to have a reasonable idea of what's ailing you before you go to the doctor. A friend of mine complained that she couldn't sleep at night because of the sensation of ants crawling under her skin. 'Yuk,' I said, 'Have you googled it?' She did, and before going to the doctor she had a pretty good idea what she might have. With over 44,000 hits, at least she knew it wasn't her imagination. She wasn't the only one and she wasn't going mad. She preferred menopause to diabetes, but hey, this isn't a choose-your-own adventure.

To sum up then, we do death differently now and therefore it's no surprise that we talk about it differently. First, there's less death around. As our financial advisers are continually telling us, we're lasting longer than our superannuation is. At the other end of the three-score-and-ten-or-more, there's less infant mortality, fewer deaths in childbirth, fewer deaths from fatal infectious diseases. There's even less death in war. The only statistic that is rising is death by suicide, and this is still stigmatised and therefore not openly discussed.

Second, we're more secular. We live less in awe and faith;

we give more weight to the rational and the scientific. We don't skirt around the topic of death lest we seem to be inviting the Grim Reaper in for coffee.

Third, we live in an age of plain and candid speaking. Euphemism, flowery language, indirect and oblique approaches are not how it's done anymore. Even eulogies give a more rounded version of the dearly departed, a warts-and-all approach seemingly far more realistic and appealing. Today death is spoken about, even planned for: you can take out a funeral plan, buy a plot with a view, pay now, die later. For all these reasons, the verbal management of demise and death have an altogether different tenor than they had in yesteryear.

∿ 23 ∿

Consumption, hysteria, ticker and coming out

ONE COULD MOUNT A VERY COGENT argument in favour of modern candour in language. Certainly, there is much about contemporary ways of communicating that is refreshingly frank, direct, efficient and honest. Even conceding that, however, it's possible to have the odd tweak of a nostalgic yearning for some irreplaceable items from the often oblique lexicon of yesteryear. I'll explore just four here.

The first of these is 'consumption'. Now we know from opera that the most tragic and catastrophic events can be rendered exquisitely in music and song. And when Nicole Kidman's character Satine in *Moulin Rouge* starts her demise, hinted at in the coughed-up bloody phlegm, we know she'll end up dying romantically in her lover's arms. A moment's thought would temper the tragedy—after all, things could be worse; for instance, she could have languished to her end abandoned and alone.

Back then, tuberculosis (TB) was called 'consumption', apparently because of the inevitable, slow, wasting-away death, whereby one was apparently 'consumed' by the disease. And you can appreciate why there might be a good deal of associated spin—typically, fear of infection generates taboos around disease and these taboos become realised in language. It seems absurd from the hindsight of today, with our antibiotics and quarantine procedures, but somehow TB was construed and constructed as almost glamorous. Considered the purview of delicate young women, writers and artists, consumption was believed more likely to attack those blessed with a refined sensibility. There's perhaps something of the same misunderstanding surrounding today's chronic fatigue.

Consider Ralph in Henry James' *The Portrait of a Lady* and characters in Thomas Mann's *The Magic Mountain* going off to warmer climes such as the Riviera around the Mediterranean, or to a secluded sanitarium atop a pristine Swiss mountain. Even the poet Keats—who, ironically, was himself to die of the disease—perpetuated the myth of the feverish romantic in 'La Belle Dame Sans Merci'. The poem's heroic knight-at-arms is constructed as sick with (consumed by?) love: he is 'alone and palely loitering', with 'anguish moist and fever dew', and other symptomology more closely aligned with TB than unrequited passion. Though come to think of it, there's no reason why you can't be simultaneously consumptive *and* lovelorn, is there?

The truth of the matter is that while the refined classes (read people of means) were able, precisely because of those means, to last longer, or to waste away more slowly (and certainly more comfortably), TB was really the scourge of the poor. Thriving in conditions of poverty, like overcrowding and poor hygiene, it accounted for the 19th century's dreadful mortality statistics—110,000 reported cases of the disease per annum in Britain alone. Certainly the Industrial Revolution dramatically changed the world, arguably for its ultimate betterment, but it did so on the backs of generations of working-class wretchedness, to whom TB offered the Grim Reaper as constant companion.

Today, in the First World at least, we know more about the disease, we have weapons with which to fight it from early diagnosis to treatment, and we are less frightened of its power. So we're able to call it by its name, though it might be argued that the abbreviation 'TB', in some small way, continues the euphemistic tradition of avoiding calling a spade a spade. 'Tuberculosis' sounds a whole lot more serious than TB. But then you don't see the 'Fried' in KFC anymore, either.

And anyway, if 'consumption' continues to be used as a word in the well-heeled English-speaking West, it definitely has more to do with the material-cum-mental disease of 'gotta have the latest', for which retail therapy may be less the solution than the problem.

Of course, 'consumption' is not alone as a name for a disease characterised by an avoidant imprecision, somehow designed to take the edge off the harshness. When was the last time you heard someone referred to as having 'the vapours' or 'hysteria'? Until relatively recently, such words have long been a major means of fobbing women off. Whenever some superior male physician, often *mit* monocle, had no satis-factory answer for a set of female-presenting symptoms, and was disinclined (for this often went hand in glove with the fob-off) to use those awful words 'I don't know', then 'hysteria' of one kind or another was a mightily convenient one-size-fits-most catch-all. It helps, too, that 'hysteria' comes from the Greek *hysterikos*, 'of the womb', and hey, funny that, men don't have one of them.

Other medical problems of a mental or emotional nature were 'lethargy', 'melancholy' and 'frenzy'. Such ailments were considered the province of women who, in the minds of a male-dominated medical fraternity, were constructed as differ-ent (read deviant) from the (masculine) norm. And if you start with the premise that the masculine norm is rational, then any deviance from this is easily pronounced as irrational.

Let's look a little closer at this 'hysteria'. Before it had this name, it was known as 'Fits of the Mother' (or just 'The Mother' for short), believed to be caused by the womb (what else?) being pushed upwards by malign humours from below (where else?). This, of course, was before the advent of feminine hygiene products. It must have seemed logical then that the womb needed to be constricted so as to restrain those nasty humours. Such restraint was imposed by applying the inward skin of a silver eel on the lower belly of the woman and fastening it behind, on her back, presumably pulled tight, to create the required constriction. As the eel skin dried it tightened further, increasing the patient's discomfort for a span of five days, after which it was removed, causing (hey presto!) instant relief that was no doubt deemed to be the ailment's remedy.

At the same time, the woman was given some nasty medicine to smell (as a kind of shock treatment) and some white wine to consume. The wine was filtered through horse dung produced by an uncastrated stallion, presumably for the restorative powers attributed to testosterone. Shocks all round, I'd say. Nothing like unbridled maleness to correct a female condition.

Without doubt, the subtext of these world views is largely misogynistic. Take, for example, another remedy, a kind of amulet that offered another male-based antidote to female medical problems. This amounted to a pair of fox's testicles, dried and kept in a bag, to be hung around the woman's neck, so that the bag lined up with the woman's navel and womb, enabling the fox's auspicious privates to influence by propinquity. Someone's obsessed and it's not the woman.

Through the Victorian Age, words like 'hysteria', 'vapours' and 'nerves' continued to be the words used to describe episodes of female depression and malaise, perceived by the outside world to be tiresomely recurrent. Today, such clearly hormonally based fluctuations in female health might be attributed to premenstrual syndrome, menstrual discomfort, postnatal depression or menopause. We're too politically correct even to name the nasty female vapours, for which in any case we now have any number of deterrent sprays. And eel wrapping, let praise be given, has gone the way of stallion dung.

In 'consumption' and 'hysteria' we have words that used to be common labels to describe various real and apparent medical conditions, and they probably began in the way doctors spoke to and about patients. However, there are also changes in the way patients talk to doctors. Indeed, there have been massive changes in the kind of discourse that goes on in medical consultation rooms. We simply don't talk to the doctor the way we used to, no doubt because our relationship with the doctor is altogether different from in the past.

Doctors once had a much more holistic perception of their patients. The doctor likely knew the immediate family of the patient, something of the patient's life and context. They knew what work you did, what hours you kept, and maybe something of your concerns, fears, anxieties and hang-ups.

Not any more. I submit that it all started to change when doctors stopped doing house calls, stopped taking calls after hours and stopped sending out monthly accounts. From then on, whereas once you were a person who went to visit your doctor with an infected throat, now you're an infected throat that goes to get a doctor's script.

There once was trust. You trusted that your doctor had the answers, no matter what the question was. You would never have considered seeking a second opinion, and if by chance you did, you would have done it clandestinely. The doctor had expertise that should not be questioned. The TV program called *Father Knows Best* could have had a twin called *Doctor Knows Best*.

One aspect of the old way of talking to your doctor reflected the asymmetry of the relationship. He was the doctor (it was usually a 'he') and he had the knowledge. This meant he had the power. You were the trusting patient come for some relief. The relationship echoed a parent–child connection, and for this reason it's not surprising that the language in part was infantalising. The patient, for instance, tended to use deflecting slang for parts of the body, terms we hear much less these days. Your 'ticker' was your heart; your 'noggin' was your head or skull; your 'grey cells' meant your brain; your 'pegs' were your legs; 'the plumbing' or 'water-works' referred to the urinary system; 'women's business' was largely gynaecological; 'nuts' and 'balls' were slang for testicles; 'bag' meant scrotum; 'gob' meant mouth; 'guts' were intestines; 'gut' was stomach; and 'bellybutton' was the navel. Even a grown man might use bellybutton with his doctor.

These days we're far more likely to use the correct name for the body part we're dealing with. This is partly because the patient *qua* patient is now entitled to know. Information about the body, health, medicine, symptomology and wellbeing is far more available, and as the dissemination increases, largely through the internet, a parallel decrease occurs in medical mystique.

We're also less likely to escape into euphemism through timidity or embarrassment. We know more about our bodies and we know more about our rights, and these knowledges create a more balanced symmetry between patient and doctor.

In fact there are two core changes that have an odd parallelism. We know our bodies better and we know what we're entitled to. And we know our doctors less well—depending which surgery you attend, you may see a different doctor each time. S/he knows nothing about you except what's on your chart, and depending on the handwriting, not even that. No big surprise, then, that the language has changed.

The last of the four old-world words to be discussed here is 'coming out'. Unlike the other three, this one has no medical associations; but like the other three, its use and function were essentially euphemistic—saying one thing by means of a more delicate turn of phrase.

A girl's 'coming out' at eighteen was her formal introduction to what used to be called 'polite society'. And polite society was that social element who were particularly adept at the use of language, so much so that they could insult others without ever betraying an iota of anger or displeasure. I gather that now such events are, if not quite extinct, then fairly moribund. One comment I heard was that private schools in the country have almost abandoned the custom because the quality of debutante (and presumably the parents) was below the minimum standard of acceptability.

Coming out, when it was first instituted, was meant to denote that the young (emergent) woman was eligible for marriage; and marriage was a very serious business, with 'business' being the operative word. The coming-out tradition allegedly arose in a post-feudal world, when asset-rich, cash-poor noble families started to see, in an alignment with the new cash-dripping industrialist class, an answer to all their financial woes. It was win–win all round, actually, because the bourgeoisie would give their eye teeth for just a whiff of nobility. For the latter, marriage into the wealthy bourgeoisie could mean welcome infusions of ready cash. And ready cash was precisely what you needed when the serfs whom you used to own no longer produced the goods that underwrote your expenses. All told, everything was so much easier when you didn't need to include the cost of serfs in your overheads.

In the United States, the coming-out event is alive and well, though more as a formal social event than as a display of a new crop of maidenhead. There it is called 'cotillion', a French word that arrived in American English in 1766, derived from Old French meaning 'petticoat'. A secondary meaning of 'cotillion' is a particularly lively dance originating in 18th-century France. My dictionary of etymology notes that the 'application' of 'cotillion' (skirt) to 'dance' is 'obscure.' All I can say is, that lexicographer mustn't have had any daughters because a dance, to a girl, is all about the clothes.

In the American context, the Cotillion (they give it a capital) has become an institution, an annual formal charity dance—which boosts consumer spending enormously, from the dress-the hair-the shoes to the dance lessons, and that's not even half of it. You can click onto a calendar of all the Cotillion events planned for the current year across the United States, and you can home in on any particular state for more details—like Wichita, Kansas, San Diego or California. Like many social events, a swathe of satellite service industries has grown up around it. For instance, you can enrol your child in a special course of 'the complete etiquette experience', a menu of learning opportunities that includes ballroom dancing, table manners, deportment, poise and social graces.

We don't have to go very far to appreciate how obsolete 'coming out' as a social marker of marriageability is. To make yourself available—dare I say, to market yourself—more and more people today turn to the personals on the internet or in newspapers. There the language may be anything from coy to explicit, but irrespective of the language used, the very fact of its appearance as a personal ad indicates your availability. This may not mean the same as marriageability, but it may come to that in the end. One thing's for sure, though—the chaperones and corsages are long gone.

'Coming out' today refers to something entirely different. It means announcing openly and publicly one's homosexuality. The person who 'comes out' effectively emerges from the 'closet', which is the metaphoric place they have been while discovering and becoming accustomed to being gay. As long as such a person has chosen to keep their sexual orientation a secret, they are not 'out'.

The overlap of linguistic form is by no means accidental. There is a winking reference in the new, gay coming out to the old debutante coming out. In both cases there is an emergence into a wider society; in both cases there is a 'public' dimension to the act; and in both cases the issue of gender identity is central.

There's also the newish verb 'to out'. Whereas 'coming out' implies an active choice on the part of the person coming out, the verb 'to out' removes that choice. 'To out' someone is to expose them as homosexual and thrust them into the kind of public scrutiny for which they are probably neither ready nor willing to face. An 'outing' refers to such an event and the surrounding adverse publicity that accrues. This kind of 'outing' is about as far as you can travel from the old-fashioned outing—your 'day devoted to an outdoor social gathering'— like your picnic in the park with family and friends.

However, there is one big difference between the event of coming out à la debutante and coming out à la homosexual, and this has to do with the nature of the actual coming-out event. While the big dance is a formal occasion with a beginning, a middle and an end (even taking into account that preparations can start a year in advance), the gay coming out does not entail the same binary relationship that the terms 'come/be out' suggest.

Most gays don't go overnight from being entirely in the closet to being entirely out of it, for the process of taking public the ownership of one's sexual identity is rarely so simple. Rather it tends to be a gradual process of coming out, where the coming out happens at different times with different circles of people. For instance, you can be 'out' with your friends, but not with family or at work. People intuitively know that coming out at work may have repercussions on how they are perceived and how their work contribution is assessed. Of course, this largely depends on the kind of work involved. I heard some time ago about a case where a man was fired (and subsequently awarded damages for wrongful dismissal) because his employer discovered he was *not* gay. He was a restaurant waiter in a gay area and his employers argued that the assumption was made at interview that being gay was an asset.

In the gradual process of coming out, very sadly, family is usually the last to know, with gay children rightly fearing that the information will change forever the way their parents see them and the way they see themselves.

Once 'coming out' evolved from its debutante sense to its use in the gay world, it didn't stop there. It grew legs and moved on. Of late it's started to assume the wider quality of going public about something you previously kept secret. The added dimension is that the nature of the true-new-you in some way renders the old-untrue-you somehow compromised or fraudulent. Such as when a supposed vegetarian emerges as an actual meat-lover. Or when an armchair leftie emerges as a hard-core right-wing conservative, or at least a Howard-voter. The sense isn't simply that someone changed their views, but rather that hitherto they had held the two contradictory views simultaneously, and hence dishonestly.

And as it continues to develop, the meaning of 'coming out' becomes even more free-ranging in its possible scope of reference. It can have a number of meanings simultaneously, resulting in a depth of texture that has even a TV program looking multi-dimensional. Take for instance, this blurb from a TV program announcing a movie called *The International Madam*: 'Margaret McDonald, the world's most successful madam, is coming out. After doing time in a notorious women's prison in Paris for pimping, Margaret has agreed to tell her story.'

~ 24 ~

Black dog

DEPRESSION WAS NOT SOMETHING that people used to talk about. Along with other forms of mental illness, if it was recognised it was put in the vault and left there. It was as if denial or neglect, one or the other or both, were kinds of treatment that might make some sort of difference for the better. Perhaps it was part of the cultural tradition of 'out of sight, out of mind'—that extraordinary capacity for which the British are renowned, where you can fool yourself into a certain way of thinking so long as there is no visible evidence to the contrary right in front of you.

We had hundreds of names for the people we stigmatised by their mental frailty. They were loonies, crazies, psychos or just off with the fairies. Whatever we called them—they belonged in the loony bin, and when they were taken there it was always by the men in the white coats, who would come to get you in the green cart. White coats I understand, but a green cart?

There were plenty of jokes. Humour was a great way to objectify the problem and place distance between it and oneself. Humour was also a way of coping with the fear of the unknown. Laugh at it; then you don't have to deal with it. There's not too much wrong with the humour, so long as it's not the only response given.

We locked some crazies up and threw away the keys. Given the level of denial, it makes you wonder just how crazy someone had to be to be actually put away. But mostly we didn't physically lock them up; rather we shut the door on the problem, and threw *that* key away. There was always a lot of crying, drinking and abuse connected with what we now call depression. Sometimes it involved silence and sometimes violent screaming bouts, as though a wild animal had been let out of its cage. And maybe it had.

Even those who worked with the mentally ill suffered from the stigmatised associations. Psychiatrists were often the butt of jokes that deemed them as unstable as their patients. People were cautious around psychiatrists, almost as though they feared they were infectious. 'Mad' was a word that was often put alongside 'psychiatrist'. Psychiatric nurses got a very harsh press—remember Nurse Ratched in *One Flew Over the Cuckoo's Nest*? But for a sign of how times have changed, compare the representation of the psychiatric patients in Ken Kesey's novel (and the film of the same name), with the much more sympathetic, even romantic, treatments of various mental conditions in films like *Rain Man* (autism), *As Good As It Gets* (obsessive-compulsive disease) and *A Beautiful Mind* (schizophrenia).

Mental disease often had its own ugly accompaniments, such as alcohol and domestic violence, which might be considered the fallout. There were always ways and means of explaining away the fallout—wives tended to be very clumsy with the stairs or, alternatively, they stupidly ran into doors. Everybody knew what that meant, but it sure wasn't something that anybody talked about. We didn't even have the term 'domestic violence' back then. What we did have was the 'rule of thumb', a term allegedly and controversially derived from a line in Common Law that supposedly allowed a man to beat a cantankerous or difficult wife with a piece of wood no thicker than his thumb. Handy that. You can always find a plank or two lying about, and you've got your thumb with you wherever you go for a handy rough measure.

It wasn't called 'depression' then. You were 'in a mood', which sometimes involved anger, sometimes sullen, silent, morose withdrawal and often a whole lot of alcohol. Women spoke of being 'teary' or 'down in the dumps'. Men didn't speak. For them it was expressed as stoicism, the stiff upper lip. Any weakness and they urged each other to behave like a man, to get over it, to stop acting like a girl. Anything other than coolly rational was characterised as female. Don't be a silly girl or an old woman. Irrationality, hysteria, indeed any shows of emotion were certainly not valued as ratified male responses. There weren't any counsellors. No therapists of any kind. Psychology was voodoo, or might as well have been.

If it was a matter of a mood, then it was transient. Although it was not actually your fault that the mood landed on you, it was up to you to get rid of it. Staying in that place was selfish and self-indulgent—a hallmark of moral weakness. It was inexcusable for men to be 'flat', and although women had some limited dispensation because of the hormonal fluctuations known to affect their emotions, that was a few days' allowance at best, and even that latitude was granted under sufferance. You were told to snap out of it. You might even have tried to snap out of it. On occasion the snapping may even have worked. Or the pretend-snap that gave a surface semblance of normalcy returned.

'Snap' is an interesting word, especially when applied to a response to emotional disturbance. It means to break or cause to break with a short, sharp movement and accompanying sound. A click of your fingers simulates the sound of a 'snap'. Things that can be snapped in two are a twig or a piece of wood or a pencil. You wonder what it is about the perception of the 'bad mood' that encouraged people to think of saying 'snap out of it'. It tells us a lot about how emotional fluctuation was perceived—as something that was easily fixed with the right attitude. Nice little Catch-22 there. If you had the right 'attitude' you may not have had the 'fluctuation' in the first place, in which case you wouldn't need to be snapping out of it. Then again, 'snap' is a bit of a double-edged sword. We talk of snapping out of a mood, but there's another sense to 'snap', and that's when someone is or feels pushed beyond their point of endurance. Then they just snap, and that might be the time to call the little men in their white coats and their green cart.

It was probably the most articulate and literate people who feared mental illness the most. Perhaps this is because mental illness seems so closely related to creativity that intro-spective or creative people were fearful of where their mental processes and insights would lead them. Or perhaps they feared that their moods were intimately linked with their creativity—touch one, you may ruin the other. Hence much of the silence, avoidance, denial, euphemism, shame and stigma. Families with a medical history of mental instability were particularly sensitive on the subject.

It's called 'depression' now. Even though some of the stigma remains, and diagnosis is often much delayed—mostly because people feel ashamed to present their symptoms to a doctor—there's less of the view about that it's a snapoutof-able condition that simply requires a good attitude. Every other day someone in a prominent position, usually a man, quits his position, and the reason given is 'a battle with depression'. Invariably some other prominent person will commend the honesty and call the person 'brave'. Then again, usually another prominent person will put forward the argument that the person should not have quit but rather shown that it's possible to hold down a responsible job and seek medical attention for the condition at the same time. Whatever the contentions, there's no doubting the courage involved in going public with a stigmatised medical condition.

Today it's 'black dog'—the term that originated with Winston Churchill, and an image that seems to have captured people's imaginations. There's even an organisation by that name, plenty of books on the market, self-help manuals and support groups everywhere. These days it's vogue to cite famous men—Abe Lincoln was one—known to have been afflicted by depression. No doubt standing in such company helps with the esteem issues that are all wrapped up with depression. I'm reminded that the same myths grow up around left-handedness. Having a left-handed child, I often came up against remarks, usually made by other left-handers, who would say, as if we had reason to need to feel better, that, for instance, did we know that Napoleon was left-handed, and so was Alexander the Great? To this day I haven't worked out why that information, even if true, should have any effect on any left-handers. Perhaps it's a celebrity thing, or a respectability thing, or an identity thing.

In fact, while not exactly 'in vogue', depression is certainly in from the cold. There's even a certain glam element associated with it at times—some kind of badge of honour, evidence that you're an interesting and complicated person. So boring to have had an ordinary happy childhood. There are some socioeconomic associations as well. For example, in the then West German TV series *Derrick*, which dealt mostly with crime among the uber-rich, there was hardly an episode where the family under scrutiny didn't have a member, often half-secreted away in a top room without a balcony, with some mental affliction.

Nowadays, everyone knows someone who's fallen prey or is on Prozac. Antidepressants are household names; they lurk in many a family medicine cabinet. You can even get pet Prozac if your dog or cat, bird or fish is suffering emotional disturbances. Indeed, pet owners are warned that their own medical conditions can be reflected in their pets. People openly admit to being 'on' antidepressants, or one of their derivatives. One in four of us, allegedly, will have suffered at least one episode of major depression by the time we are eighteen years old. Makes you wonder if anyone can escape an episode over the course of a lifetime. It's probably always been so, but now it's less shameful and more scientific. It's less a defect of character and more a matter of neurotransmitters and serotonin uptake, all of it hard-wired into your DNA. Careful how you choose your parents.

∼ 25 ∼

Bad

Life does not always work out as one hopes it will. In fact, if you're a glass-half-empty kind of person, you'd say the real thing falls short of the mark most of the time. Yet, however full or empty you perceive your glass to be, even the most dyed-in-the-wool optimist has times when things don't work out, when regret or recrimination or blame seem appropriate responses to misfortune.

Today, people draw on a core bank of swear words to express their frustration or disappointment. We use verbs-become-adjectives, like 'fucked up' and 'buggered' or nouns like 'fuck-up' and 'stuff-up', or we might say 'what a bugger' or 'what a bastard'. No doubt swear words have always furnished, and will continue to do so, those who need them with a ready, vivid, if restricted supply of words uniquely suitable for their purpose. However, in the days before the f-word was attached so liberally to anything or anyone, there were other phrases and expressions to express a similar state of affairs. These too have become victims of modern candour and we can expect them to gradually head their way to the Hospice of Fading Words, if indeed they're not already firmly ensconced therein.

Some years ago I put in a development application to my local council to close in part of my front porch so as to build an ensuite to the main bedroom. Pretty simple and straight-forward all round, one would have thought, and it was—until a man across the street protested to council that the drawings suggested to him that the development would look like 'a dog's breakfast', and he certainly did not want to look across his balcony at a dog's breakfast every morning, especially, I gathered, over his own breakfast. The tragedy was that he moved out shortly after lodging his objection, and probably never gave anyone else's breakfast a second thought. But his objection stayed in place, in his absence, and continued to hold up the application for another two years. But then, bureaucracy is a self-perpetuating nightmare that spews out its victims, laughing uproariously all the way to the bank to deposit the building application fee, and then sitting on its hands, refusing to untie the red tape, without a thought to the citizen, other than in the week leading up to the next local government elections.

A dictionary will tell you that 'a dog's breakfast' denotes a mess or a state of confusion or turmoil. Sometimes, it was the dog's dinner that was so described. All this no doubt came from a time before pet food came in neat little tins at the supermarket, but rather was anything and everything that was leftover and one step from being thrown out. Sometimes, even the dog got dropped and was replaced by 'a madwoman'. Such as being 'all over the place like a madwoman's breakfast'. Here the assumption would seem to be that the mad woman in question, wildly dishevelled and unkempt no doubt, would lack any semblance of order in her person or her life, let alone her breakfast. This may be unwarranted. I have seen one quite deranged homeless women whose collection of bags was fastidiously neat, and this description might also have applied to her breakfast.

There used to be a whole grab bag of expressions that might collectively be called 'soft swearing'. This was language that would emerge when you 'let loose' or when some provocation caused you to 'spit chips'. One category of oath-like phrases is clearly religious in origin: 'Holy Moses', 'Ye Gods', 'Jesus, Mary and Joseph', 'Holy Mary, mother of God', and 'Heavens to Betsy', though just who Betsy is remains a mystery. Another category is derived largely from religious epithets of the past, and in terms of meaning, mix various quantities of surprise and disgust. 'Struth' comes from 'God's truth'. 'Cripes' is a euphemistic variant of 'Christ'. 'Crickey' seems to me to be a derivative of 'Christ', though I can find no evidence of this, even on the website (www.crikey.com), tagged as 'what you need, when you need it.' 'Jeepers creepers' is an American-English expression of surprise, and is a euphemism of 'Jesus Christ'. 'Sugar', as an expletive, is a euphemistic avoidance of 'shit!' Annoyance could equally emerge in phrases like 'pig's bum and cabbage' or 'damn and blast it'. And 'blinking', 'blooming' and 'frigging' were useful substitutes for more offensive terms, but conveniently adjectival and available for attaching to any damn noun you chose. A classic put-down to someone overengaging in soft (or not-so-soft) swearing was 'keep a civil tongue in your head', or 'wash your mouth out' (with soap), which quaintly seemed to attribute politeness and its opposite, as well as the power to know the difference, to the whims and wishes of the tongue.

A term for this subgroup of euphemism is a minced oath, the kind of thing you're liable to say if you hit your thumb with a hammer when great aunt Eunice is within earshot. And while we continue to recycle and generate fresh euphemisms for human behaviours that aren't going anywhere, the actual taboos on discussing God, death, disability or sexual preference have weakened, loosening the restrictions on swearing out loud when you're surprised, frustrated or just plainly emotional.

There are some long and rather convoluted soft-swearing expressions that are fixed or hardened into a conventional form. This is quite clever because it allows the speaker to use the expression while not really owning it. After all, everyone knows that the expression exists in its own right, was not manufactured in your mouth, simply used you as a conveyer belt. Of course, being the vehicle of the words, not their author, the speaker has a certain immunity from prosecution, in the way perhaps that the spokesman for the minister's office may deliver the minister's words or represent them, but at core, is not responsible for them. It's as if the words are laminated and touch not even the lips of the non-authorial speaker.

Nancy Keesing tells a lovely story about an elderly lady who never swore, but on some occasions 'such as kicking off a pair of smart uncomfortable shoes or relaxing in a loose housecoat on a hot day', she would say: 'Ah that's better, as the old woman said when she removed the French letter that had been there since Armistice Day.'

PART V

A NEW CENTURY WITH ITS OWN
SENSIBILITIES

∾ 26 ∾

Body bits

....

WHEN TWENTY-YEAR-OLD Kate DeAraugo, a swimming instructor raised in Bendigo, won the third series of *Australian Idol*, it was a win all round—for Bendigo, for regional Australia and well, I have to say it, for tuckshop arms.

How come? Well, young Kate had had a rather traumatic lead-up to her final win. One of the judges had unmincingly suggested she lose the tuckshop arms if she really was serious about achieving her fifteen minutes of fame. It was a resounding blow. Women across the nation felt they'd been personally slighted. Ironically, but predictably, Australian fans rallied behind the underdog, giving her the needed boost of confidence, and then some, not to mention the requisite votes.

Tuckshop arms. Now there's a term that came out of the blue, and one many of us had not heard, or at least not for quite a while. The last time I heard it, I was too young, slim and well-toned to register it on the radar. Things pass you by when they have no relevance to your life. Two-thirds of my life passed me by, for example, before I made sense of 'superannuation'.

The thing is that tuckshop arms can exist outside of tuckshops. There is nothing holding them down to that pokey little room-without-view. Yet, the truth is that if they have a home, a habitat, an archetypal association, it's got to be the tuckshop.

Or more correctly, it's got to do with the gender and stage of life of the volunteering staff readily (wo)manning your average school tuckshop.

Then again, it's also the hole-in-the-wall point of contact between the child-purchaser and the adult-seller. To the young eye, that space must rather unseemingly fill up with underarm flab. Still, if we go the way of the United States, we can expect McDonald's franchises to take over school tuckshops (will they still be called 'tuckshops'?), and there's rarely a tuckshop arm to be seen among the demographic that stands behind the counter and says, 'Do you want fries with that?'

Let's skip past the tuckshop itself and focus on those arms for a moment. We're talking about the upper arm, the flabby tricep. Well, in a young person, it's 'flab' as in overweight. In an older person, it's 'flab' as in overweight plus (as cosmetic surgeons like to say, and I did check a few websites) the wasting quality of ageing skin. It's no wonder the aged feel they're past their use-by date, when words like 'wasting' are used apropos a very natural process. I prefer 'evolving', myself.

Note how hard I'm trying to be gender-neutral. Out of fairness and in defiance of the *Macquarie*'s entry 'the arm of an overweight woman having flabby triceps'. Does this mean that men don't do flab? Or that they don't do skin-tone loss? Or is it simply because only an infinitesimally small number of men ever volunteer for tuckshop duty?

Of course the culture's age-old gender bias is reflected in, conveyed through and perpetuated by language. Ever since Eve, and notwithstanding the form-fitting fig leaf, a woman's appearance is far heftier a factor in everything than a man's. For the female, it's 'I appear, therefore I am.' As far as I'm aware, the notion of 'vanity sizing'—adjust the size label so that it's less an indictment—is as yet applied only to women's apparel, not men's. It's heartening, though, that with men's grooming products beginning to compete for space in the smell-sweet market and the wider influence of metrosexuality, the see might be finally beginning to saw. But expect glacial speed.

There are many alternatives to the 'tuckshop' label. Try these for size: 'floppy arms', 'piano arms', 'auntie arms', 'bingo wings', 'bat wings', 'wobblies', 'bye-nows', 'goodbye muscle', 'nannas', 'reverse biceps', 'ta-ta flaps', 'widow's curtains'. Yep, my thoughts exactly. This lot makes 'tuckshop arms' seem almost endearing. (I said 'almost'.)

Now all of these terms, along with 'tuckshop arms', were common in the past but are not heard much in public these days precisely because they're associated with women, and often with age. There's a new delicacy about expressing discriminating and hurtful remarks against specific groups in society, of whom women and the elderly have traditionally had a rough time of it. While many past expressions have gone to the Hospice of Fading Words as Victims of Modern Candour, a discrete subset of words has been elbowed out of the lexicon precisely because they're too candid. Or rather, too prejudiced. In some domains, euphemisms have thrived, and grown siblings.

So if 'tuckshop arms' are fading, it's not because gyms and cosmetic surgeons have totally rid us of underarm flab. Nor that mum-staffed school tuckshops are on the way out, mums being out working in real (i.e., paying) jobs. Rather, it's that these days we are less likely to talk about the tuckshop arm quite so openly or cavalierly.

This is an outcome of the so-called politically correct movement. I say 'so-called' because the label 'politically correct' (or PC) was superimposed on a group of well-intentioned people (it's not what they would have called themselves) and, unfortunately, it stuck. Along with 'the thought police' and 'attitude nazis'. It's been generally forgotten that the motivation behind the early attempts to clean up the language of prejudiced terms was whole-heartedly in the evolving tradition of Western liberal humanism that began with the Enlightenment and has been developing, in fits and starts, ever since. To call someone a 'nigger' or a 'chink' is so much worse than suggesting that they use neutral terms for minority groups, terms that such people themselves would use about themselves. When they asked the so-called Red Indians what they wanted to be known as, you can be sure it wasn't 'Red Indians'. Indeed, it was entirely consistent that those who damned the PC movement were the same as those who couldn't see what the fuss was all about— after all, a nigger is a nigger is a nigger.

But cultural change happens best when it happens slowly, and when it comes from within rather than being imposed from outside. The so-called PC movement was perceived to be composed primarily of left-leaning, female agenda-dominated university types with at least one foot in the intellectual clouds and little understanding of the cut-and-thrust of ordinary reality. For decades they were mocked and ridiculed and satirised, and the ugly PC moniker stuck fast. I remember a comedian in the 1980s suggesting Paul Newman change his name (or risk having it changed for him) to Paul Newperson.

Certainly, the earnestness and idealism of the early so-called PCers left them open for the slings and barbs of satire and mockery. They were readily portrayed as humourless, doctrinaire and themselves intolerant of difference. And also without doubt, some of their number went too far and expected too much change too fast. Currently, 'fatist' attitudes have led to suggestions for euphemistic alternatives like overweight, weight-challenged, or 'person of substance', echoing the antecedents of 'person of colour' and 'person of faith'. Facilities catering for such people are being called 'size-friendly' or 'generously cut'. A series of books on politically correct nursery rhymes hilariously converts the well-known traditional tales into supposedly more neutral and less offensive language. For example, the story 'The Three Codependent Goats Gruff' begins thus:

> Once on a lovely mountainside lived three goats who were related as siblings. Their name was Gruff, and they were a very close family. During the winter months they lived in a lush, green valley, eating grass and doing other things in a naturally goatish manner. When summer came, they would travel up the mountainside to where the pasture was sweeter. This way they did not overgraze their valley and kept their ecological footprints as small as possible.

In another example the story 'Peter Pan' opens with: 'This is the story of Peter Pan, a temporally trapped, pre-adult male who had never grown up owing to a severe self-image problem brought on by rich overprotective parents.'

Art critic and cultural commentator Robert Hughes argues that names and labels make no difference. Black people in the United States are treated as badly whether they are called African American, niggers or persons of colour. He says that words make no difference, any more than the Five-Year Plans turned Stalinism into a triumph:

> We want to create a sort of linguistic Lourdes, where evil and misfortune are dispelled by a dip in the waters of

euphemism. Does the cripple rise from his wheel-chair . . . because someone . . . decided that, for official purposes, he was 'physically challenged'?

It's true that a new label won't restore mobility, or even improve the circumstance of disability. No one in the so-called PC movement would have argued that it would. The very minimum the abled world can do for the disabled is naming them with neutral words. Everyone laughed at the 'Ms' label when it first came into use. Now, a prospective employer cannot question a female applicant on her marital status, baby-making plans and maternity leave and child-care expectations.

In her excellent book *Verbal Hygiene*, applied linguist Deborah Cameron deftly exposes the holes in Robert Hughes' position, which she sees as 'breathtakingly arrogant'. For example, she argues that people have the right to be called by their preferred term. If George introduces himself as George, it is socially rude, bizarre, potentially hostile, as well as patho-logical, to call him 'Bill'. Why should Robert Hughes' opinion 'about the relative merits of two names [matter] more than the opinion of the people whose name they are?'

Proponents of so-called political correctness are some-times called the 'thought police', an appellation that is effective as an attack weapon but wholly incorrect. No one can force you to have certain thoughts. Even under duress or torture, you may state that you have given up certain views (e.g., a different faith, political ideology), but we're talking at best about professed opinion, not actual inner thoughts. Inside your head, you can think what you want. As a child once put to me, 'I'm the boss of me inside my own head.' And in the privacy of your home you can use what language you want, a point poorly understood by the owner of a bed and breakfast in northern England who whispered to me in a deserted corridor that she 'didn't like all the Moslems flooding into Britain, but you're not allowed to say anything, of course.' You can have your thoughts or your speech acts in private. But in the arena of public or social life, it surely is a good thing that we strive for a respectful discourse towards everyone, including members of minority groups, and I include here women (where half is hardly a minority) and even the aged (though they are fast becoming numerically important in the population-dwindling West).

Deborah Cameron also relates an incident that happened in California in the early 1990s. A newspaper had inadvertently referred to 'a plan for putting Massachusetts back in the African-American.' The subsequent correction that was printed indicated that the phrase should have read 'back in the black'. What had happened, of course, is that, following in-house guidelines about appropriate labels, the newspaper's computers had automated the correction of 'black' to 'African-American', without differentiating between the various uses of black. As Cameron points out, there is a special irony in the fact that 'being in the black' is one of the few idiomatic uses of black that connotes a positive meaning.

Still, three decades have also born witness to the substantial impact PC has had on the language. Starting back with 'Ms' as a marital-status-neutral Miss/Mrs, the female equivalent of 'Mr' which is now unmarked and normal, with people now wondering what all the fuss was once about. More recent controversies have centred on appropriate ways to refer to those associated with the Islamic faith.

So, 'tuckshop arms', 'bat wings' and 'bingo arms' are leftovers from a previous era. The tuckshop suggests undervalued voluntary work by people-who-don't-matter. The bat conjures up the image of ugly hideous pests with not a single endearing quality. The bingo brings its cache of negative associations— old, low-class, unemployed or pensioned, marginal. With all the grey of 'Grey Power' but none of the power.

Effectively, we've had our consciousness raised about people's multiple sensitivities. It's a new awareness of what we can and cannot say in public, which thoughts are allowed to percolate up to the surface, and which are best kept unspoken. It has been a major force of influence driving linguistic change and is responsible for multiple admissions to the Hospice of Fading Words. The *Australian Idol* judges, they of the tuckshop scandal, could have thought what they wanted to think. It was altogether another thing to say it, directly, and on national television.

~ 27 ~

Mad

....

WE USED TO GET 'ANGRY' or 'mad'. Now we have 'rages'.

It started with 'road rage' and grew from there. In the last year, quite a few have been added, like 'pump rage' (fury at the rise in petrol prices) and 'roast rage' (an attack of the angries around Christmas time).

A rage is qualitatively different from the experience of 'getting angry', and a number of features contribute to this difference. First, having morphed into a noun, getting angry or mad has accrued a more substantive character. Getting angry, for instance, can be over in a moment, but a rage has to last long enough to be recognisably what it is. I mean, it's got to have a beginning, a middle and an end, as countless English teachers have told essay-challenged students.

Second, a rage has to be public. There's no use trying to have a rage on your own. You need an audience, people to appreciate the effort you're putting into things, people who will duck for cover when it happens, but spectate greedily for the duration. Later they'll recount the experience to anyone who'll listen, each time embroidering the telling, as you do. In this way, the experience gets reified: the fact of the rage spreads, and in spreading, takes on legitimacy.

Third, a rage is not something that happens only to you. It is, almost by definition, a social thing. You get to share it with others who are similarly provoked. In other words, it has to have the status of a syndrome before it can qualify as a rage. We don't have 'laundromat rage' or 'lost-sock rage' because not enough people get so incensed at missing an item from their wash that they will boil over on cue. This is not to say that it won't happen someday, or even next week.

Fourth, a rage may be explosive but the fireworks actually mask the slow build-up that predates it. Pump rage didn't happen after the first price hike, or the second or the third. Each time, however, the unexpressed anger builds on existing anger, until finally, all those spikes mean the cup floweth over.

But before we had road rage and all its offshoots, we had a one-size-fits-most kind of word. 'Mad'. Mad covered most contingencies. Someone might be described as 'mad as a cut snake' or 'mad as hell', and you didn't need to have lived in the bush or to have read Dante to get the gist. But mad had, and still has, blurry borders. With one foot in the angry camp and the other in the crazy camp, mad clearly wants it both ways. Of course, as ever, context is the best determiner of whether the intended meaning is veering towards rage or towards insanity.

Shakespeare's King Lear remains the archetypal symbol of mad-cum-insane, with the theme of madness dominating the play's language and action. Lear himself, speaking of another, says: 'We are not ourselves/When nature, being oppress'd, commands the mind /To suffer with the body.' For years high school students have tossed about various issues of Lear's condition—When exactly did he go mad? What caused it? What pushed him over the edge? What insight did it bring? Was it ultimately redemptive? What can we learn from it? Does it matter? Does anything?

At least Lear could gain some solace from the Elizabethan explanation of the humours by which belief you could account for how temperament and behaviour were shaped. According to the thinking of the day, Lear's madness may have been triggered by family events (daughters will do that to you), but at root there was an imbalance of the humours. In fact, conveniently, you can get a feeling for the state of the main character's humours by the weather forecast. The stormier the weather outside, the stormier the humours within. And all things considered, it's not too big a leap to our current pass-the-Prozac-paradigm of chemical imbalance. And in terms of weather forecasting, things haven't changed that much. Ask any childcare worker what it's like on a rainy day. Or try teaching the niceties of literature to an unruly class of fifteen year olds on a windy Friday afternoon.

When 'mad' means your reality is out of touch with everyone else's—think Russell Crowe's character in *A Beautiful Mind*—we have no shortage of expressions to fall back on, some of them more kindly than others. 'Off with the fairies' is as gentle an image of insanity as may be possible; and even 'mad as a gum tree full of galahs', which I've never heard said by a real person, suggests a noisy camaraderie rather than anything sinister.

Quite dated now is 'mad as a March hare' which, while being seasonally out of antipodean whack, calls on a bucolic image of randy rabbits going off their little heads during their high-peak mating season, though my understanding, forged from the experience of having had pet rabbits, was that they are good for it any time. Still, the March-hare notion of madness is rather benevolent. It spells an erratic, unpredictable excitability perhaps, but it attributes no blame. After all, if it's meant to be seasonal, then it's species-programmed, not an individual affliction. The defence's argument: the season made me do it.

Then again, not everyone agrees about the rabbits. Martin Gardner reports that two British scientists, having researched the spring behaviours of hares, found no evidence that male hares go into a seasonal frenzy. They concluded (just as I did, with no empirical research) that March is no different from any other month: 'The main courtship behaviour of male hares during the entire breeding period . . . is chasing females and then boxing with them.' One could try to extrapolate something from this to wider human behaviour, but this would take us into domestic violence and we'd be way off topic.

Then again, the issue may be less one of month or season and more one of locality. Another claim has the Dutch Renaissance scholar, Desiderius Erasmus, using 'mad as a *marsh* hare', and this was centuries before Lewis Carroll was alluding to the month of March. Who would have thought that a 'sh' and 'ch' consonant cluster could be so semantically apart?

Less benevolent and certainly less bucolic is 'mad as a meat axe', which I used to hear as a child, though why a meat axe should connote insanity is anyone's guess. Perhaps it's the association with the savagery one expects goes on behind the closed doors of an abattoir. After all, there's a reason we're comfortable with the more esoteric French 'abattoir' in place of the totally in-your-face English 'slaughterhouse'. We'd really rather not think about what goes on in there, not while we're still into our steaks. The ethics of what we eat is topical, yes, but on the whole it hasn't yet made serious inroads into what goes into our shopping trollies.

A classic phrase, and one hardly heard any more, is 'mad as a hatter'. Immortalised by Lewis Carroll, of course, the kind of madness experienced and symbolised by the Mad Hatter is a far cry from the meat-axe variety of mad. Mad as-in-hatter is a whole lot closer to jolly as-in-clown than it is to mad as-in-slash-slash (I'm thinking here of the shower scene in Hitchcock's *Psycho*).

Two competing theories exist to account for the calumny of hatters as an occupation allegedly given to producing or experiencing madness. The first one, which we'll call the mercury theory, hails from the dark factory days long long before occupational health and safety changed the way we work. In the bad old days, a complicated set of processes was involved in the manufacture of hats. The cheap felt variety of hat was mostly made from rabbit fur (there's that rabbit again), and among various other steps, the fur was brushed with a mercury-compound solution, the fibres were immersed in boiling acid, and the felt was finished off with steaming and ironing. Poorly ventilated factories meant hatters inhaled the mercury compound, among other noxious gases.

The phrase 'mad hatter syndrome' is today all that's left of those nasty times when mercury poisoning was an occupational disease. Not that back then mercury was known to be dangerous. Some of the nervous disorder symptoms—trembling, twitching, slurred speech and various personality changes—made the mercury-poisoned sufferer appear quite demented, though with our 21st-century minds, and our computer-driven epidemiology, it's hard to believe that hundreds of hatters could be perceived as mad without anyone twigging to the pattern. In any case, with this historical perspective, suddenly 'mad as a hatter' isn't nearly as whimsical as its Lewis Carroll associations might suggest.

Then again, according to the second interpretation, what I'm calling the snake theory, Lewis Carroll was nowhere near as innocent as might be thought. Mad apparently also meant 'venomous'. Yes, venomous as in 'snake'. This is perfectly consistent. In fact if you combine the features of anger and irrationality, you get something like a venomous fury. Now why should a hatter be venomous? Because, according to this second theory, 'hatter' has nothing to do with hats, felt, rabbits or mercury. Rather, it's a corruption of 'adder' (yes, adder as in snake), so that, according to *A Dictionary of Common Fallacies*, 'mad as an atter' originally meant 'venomous as a viper' (the Germans use 'natter' for viper—Edwards, 1901). With his penchant for linguistic games, there is no way Carroll could have not known this.

There are other less nature-dependent ways of referring to 'mad' (insane). Terms like 'loony', 'nuts', 'psycho', 'bonkers', 'off one's rocker', 'berko', 'maniac', 'spewing', 'spitting the dummy', 'going troppo'. Although so-called political correctness took a while to find the domain of mental illness ('neurological diversity'), it has no doubt had an influence on the language, compromising the open candour that has broadly replaced the ornate and flowery language of the past. Today we are cautious about calling someone mad outright. Ironically, we still use 'loony' or 'nuts' or 'bonkers', but usually the targets here in fact aren't clinically insane at all. When confronted with truly insane people, we now tend to choose our language more carefully.

Similarly, we don't have lunatic asylums or 'loony bins' any more, and we don't talk about 'throwing away the key'. Instead we talk about humane treatments and rehabilitation; about mental health options and, at worst, 'psychiatric facilities'. All round, we'd rather have fewer incarcerations and more community-based living arrangements. We've invented new language, too: manic depressives are now 'bipolar', for instance. Partly because of this relaxing of the stigma associated with mental illness, and the suppression of the cruel and dismissive language that used to be used, people are more prepared, as we have seen, to own up to suffering from depression, to seek treatment, and to feel hopeful about getting better.

Advocates for the mentally ill would have more of us affected by the changing public awareness. A spate of recent television advertisements equated schizophrenia or obsessive-compulsive disease with physiological conditions like diabetes, calling for greater understanding and less ostracism of the mentally ill. In the United Kingdom, in particularly in-your-face language, the 'mad-not-bad' movement similarly tried to raise public awareness. Some advocates in particular targeted the media and tried valiantly to change current nomenclature practices and convince people involved in ethical practice in journalism to go for a fairer, less damning manner of representation.

Under the influence of so-called political correctness, the language may turn back the clock and return to favour some of the expressions that once freely called on Nature's resources. You can surely see the attraction. There's a whole lot less offence in calling someone mad 'as a wet hen', 'as a hornet', 'as a cut snake'. While in all of these the sense is of anger turning insanely nasty, all things considered, there's some comfort in seeing a parallel between the natural and the human world. So long, of course, as that cut snake is not heading in your direction.

~ 28 ~

Stupid

....

IF SIDNEY BAKER IS RIGHT that all languages are amply supplied with ways of referring to the good and the bad in life, then he's also right that the stupid are not left far behind. Making reference to people or behaviour that is perceived as stupid brings us very firmly into the terrain of euphemism, which allows us to talk, usually indirectly, about what we're no longer comfortable talking about directly.

Every generation seems to develop its own lexicon for managing talk about stigmatised or taboo topics. These get recycled or replaced every so often because, sooner or later, and increasingly sooner, the stigma catches up to the euphemism and makes a new and fresh word necessary. It's hard to believe now that 'senile', like 'geriatric', was once a euphemism for 'old', introduced because 'old' was considered too blunt and in-your-face. Well, eventually the stigma caught up and re-infected both 'senile' and 'geriatric', and it may take a few more generations before they can be recycled successfully. Meanwhile we'll have to manage with 'aged', as in aged care (not aged beef), and 'senior' as in senior citizen, the latter having been first used in 1938.

The cluster of euphemisms that develops around a concept provides ample linguistic evidence of uneasiness. Consider our dis-ease with the concept of old age: we have 'retirement village', 'advancing years', 'the golden years', 'the grey vote', 'the twilight years', 'dependent living'. And we have plenty of jokes of the Paul Newperson character—such as the name-changing by the non-ageist press of Hemingway's classic to *The Senior Citizen and the Sea*, and Coleridge's famous poem to *The Rhyme of the Chronologically Gifted Mariner*.

What euphemisms do is allow a compromise between the needs of expression and politeness. Very handy, in other words. Linguists Keith Allan and Kate Burridge, for instance, devoted an entire book to the staying power of taboo topics that require a constant generation of new euphemisms to outstrip the pace of stigma.

It's not surprising to find, then, that words that were used in the past for any area that falls within cooee of a stigma would be likely to have changed somewhat over the years. For a while back there, 'a late bloomer' was someone who didn't keep up, who would, one hoped, be able to flower later, at their own pace. Today we might say 'developmentally delayed' for someone whose mental level is below that of their age-peers; or you can avoid the topic even further by mentioning that the person goes/went to a 'special school', or has 'special needs'. That ubiquitous 'special' says it without saying it.

Stepping around difficult topics is nothing short of an art form. Consider the expression 'not the sharpest tool in the shed'. This is a beautiful example of a phrase having evolved to allow a speaker to say something perceived to be unpalatable while in the very same moment demonstrating the required tact. Even though the remark is generally third person—said about someone rather than to the person being described—it still displays evidence of a perceived need to step around the topic rather than go at it head on. Ultimately, it's evidence that we live in a social world and that we need to be on our guard about how our choice of language might impact on others around us.

In fact 'not the sharpest tool in the shed' achieves its attenuating quality in three ways. First, through the convoluted negative. Instead of a possible 'the bluntest tool in the shed', it's inverted to become 'not the sharpest'. The negative has a distancing function, moving the proposition from here under our noses to over there, in the shed. Anywhere but not here. It also allows the speaker to avoid the word 'blunt' which is too direct and uncompromising. Further, it facilitates an indisputable quality of imprecision—'the bluntest' is definite and precise, being right at the bottom of the hierarchy, while 'not the sharpest' is anywhere on the hierarchy except right at the top.

Second, the very use of a metaphor (sharp tools in a tool shed) removes the issue (mental acuity) from the centre stage of attention. It enhances the distancing function of the negative by locating the issue elsewhere (Where? In the tool shed of course!). The metaphor, at least momentarily, risks being obfuscatory, because it is literally false (a human being is not a tool) and, as a result, its central proposition is potentially up for grabs. All this befuddlement helps in the attenuating process. The unclearer you are, the less likely you will be to cause offence. In fact, verbal dithering is a powerful weapon in the arsenal of those whose job or life requires copious, if unpredictable, amounts of deniability.

Third, 'not the sharpest tool in the tool shed' is attentuating because, even while being disparaging in its implied meaning, the 'tools in the shed' concept suggests warm-and-fuzzy notions, like collaboration and team work. There's the added nostalgia for a time when every house had a shed and real men retreated there to fix a range of items, and not just mechanical. That was before men's groups or Jungian therapy. An additional layer of inference is a world view that offers a place for everyone. People are different, not worse (not every tool needs to be sharp). Diversity, equality, fraternity, humanity. Definitely warm and fuzzy, even, in the right context, bordering on endearing.

Of course, metaphorically speaking, varying degrees of sharpness of shed tools is one of many such expressions. Like our less-than-optimally-sharp tool, these now-fading expressions allow one to point indirectly in the direction of a deficit. Consider 'a bob short of a pound', 'not the full quid', 'one snag short of a barbie', 'a sausage short of a picnic', 'a shingle short of a roof', 'a joker short of a deck' and 'a couple of lamingtons short of a CWA [Country Womens' Association] lunch'. In fact, when you survey these expressions, the impression is that hardly an aspect of life is excluded in these elaborate ways of highlighting deficit. It goes on and on: 'a few ants short of a picnic'; 'one rose short of a bouquet'; 'a few stubbies short of a sixpack'; 'a fortune cookie short of a Chinese dinner'; 'a pane short of a window'; 'a clock that's missing some numbers'; 'a few trees short of a forest'; 'a couple of eggs shy of a dozen'; 'not the brightest bulb on the Christmas tree' (or 'the brightest light in the harbour'); 'not the sharpest pencil in the box'; 'some bacon short of a BLT [bacon, lettuce and tomato sandwich]'; 'a golf bag without a full set of irons'; 'a few bricks short of a wall'; 'a few pages short of a book'. Or 'not having all one's dots on one's dice'. Or 'all wax with no wick'. Sometimes deficit is more like absence: 'If you stand close enough, you can hear the ocean'; or 'If he had another brain, it'd be lonely'; and 'If brains were taxed, he'd be getting a rebate.'

At times, the deficit is alluded to by implying some kind of malfunctioning. We have expressions like 'the cheese has slipped off the cracker'; 'the mouth's in gear, but the brain's in neutral'; 'doesn't have both oars in the water' or 'both oars in the water, but on the same side of the boat'; 'the elevator is stuck between floors'; 'needs a few screws tightened'; 'the lights are flashing and the gate is down, but the train isn't coming'; 'the belt doesn't go through all the loops.'

Other times, the expressions make implicit reference to the head as the source of the problem, like saying someone is 'not all there in the top paddock' or that they have 'a leak in their think tank'. Or perhaps their train is 'missing an engineer'; 'the porch light isn't on'; they 'have two brains— one's lost and the other is out looking for it'; or they 'forgot to pay their brain bill'.

Then there are the times when the hint is that the problem is congenital. Such as describing someone as 'swimming in the shallow end of the gene pool'; having 'too much chlorine in their gene pool'; having 'got into the gene pool when the lifeguard wasn't looking'; or as being 'the result of years of careful inbreeding'. And if not a birth defect, then a childhood misadventure—such as 'played too much without a helmet'; was 'not quite strapped in during lunch'; or 'fell out of the family tree'.

These phrases are vividly inventive, sometimes graphic and colourful, with varying degrees of obliqueness built into the mix. Some are blindingly unambiguous ways of referring to matters of reduced mental acuity. For instance, there's not much that's attenuated about 'thick as a brick', which stands as contrasting evidence of how cleverly contrived some of the euphemisms are. Of course, much depends on whether you're saying the expression to the person or about them, behind their back. Used directly, that is, hurled at the face of the person being abused, they constitute verbal assault.

On such occasions, the very indirectness would be salt in the wound.

Whether they're employed euphemistically or dysphemistically, they're fading. My impression is that we're hearing less and less of this kind of colourful language. It's rather as if the expressions have all got run over by the PC train. If so, it's an irony because so-called political correctness was intended, as we have seen, to bring caution into the language about ways of expressing oneself that are potentially hurtful to others. The indirectness and circumlocution of the colourful expressions were intended to do precisely that—to say 'stupid' without saying 'stupid'. These days they seem all to have been swept under the 'special' carpet. The last time I can remember anyone using the gene-pool metaphor, for instance, was by way of explanation following a particularly loopy anti-science remark made by Prince Charles.

~ 29 ~

Ought

....

STAND BACK FOR A MOMENT and have a long, cool, hard objective look at 'ought'.

Of all the modal verbs—the species of verb that allows us to make meanings around such notions as possibility, probability, permission, obligation, desirability—'ought' is the one least used, and as time goes by, less and less. Sure, it gets the odd run in some fading upper-middle-class moments but few would doubt that today it's wheezing on a respirator. The kissing cousins—'should', 'have to', 'must'—have ducked in to fill the void and they're doing well in the 'acting' position. It may be that as they start to take up the slack being left by 'ought', that they too will be phased out. As with all conjecture regarding lexical evolution, only time will tell.

'Ought' has an interesting history. It is derived from an Old English word *ahte*, which is a form of the verb that meant 'own', 'possess' or 'owe'. By Middle English, it came to have the sense of 'possessed' or 'under obligation to pay'. The most important point to note here is the creeping in of the notion of obligation, which, as the word moved forward into its modern era, came to be its main denotation.

You have to agree that 'ought' is an odd-looking word. Not only because of the dissonance between how you write it and how you say it, though of course English is replete with this, but also because it seems to hark from an age when boys called their father 'Sir', when children asked to be excused from the dinner table, when their ears got easily 'boxed', and when they were, by and large, generally best neither heard nor seen. A time when children were owned as chattels by parents who were anything but child-centric. 'Ought' comes from that era, and perhaps because of its uncompromisingly finger-pointing quality, it's some years since it got trampled by the zeitgeist.

Yes, I concede that these are quite sweeping statements and it's best I qualify them early on. When I say that 'ought' is fading, I am not referring to public discourse, where formal authority (which means anything from the boys in blue to the bank manager to the local school headmaster) tells people what to do and how to behave. And there's no shortage of orders coming down from on-high. If the BBC's Grumpy Old Men are right, the quantity of public prohibitions is increasing—no smoking, no standing, no stopping, no loitering; take a number and wait your turn; left lane must turn left; exact change must be given; these seats must be vacated for the elderly or infirm. It goes on and on.

I'm reminded of a sign I once saw at a small harbour-side beach in Sydney, where I'd taken my young son for a bit of fun and relaxation. The sign—a Municipal Council Notice, with a 'by order of' and a penalty 'not in excess of'—admonished anyone about to enter the area that the following were strictly prohibited: dogs, bikes, skateboards, balls, frisbees, camping equipment, overnight stays, loud music, beach games, nude bathing, and that's all I can remember off the top of my head. It was a long time ago and my point is that the list was a long one.

It wasn't only the length of the list that impressed me. It was also the choice of words. They could have said 'None of the following is permitted here', but they didn't. They opted for 'All of the following are prohibited here'—and this was followed by a long bullet list where each item was quite tauto-logically preceded by a big black 'NO'. As if you hadn't already got the message. At the end of the reading of the list, the word that was imprinted on your brain was, you guessed it, 'no'. Not an accident, I thought. I recall saying, when I got to the end of the list, 'Well, we'd better go home then, hadn't we?!' There seemed nothing left to do that wasn't *verboten*. The thought also popped into my head that the council could have saved itself some funds with a simple sign that said 'No Fun To Be Had Here.' The Grumpy Old Men refer to this hyper-regulated lifestyle as 'the nanny state'—a term that I think was invented for Singapore where, I'm told, if you chew gum, swear or write on walls you take your life in your hands. Drugs—using or selling—constitutes the purest form of suicide. Still, weird things happen. I was once in an elevator in Singapore and a man got in with a lit cigarette that he held against the side of his leg. I pointed to the sign in the lift that advertised the fine for smoking in the lift. He replied with 'I'm not smoking.' Ah, a literalist of the best kind.

I wonder if there is some kind of symmetry here? Is there a relationship between the nanny state and the domestic abdi-cation of authority? Has the state become more invasive in our lives in tandem with, and because of, the decline in the status of home-based authority? Is it a case of, the more parents relinquish authority over their children, the more the state assumes the right to intervene in matters of conduct and comportment? I mean, just the other day the Chief Justice of the New South Wales Supreme Court was talking in public about the falling standards of polite discourse, and how he always knew the telemarketers were on the phone because they were the only ones who asked for 'Jim'. The Prime Minister became embroiled in the same discussion (would telemarketers based in Indian call centres really be ringing the PM's residence?), making you wonder whether this was one of those no-news days when news programs reach into those deep, dusty side-pockets for faux-news stories.

Still, I concede that my point about 'ought' ought to be honed. Perhaps it's more properly rephrased as an item of language that is disappearing from the discourse of parents to children. 'Ought' hails from a time when parents openly admonished their children and explicitly pointed to valuable lessons to be learned. 'Don't count your chickens before they hatch' was a warning about making rash assumptions about results and outcomes, before they're, well, fruited, to mix a metaphor. 'Don't burn your bridges' was a warning to temper your responses as you never know when you may need allies in the future. 'Take care of the pennies and the pounds will take care of themselves' was a line that sung the praises of frugality, an ethic no doubt clad in the iron of the Depression. 'Take pride in your work' hails from an era of artisans and craftspeople, long before your job was to fix a knob onto a sheet of metal, time after time after time. Similarly, 'mind your manners' assumed that manners were taught, known and abided by. Now we have reminders in the bus telling schoolchildren what they ought to have learned at home.

Many aphorisms, such as the ones above, begin with an imperative, a command verb that orders you to do—or not do—something. Here the tone is an authoritative one, and the act is a dispensing of ancient wisdoms. It's not an invitation to a discussion of viewpoint, a sharing of opinion. On the contrary, it's a handed-down gem of wisdom that brooks, and is known to brook, no resistance.

Even further up the incline of non-negotiability are aphorisms with 'ought'. These are very firmly positioned on the high moral ground, tending to speak to the tune of universal truths and moral principles. Here's a famous one by Abraham Lincoln: 'The probability that we may fail in the struggle ought not to deter us from the support of a cause we believe to be just.' A painstakingly crafted, noun-heavy sentence, if ever there was one, able to be cited whenever principle is being urged over expedience. And here's this ancient one by Epictetus, the Greek Stoic philosopher: 'A ship ought not to be held by one anchor, nor life by a single hope.' The metaphor offers universality while the 'ought' leaves no doubt as to the recommended pathway. It's the kind of thing a financial advisor would say to encourage you to diversify your portfolio—that is if financial advisors had a classical education, which they mostly don't, so they're far more likely just to say: 'Do it.'

Parent–child discourse was once an ought-friendly zone, where the word was thrown about liberally and unselfconsciously. It was as if the dispensing of advice and wisdom were written into the parental job description. It was part of the contract parents had with society. But no one tells kids what to do any more. Certainly it's not the straightforward task that 'ought' once facilitated. 'Ought' was the kind of word that functioned well in an explicitly structured society which consciously invested authority in certain figures—such as parents.

The bang's been bleached out of the buck now. Its currency has been inflated to the point of meaninglessness. It's been blown out of the water. These days, before you say something to your teenagers you need to first consider the language you're going to clothe your sentiments in. You won't be making any appeal to positional authority ('I'm your father and you'll listen to me.') In lieu of such, we have the much-vaunted emotionally honest 'I statements'. Like: 'I feel upset when you play your music very loud.' Not, 'Your loud music is driving me up the wall.' The problem is not in the decibels; it's how you choose to feel.

Parents are now in that limbo land, observing accidents and tragedies on the point of happening, but with their hands tied behind their backs and masking tape across their mouths. I know a woman who felt the visceral need to say something to her teenage daughter who was about to go out clubbing, again, with a bunch of like-minded and like-attired friends. It was a formula for maternal angst. After all, it's an Attenborough-like principle of the human urban jungle that bronzer + sparkles + glossiness + stilettos + grog = cause for worry. She anguished over what she might say to her daughter, what might be valuable, what might serve her. Nothing that starts with 'don't', such as, don't drink too much, don't let your drink be spiked, don't go off alone with anyone you don't know, don't get into a car being driven by someone who's been drinking. And even if 'don't' were allowable, there are just too many to say in too few seconds the daughter passes through the hallway to the front door.

Yet parents are supposed to worry. At one school–parent meeting, the parents were told by the principal: 'Whatever you fear your kids may be getting up to when you're not around, it's worse—worse than you think.' The *Good Weekend* ran a spread that many parents would have read in dread, fast turning to pure horror. You're supposed to worry, you're supposed to know where they're headed (if only to be able to tell the policeman the next day something in response to the question, 'Where did she go?'), but what you're not allowed to do is use 'ought' when you speak to them. Because they don't like it. Because it doesn't work. Because it's likely to steer them defiantly in the very direction you don't want them to go in. Parents have to be chess players, while also being cool.

So what does that leave? A woman I was told about actually plans her utterances with her now grown-up, married-with-children daughter so that they never sound anything remotely like 'advice'. Essentially, it's a hyper-dishonest endeavour. Typically, she'll bury them into some mild-sounding, irrelevant-seeming, supposedly vacuous remark made about something unthreatening—like something she saw on *Better Homes and Gardens* last week. She'll direct her gaze indiscriminately into the vague mid-distance. The purpose of this crafted performance of nonchalance is to ensure that her very esoteric point might land in her daughter's consciousness without having been filtered out by the automatic spam defence system that rejects anything remotely like mother-to-daughter advice. This woman's husband occasionally overhears one of these constructions and is alerted to the artifice by the style of speaking as much as the bald-faced lies he occasionally picks up on (she never watches *Better Homes and Gardens*, for instance). Why is she rabbiting on about that, he thinks, and then realises that it's strategic: to make a certain point that might influence the thinking of the daughter.

The danger, of course, is that the remark is so nuanced, so velvet-gloved, so embedded, so camouflaged, that it's not taken up as intended. Can't be. It might have been heard but it wasn't understood. Not really, not fully, not as intended. At the end of the day, it's almost guaranteed not to be heeded. A state of affairs that, some might say, looking at the circumstance with the wisdom of distance or hindsight, ought not to have happened.

~ 30 ~

Honey

....

MOSTLY—AND I HAVE TO SAY, ideally—whispered sweet nothings are heard only by the participants involved in the communication—one each of speaker and hearer. There are no eavesdroppers, no one at the keyhole as it were. If beauty is in the eye of the beholder, then 'sweet pea', 'schnookums' and other such terms all hail from the same place—and that's a darkish, warmish, moist-ish kind of place where the goings-on are intimate and private. Say no more. No one else needs to know. Valvoline. You know what I mean.

Of course, once a year, on Valentine's Day, all those rules of discourse (and other –courses) go out the window and everyone's into sharing their schnookums liberally around to anyone who wants to voyeur or ear-eur. It's not that all these terms are born on 14 February each year. It's that on this day they have permission to rise to the surface, come out of the closet, march in the streets, and stand tall and proud. For one whole day, the silly, over-the-top mushiness that is the hallmark of couples in love is tolerated in the wider arena. It's their special day, and fair enough. Give them one day to get it all out of their system. Then things get back to normal on the 15th —the streets are hosed down and, within twenty-four hours, all evidence of the riotous behaviours of the day before have vanished. Schnookums has gone back to where it came from.

But on this one day, according to Roger Rosenblatt, endearments 'spread like nougat over the continents' and cause the earth to 'heave and deflate in one vast swoonish sigh'. As an anthropological event, the annual Valentine outpouring is on par with the yearly pilgrimage to Mecca or extravagantly noisy and dragon-centric Chinese New Year festivities. Potentially, it's another field day for the –ist brigade: anthropologists probing the underlying belief systems; linguists taxonomising the verbal patterns; psychologists investigating the motivations; sociologists pondering the distribution of power and the wider social meanings.

Sweet nothings may be considered pillow-talk between intimates, but what you call your beloved in private can end up being very important. This emerged during the palimony trial of film-star tough-man Lee Marvin when he was sued by former lover Michelle Triola. Marvin and Triola shared six years of not-entirely-smooth cohabitation, which ended when Triola was given the boot in 1970. Stunned and enraged, she sued him for palimony—a new word back then, combining 'pal' and 'alimony', and meaning: 'compensation claimed especially by the deserted party after the separation of an unmarried couple living together.'

In the court case, Triola's lawyer had the unenviable task of seeking to establish that Marvin had indeed loved Triola. He presented as evidence a letter from Marvin that ended with the line: 'Hey baby, hey baby, hey baby, hey baby, hey baby, hey baby.' Drawing a rather long bow, the lawyer claimed the letter was evidence that Triola had served Marvin as 'companion, homemaker, housekeeper and cook'. When asked to explain what his 'hey baby' line meant, Marvin couldn't, or wouldn't, oblige.

That was the end of that. Instead of 50 per cent of

US$3.6 million, Triola was awarded US$104,000 for 'rehabilitation'—an interesting use of the word, I must say—most of
which probably went to the lawyer. Still, a new word was added
to the language and henceforth celebrities, and others in like
circumstances, were savvy enough to get it in writing before
anyone went anywhere. A lesson Sir Paul McCartney may
have wished he'd heeded, though I have to say I find it quite
endearing that Sir Paul rejected a pre-nup on the grounds of its
being 'unromantic'.

Of course, making the whole case rest on 'hey baby'
(albeit, six of them) was a tenuous approach because what,
after all, can we say 'hey baby' means? While nothing means
anything definitive outside of its context of use and in the
absence of information about the participants, the circumstances, the history and the immediate co-text and context,
there are some explicit text-heavy utterances that may achieve
something meaningful on their own. But 'hey baby' is not
among them. 'Hey baby' can mean anything you want it to
mean. Fortunately for Marvin and his intact millions, it was
vague enough that on being quoted out of context, it
was, well, just vague enough to be meaningless, certainly as
evidence of love.

The curious thing about endearments is their universality. That is, most known peoples have found linguistic ways
of expressing their fondnesses. Of course, different languages
and cultures have their own specialities. English seems to have
concentrated on the edible (especially the sweet) and small
cute furry animals that hail from a Disney zone rather than the
animal kingdom. During research for the film *The Queen*,
starring Helen Mirren, it was discovered that the Duke of
Edinburgh uses 'cabbage' as his term of endearment for his
wife, the Queen.

But that's in English; it varies further afield. As well as cabbages, the French call their dear ones rabbits and casseroles. The Italians, little eggs. Nigerians refer to lovers as tigers, which may be ecologically understandable, and as bedbugs, which are evidently cuter in Nigeria than they are elsewhere. The Chinese use the term little dog, and the Germans, little treasure.

An underlying pattern is size, and the key word is little. Couples-in-love tend towards expressions that, without being reflexively belittling, make little of their sentiments, often through a diminutive suffix ('mousey') or an infantilising variation ('schnookums', 'Dodo loves Bebe'). Perhaps this feature demarcates the language as special and lends it (and them) some legitimacy—a kind of 'we're in love so we're allowed to be silly.'

A hardline feminist view might be that the diminutions assert one partner's possession of and/or superiority over the other ('my pet', 'my baby'), and serve as a vehicle for ongoing subordination and exploitation, thereby reflecting and recreating the broader patriarchal regime within the coupled microcosm. Well, such a conceptualisation might carry some water if the diminutive terms of endearment were consistently and unreciprocally one-way. But evidence suggests that the 'littling' and the silliness are mutual, two-way expressions. The feminist line sounds neat, if unempirical, but in any case, I rather prefer Roger Rosenblatt's verdict: 'The effect diminishes all parties. We have created these words as verbal comforters, warm safety zones, wherein anyone, no matter how high and mighty, is free to sound like a nitwit.'

Just as expressions of endearment vary across cultures in space, they also vary across cultures in time. By this I mean that the cultures (plural, because of course there's not just one) of Victorian England, for instance, could hardly be expected to be the same as the cultures of Blair's England in 2006. We don't expect Victoria and Albert to schnookumise (to create a verb of it), as perhaps Tony and Cherie might. This is where we need to call on the research of a historical lexicographer with a special interest in the language of personal endearment. Dr Julie Coleman of the University of Leicester's Department of English is one such scholar who has tracked the development of words like 'schnookums' across the centuries with the aim of noting the changes and what, if anything, such changes mirror of society.

Coleman's study is called *Love, Sex and Marriage: A Historical Thesaurus*, and in it she charts the changing forms of verbal endearment from the Anglo Saxon period through the Norman Conquest, the later Middle Ages, Victoriana, and up until the present day. There is no shortage of words to work with because of the plethora of euphemisms that have grown up around words deemed coy or lewd. The fact is that people do want to be able to talk about matters intimate and sexual, so to get around the various cultural and linguistic taboos of different eras, they resort to a euphemistic code which amply supplies them with the lexicon they need to express their endearments. Yet even within the retreat into euphemism, Coleman found that terms of endearment reflect social values.

Comparing modernity with previous centuries, Coleman found that terms of endearment in the modern era have characteristics that mark them off from previous eras. We tend to be more sexually explicit while also seeking out words that disguise the emotions. We go in for childish words, or even insulting ones, to express our affections, often resorting to, adopting or adapting names of characters from children's books or TV shows. We tend to use words that do not distinguish between being married or single, reflecting the declining significance of marriage. Not surprisingly, the language we use tends to shun terms emphasising the link between sex and procreation. After all, being no longer at the mercy of our fertility, we're able to conceive (sorry) of sex as pleasurable rather than as functional.

These are the patterns that distinguish modern usage from the Victorian period that preceded it. But even within the last century, different social mores have found their expression in different terms of endearment. Baby boomers growing up in the decades following World War II would have heard their parents address each other pretty uniformly as 'darling', 'honey', 'dear', 'love', 'sweetie'. This would have been roughly the same on *Leave it to Beaver* or *Father Knows Best* as it would have been in suburban Melbourne. Further, these are the pet names a child might be called by shopkeepers or parents of friends.

Anecdotal evidence suggests that generation Xers and Yers are more personal and creative in their endearments, tailoring them more closely to the context of their relationship. If 'darling' and 'honey' are typical of the anodyne nature of endearments that are attachable anywhere, any place—to wife, husband, child indiscriminately—then one thing that marks out gen Xers and Yers is that their endearments are not one-size-fits-all. Some examples here are 'mookie', 'bubs', 'cookie', 'plum', 'heart', 'cake'. One couple I was told about use 'face' as an endearment to each other. For example, 'Love you, Face' or 'Face, can you take the garbage out?' Clearly, 'face' has come out of some shared experience. A man I interviewed said a former girlfriend alternated between calling him 'brain' and 'dog', each of which apparently was equally endearing. Another couple reported using 'schnitzel' (for him) and 'strudel' (for her), but they were reluctant to clarify the Austrian connection.

Linked to the personal quality that endearments have been acquiring in recent years are the new proscriptions on use. If once you called not only your partner 'honey' but everyone else besides, then it was a generalised endearment, one-size-fits-all, universally applicable across the board— lover, friend, co-worker, customer, neighbour, child, dog, you name it. But once the endearment is tailor-made to the lover (like 'face' and 'brain'), then it loses its universality and appropriacy, and arguably, too, its piquancy. Thus one is expected to refrain from calling a subsequent lover by the name once allocated to someone else. In other words, the endearment is meant to be one-size-fits-only-one.

Another feature of recent endearments is their monosyllabic nature. It's 'hon' over honey, 'babe' over baby, 'darl' over darling, 'pet' over petal, 'bloss' over blossom. One commentator responded to this pattern by suggesting that the shortened forms seem to confirm the modern love of brevity. 'Maybe', he mused cynically, 'modern love is a fleeting experience.'

Language change is not surprising at any time, but especially not in a period of time that has become particularly conscious of the associations that words can have. The workplace has seen a dramatic reduction in the free use of endearment, especially gender-based endearment. A survey in the United Kingdom, conducted by Fish4Jobs, the UK's largest job board, looked into affectionate terms used in the workplace. It claims two out of five workers in the UK say their co-workers call them by a pet name, the ten most common of which were love, mate, duck, babe, sweetheart, honey, pet, chuck, darling and lover.

The UK study found mixed reactions to pet name-calling. Some thought the custom warm and friendly; others found it unprofessional and patronising. Women tended to have stronger views and were more likely to react in a hostile way, probably because they linked it, and not unreasonably so, to their lower status in the workplace. And with the increasing awareness of workplace harassment, and changing social and sexual mores, many are coping by erring on the side of caution. I know of a few rather confused, older male executives who worry about holding a door open for a woman, about what terms to use in addressing women and whether any comment on their appearance is out of place. When I've been consulted for my view on workplace gender relations, I've mostly advised this as a rule of thumb: don't deal in any way with a woman employee that you don't with a male employee. But it's clear that men raised in a different era find the new rules worrying or irritating, or both.

What's significant about the use of pet names is whether they're used reciprocally. If they're used only one-way, such as down the hierarchy (the boss calling the office manager 'darl'; the office manager calling the girl Friday 'honey'), then the non-reciprocity of exchange is a fair indicator that the pet-name use is linked to status. When the name-calling is linked to status, then every instance of it is a reminder of that status. This might be nice if you're the boss, but it won't be so nice for 'darl' or 'hon' who'd rather not stay back late when the late-afternoon call for the Coalition of the Willing is given.

Then again, you can decode a lot from the endearment applied to you. A friend commented recently, quasi-bitterly, that she'd progressed from 'hon' and 'luv' and 'darl' to 'Madame', which she attributed to her changing appearance—added girth, added lines on the face, etc.

In any case, without a doubt we live in times that seem more jaded, more cynical. As part of the empirical research for this chapter, I asked a rather permanent bachelor friend of mine (two ex-wives and a stream of short-lived relationships) what he calls his partners. He said: 'I call my current partner "Missing in Action". I could tell you what I call my exes, but I think that is outside your field of research.'

There is also less personal endearment towards small children and elderly people. Let's look at kids. We live in much firmer nuclear units today; remember when it took a village to raise a child? No more: the only contact you may have with children is with your own; for many women, the first child they hold in their arms is their own. In the old days, when kids walked home from school (now they're collected in 4WD Range Rovers with tinted windows), they ran into more people, said hello to more people. I was universally called 'pet' by others as a child. It could have been pet was for 'petal' or for small domesticated furry animal. It simply served as a friendly term of address to someone whose name you didn't know, or had forgotten or couldn't be bothered to use.

But things have changed. We've had a few decades of 'stranger danger' warnings and safe-house signage and school-room drills on escaping and reporting and school visits from the boys in blue, and all in all this may have reduced the number of attacks on children, if at the same time grossly increasing parental worry. Alongside these concerted efforts has always been the worrying knowledge that most attacks on children are not from strangers but from people they know, but this is a much tougher nut to crack.

We've had parliamentary hintings of paedophile networks implicating 'solid citizens'. We've seen institutions, like the church and the boy scout movement, as well as enough instances of teachers betraying the trust invested in them, to have seriously dented our blind faith. The truth is that you don't want anyone outside the family network taking an undue interest in your child. And you don't want them wandering up and using 'pet' or 'sweet pea' or sweet anything. Parents have stopped having T-shirts printed with their child's name on the front for fear that the name creates access—anyone can approach the child and gain their trust by using their name.

Broadly speaking, while endearments are still widely used, the rules of play have changed. Endearing language outside the context of an intimate relationship is much less acceptable. You don't want to be called honey or sweetie by a bank teller, a council worker, a call-centre operator, a police-man or, in fact, by anyone clearly younger than you. What was once uncomplicated just got very complicated. So if any of the traditional endearments end up in the Hospice of Fading Words, there needs to be a sign put up over the bed, indicating that what's fading is less the word itself than the rules that govern its use. There's surely a concise 'nil by mouth' style of phrase that would say this succinctly.

~ 31 ~

Fortitude

....

WE DON'T HAVE FORTS ANY MORE. You know, those heavily armed, pessimistically designed, impenetrable castle-like places that sat on high-up landmarks such as hills so that the people in them could look out on the rest of humanity with a sense of safety and superiority—not unlike the drivers and passengers of today's 4WDs. They're everywhere in Scotland, though over there they're called castles. These days the only predictable building atop a rising piece of terrain is a Catholic Church or school or both. Yet even without suburban forts, we still have the expression 'as safe as Fort Knox', which we can relate to as if we spent our childhoods watching cowboy-and-Indian movies, and even if we didn't know that that's where the US gold reserves are kept. It's probably a safe bet, though, that they've got state-of-the-art security facilities there.

All this means is that it's possible to know and correctly use an expression—such as Fort Knox—in a language without having any experiential sense of its meaning. Nor do you need even a clue as to its etymology. You won't be surprised that it comes from the Latin word for strong, and further back, to Old Latin and even Sanskrit, where there's a connection to the words for 'high' and 'elevate'. You won't be surprised by this information and, interesting though it is, it's not needed for the skill of being able to use 'fort' in sentences, both comfortably and accurately. After all, we happily take a Panadeine Forte with not a moment's thought to the revivalist Latin.

Even a century ago, there weren't many forts. The closest most of us have come to seeing/being in something fort-like is your mock version made of wood used for children's outdoor playground furniture. The kind that encourages imaginative adventures, albeit not splinters or tears. Short of that there's your celluloid fort à la *Dances With Wolves*.

'Fortitude' is not a word with much currency any more. We still have the verb ('fortify') and the adjective ('fortified') and when they're not being used in their military sense (such as *Operation Fortitude*, the massive Allied counter-intelligence operation in World War II), they tend to mean something like a medicine or a drink that has been artificially strengthened. Indeed, that's what a tonic is—a drink that has been medicinally fortified. As regards alcohol, or so I'm told by one who ought to know, a fortified drink is the preferred drink of those drinking-to-be-blotto. Rarely anymore do we hear 'fortitude' being used in relation to strength of mind in the face of adversity. Sure, it'll probably resurrect soon as a website or an army blog or the name of a soft drink, but for the moment it's simply a word on the way out.

Not always so. 'Fortitude' once had a proud place in the language. For instance, in the city of Brisbane there's a busy, if somewhat benighted, suburb called Fortitude Valley. It wasn't always a suburb of a modern city. It used to be a fairly isolated valley, and the story of how it got its name reflects much about early colonial Australia. Fleshing this out a little will serve as a cameo introduction to the notion of fortitude, for it's a story built, in turn, on high expectations, disillusionment, despair and survival, and for this to have happened, as we shall see, fortitude was needed in no small measure.

Back in the mid-19th century, still in the heartland of colonial times, the powers-that-be in the penal colony of Sydney were looking around for somewhere else to send their very worst convicts—a rather macabre mirroring of the British transportation that used Australia to solve the accommodation problems of overflowing British prisons. They clearly didn't want them in their own backyard, and people don't, even today, want their home turf to be so sullied—hence our acronym 'nimby' ('not in my backyard') for those who oppose entrepreneurial development near where they live. Nimby is a new word for an old concept. With the same motive in mind, Moreton Bay had been founded to enable Sydney to send its overflow of undesirables, the worst of the worst—somewhere, anywhere, but not here.

Explorers who were sent up north to assess the prospects for settlement came back with good news. Then, as was the way then, the site came to be considered too good for society's dregs and was opened up for free settlers. It was a big decision at the time, but nevertheless the plan soon capsized because the free settlers failed to come in the anticipated numbers. Eventually, one enthusiastic Presbyterian minister, the Reverend Dr John Dunmore Lang, put his money where his mouth was and chartered three vessels in the first of many grand immigration schemes which brought about 630 British immigrants through the period of 1848–49. The first lot of 'Langites', as they were called, and I'm not sure if the designation was affectionate or not, were 49 souls who arrived in three ships: the *Fortitude*, *Chaseley* and *Lima*.

Migration is rarely easy, and it's worse when expectations are a poor fit with reality. The newcomers had been promised allocations of land on arrival, and no doubt it was the prospect of such ownership that encouraged them to make the risky and arduous journey in the first place. But people-transportation over long distances back then has much in common with people-smuggling today. There were few guarantees; indeed, for the price of your ticket you were opening yourself to the great likelihood of being robbed blind and dumped at the end of the earth to fend for yourself.

Such was the lot of the human cargo of the *Fortitude*. They didn't get their parcels of land, as promised, and instead settled in a place they named Fortitude Valley, which at first was a miserable shanty town. Named after the vessel that brought them there, but also most likely with a winking nod to the test of character that the experience turned out to be. Today, people drive through Fortitude Valley on their way to somewhere else and rarely give a thought to the name and its origins. As you do. We live, after all, with both feet in the here-and-now.

But 'fortitude' was an ordinary English word well before that ship got its name. And the concept itself has a long and noble history in Western civilisation, being one of the four virtue ethics that originated in ancient Greek philosophy. Along with the other three (prudence, justice and temperance), fortitude featured as the strength of mind that enables one to endure adversity with courage, and is associated with that triumvirate of philosophical wisdom—Socrates, Plato and Aristotle.

Two words that congregate around fortitude, or at least feel comfortable in the same company, are 'resilience' and 'stoicism'. All three seem to have been born in that place that acknowledges that not all of life is a bed of roses, and that certain qualities of character can be developed and cultivated to prepare you for coping if and when you have to.

The fact is that fortitude has probably run its course,

given the beating it received through the first half of the 20th century. Two world wars, interpolated by a cataclysmic economic depression were surely enough to teach you some basic fortitude. Without a modicum of the quality, you'd have very likely gone under and never come up. Millions did. And we can't actually blame their demise on lack of fortitude—as your survival prospects depended more on where you were located when the tanks rolled in and the bombs started falling. But when times are tough, there's no doubt that fortitude is considered a good quality of character. Things are hard enough without whining. It's in everyone's interests that a society *in extremis* has citizens with high readings of fortitude.

The generation born before 1946 is sometimes called 'the silent generation', a descriptor that attests to their qualities of resilience, stamina and fortitude. Workplace managers with mixed teams of 'silents', Xers and Yers are sometimes advised to use generation-specific strategies to achieve the best from their teams. For example:

> The Silent Generation born before 1946 grew up in 'Pleasantville' and adopted the values of their elders such as loyalty, dedication and commitment. Their goal was lifetime employment in a solid organisation and they looked forward to a comfortable retirement.
>
> Get the best out of 'Silents' by using their strong work ethic. If you respectfully assert your authority and genuinely use their expertise you will have success. They tend to be natural team players and supporters and will be an integral part of your team. They do however, prefer a formal atmosphere and they love to talk with real people so avoid email or voicemail and give the personal touch. Let them mix with others and publicly recognise

their achievements with overt signs such as certificates or plaques. These symbols may not mean much to you but they are usually significant to this age group.

Between the threat of hunger and of death, there was more than enough to weigh you down. Silly-sounding expressions like 'stiff upper lip' and 'chin up' begin to make sense in the context of so much gravity-bearing weight. A woman I interviewed who was a child in the 1940s said:

> Everyone felt bad. Everyone was sad or frightened or both. You waited for news but you also dreaded getting news. You were constantly fearful. And everyone was the same, trying to keep their chin up, for everyone else's sake. Not complaining was part of the effort of staying alive and part of knowing that everyone else was trying to stay alive too.

Stiff upper lip is particularly associated with the reputedly British quality of keeping your emotions contained and battened down. Holding it all together, especially in times that threaten to overwhelm you, is considered culturally worthy—as much of an individual, especially male, as of a society. We're speaking here of a highly structured and regulated society where public face is valued and respected, and where, no matter what you do behind the scenes, you must not compromise the outer poise. By all means beat up the wife and kids in a violent rage when you get home, but never betray an inkling of it while you're out and about.

Not for nothing was there the adage 'out of sight, out of mind', which brings to mind the dogged ability of a former generation of Anglo stock to clear their mind of unwanted complications that were not immediately demanding their attention. Perhaps that's how they managed to cope with such a large amount of hypocrisy and humbug.

As for the lip, that's easy. When someone is in the grip of their emotions and losing their poise, their lips are likely to quiver or tremble. Because a man's upper lip was often adorned by a moustache, any quivering in the upper lip's vicinity was likely to be easily observable. Hence the specific injunction to keep that upper lip particularly stiff.

The lyrics of a number of wartime songs stand as a testimonial to an age that had need of the word fortitude:

> Smile though your heart is aching
> Smile, even though it's breaking
> When there are clouds in the sky, you'll get by
> If you smile through your fear and sorrow
> Smile and maybe tomorrow
> You'll see the sun come shining through for you

We've come a long way from fortitude et al. to the culture of confession and disclosure, epitomised by television shows like *Oprah*, *Dr Phil*, *Jerry Springer* and *Sally-Anne*. Here the idea is to let it all hang out—all the secrets, shames, hidden bits. Put it all out there, hold nothing back. Confession is good for the soul. Don't hold it in, let it out. Don't be anal. Share it about. The airing-and-sharing will be cathartic—it'll make you feel better. And as we're talking about emotional disclosure *qua* entertainment, it'll make everyone else feel better, too, so in that sense it's a social service you're performing.

Robert Hughes wrote an entire treatise—*The Culture of Complaint*—on the subject of the indulgence of a life unguided by the solid qualities of fortitude. In a more religious era, you prayed; in today's more secular age, you get angry and make a noise and do something about it. It's the squeaky wheel, after all, that gets the oil. We live in an era of protest and ombuds-people. Stoicism and fortitude are sneered at. I have a neighbour with a yappy Jack Russell called 'Wussy', presumably because he whines at the drop of a hat. I have no sense, however, that the name is meant as a put-down. In an era when fortitude has no place, wussiness may even be esteemed.

There was a great cartoon in *The Spectator* some time ago. It showed a World War II sort of man and a more modern, contemporary-looking person. The World War II man was saying something like: 'Hmmmm, my brother got shot down over Germany—haven't heard if he's okay. Another night in the bomb shelter last night—Oh well, chin up, mustn't grumble.' Meanwhile, the other chap had seen a dead rabbit on the road and was screaming for a grief counsellor.

~ 32 ~

Modesty

....

ACCORDING TO SIDNEY BAKER, all languages have ample supplies of words for 'the good, the bad and the stupid', terms that always secure wide mention, because 'these are some of the simplest and most persistent things upon which we are inspired to comment'.

We've already had a look at the bad and the stupid, so let's focus on the good. It is certainly true that we have not had any shortage of terms to describe the good—such as when we recognise expertise, skill, talent, or a high level of knowledge or aptitude. There are many words we once used for such descriptions that today would more likely be found in the hospice.

Take, 'dab' for instance. You might be a dab hand at fixing things or a dab hand with a paintbrush. It's an easy, friendly kind of word, possibly derived as a corrupt contraction from the Latin *adeptus* (skilled, able to). But it's much more relaxed and comfortable than 'adept'.

An alternative to the dab hand is the 'wizard', or the more common shortened colloquial form, 'whiz'. Smart kids used to be called whiz kids; these days, if we don't simply ignore them, we'd probably put them in a special school for the gifted and talented, and bless the school with additional counselling facilities for dealing with behavioural aberrations. A 'swot' used to be a wannabe whiz, blessed with ample perspiration and motivation, but less up top, though when people were being honest, it was most often the case that the so-called whiz kid was also a swot. Nowadays, both groups, sadly enough, would most likely be called 'nerds' by their peers.

Other changes have happened. We've transferred the 'whiz' notion to gadgetry, such as the kitchen whiz—an all-purpose cutting/chopping/food preparation unit that purportedly can do everything save stack/empty the dishwasher or take out the garbage. The fact that it usually has something like a whizzing sound allows the trademark brand name to combine both senses of 'whiz'—the qualities of speed and smartness—in one.

We also used to say 'bee's knees' as in, she's the bee's knees when it comes to growing roses. Or cooking lamingtons. This is fine as long as you were being described as the bee's knees, but not if you yourself thought you were the bee's knees. Well, put it this way: you could think yourself such, but you'd have to keep that view to yourself and display a less boastful position in public.

One of the cardinal rules of social interaction used to be abiding by the modesty principle, which in essence meant minimising self-praise, and in case of being on the receiving end of a compliment, minimising the claim while also being gracious.

An example from the Japanese language may help here. The Japanese word *sensei* is an honorific extended to teachers, priests, politicians and other apparently esteemed folk, as a sign of respect. Sometimes *San* is added to the name, with the same effect. Both of these terms are used about another; it would be unthinkable to use them in terms of yourself. It'd be akin to a judge calling himself 'My Honour'.

However, some notable exceptions exist to the modesty principle where the rules on self-praise are, as it were, lifted temporarily. Politicians on the hustings, advertisers and promoters, and some idiosyncratic cases like Muhammed Ali's (Cassius Clay's) 'I am the greatest.' He also said 'I don't always know what I'm talking about, but I know I'm right.' Then there are in-between circumstances like talking about yourself in a job interview, where you have to juggle the two balls of self-promotion and modesty to achieve your desired goal. No one said it was easy.

A dictionary will tell you that the bee's knees means the very best, or the height of excellence. Oddly enough, height is a factor because, as we know, the bee is not a very tall creature, and standing upright (which I don't think they do), their knees are even closer to the ground than their head. Various explanations exist for the expression about bees and their knees. One claims that in 1920s America, it was fashionable to make such preposterous analogies, usually involving an animal or insect, an anatomical body part or an item of clothing. Thus we have the 'kipper's knickers', the 'cat's garters', the 'cat's pajamas', the 'snake's hips', the 'leopard's stripes', the 'pig's wings' and many others of this ilk.

Another explanation has a more insect-centric perspective, claiming that a bee's corbiculae, or pollen baskets—a good metaphor for bounty or goodness or worthiness—are located on its tibiae which, being at the mid-segment of the legs, are very knee-like. A third (and perhaps more likely) explanation suggests that 'knees' has no actual referential meaning and only works because it rhymes with 'bees'. A case of sound rules. Or a case of Occam's razor perhaps—the more straightforward, the more likely.

Being the bee's knees was another way of being 'the top banana'. You could also be 'a real pro', 'a hot shot', 'a crackshot', 'a past master', 'the tops', 'the top gun' or 'the cock o' the walk'.

These days you might be called 'a legend'. After the sudden deaths of Steve Irwin and Peter Brock, within days of each other, I received an email from my son that said: 'You may have read that a number of Australian legends have recently died. Just wanted to say I'm feeling fine, not to worry.' It took me a few moments to catch on. Other terms like 'legend' are 'the Man', or 'boss' as in 'he's a boss cook', or being told 'you rock'. The son, same one as above, once told me I rock, and it took me a few moments, again, to cotton on to the non-geological connection.

If the skill under discussion was of a mechanical or technical nature, you might be called 'handy' (good at fixing things), 'savvy' (from the French verb, *savoir*, to know, implying practical know-how rather than intellectual knowledge) or 'nifty' (mid-19th century theatre slang, possibly a reduced form of 'Magnificat'). There's also the 'all-singing, all-dancing . . .' which can mean a Jack/Jill of all trades. This one always reminds me of a spruiker I once heard outside a strip club in Times Square, New York, saying over and over: 'All girls, all nude, all night.'

Perhaps the assertion that 'there are no flies' on you was the biggest compliment of all. It meant you were alert, active, functioning vigorously, getting about, not standing still, making a fist of things, moving ahead, all at sufficient pace to deny flies a landing place. I can still remember as a kid looking for the flies, but regardless of whether or not I saw any, it didn't seem to help me make any sense of the phrase. By the time I worked out (years later, mind you) the connection with speed, activity and flies, people weren't saying it any more. They were saying they'd 'got all bases covered', or they were being 'pro-active'. Today we're likely to hear that someone's 'across all the issues', or is 'all over it', or has 'got it all going on'. I tend to think, however, that these really only go part of the way, that, even while I am no fan of heat and insects, the flies certainly had a particularly expressive something.

Having no flies on yourself is what you might want other people to say about you; it's not something you want to be saying very loudly about yourself. If you did, you'd likely be thought of as having 'tickets on yourself', or worse, as being 'up yourself'.

If being called a 'skite' or a 'bull artist' was anathema, so too was being called a 'snob'. The word itself has origins shrouded in mystery. Prior to the late 18th century it meant a cobbler or shoemaker, or the apprentice thereof. Pretty much, as low as you can go. Over time, it drifted into Cambridge University slang for 'townsman or local merchant', an indicator perhaps of the famous town-and-gown divide. By 1831, it had come to be used more broadly for a person of the ordinary or working classes. Within twenty years it had taken on the meaning of 'one who vulgarly apes his social superiors', and another fifty years later, it acquired its (related but surprisingly distinct) modern sense of 'one who despises those considered inferior in rank, attainment or taste.'

As the nose got higher, so too did the disdain. There's a peculiar, even ironic, parallelism between the semantic mobility of the word 'snob' and the actual kind of person to whom the word refers. It's as if the word started low and then forgot, or chose to forget, its roots. Is that why snobs are so disdained? For their upward pretensions? It tends not to be the cash-flow deprived families of old money who are disliked as much as the flashy new money, where money, but not manners, has been acquired too quickly.

Scorn would generally fall on anyone perceived to have tickets on themselves. These tickets are not those you'd purchase for a train trip, for example. Rather they would seem to be betting tickets that bookies scribble out and give you when you place a bet. Someone so supremely self-confident in their own talents as to bet on themselves, will have tickets on themselves, and these tickets bespeak a very public arrogance. A number of informants have suggested to me that the notion (and negative connotations) of backing yourself as a winner has links to bygone days of amateur sports. Then, the only way an amateur sportsman could earn any money for their efforts was by making a bet on themselves. Sportsmen of independent means had no need to resort to such lowly behaviour, and hence backing yourself, or having tickets on yourself, was considered ungentlemanly and contemptible.

It's worth noting that the notion of self-promotion has again shifted ground. Although it's still not on to have tickets on yourself, which you don't hear much any more, backing yourself is now linked to the newly fashionable self-esteem zeitgeist. People are now urged to 'back themselves', meaning have a go, have faith in your own abilities, bank on or invest in yourself. You can even use it to talk about yourself and do so without appearing to be 'up yourself'—for example, 'I've decided to back myself with this book and just write it.' There's a hint of the Aussie battler giving himself a go, cutting himself some slack. It is much less objectionable than the brash American confidence we're now very used to. Backing yourself is not being up yourself as much as it is opting for the chances available to you in the land of opportunity. You see it in advertisements everywhere. 'Why L'Oreal? Because I'm worrrth it!'

The kind of attitude we're on about here is best summarised in the word 'up'. 'Up', along with its various offshoots, says it all. A favourite expression, and one that endures, is being 'up yourself'—this of course being a nice way of saying being up your arse, having an inflated opinion of yourself, one that the people around you don't share. Another view is that it equates with 'wanker', someone so self-involved and egotistical, their sexual gratification is of the very solitary kind.

In fact, the metaphor of elevation, or high and low for social stratification, is deeply embedded, albeit less visible. Consider the expressions 'high and mighty' (meaning over-weening or arrogant); 'highbrow' (of self-consciously cultured taste); 'highfalutin' (absurdly and unnecessarily elaborate, especially applied to speech); 'high-handed' (overbearing in a superior way); 'high-sounding' (self-consciously trying to sound superior); on one's 'high horse' (having a tone of superiority about one's position or opinion); to be of 'high birth' (born into the high class); 'high society' (as close as you can go to the top, presumably).

A definite feudal whiff lurks about these words, and it's not too hard to conjure up an image of a monarch ruling by that most convenient of institutions, divine right, and supported on each side by the nobility and the clergy and, of course, an army to do their bidding, and then the great unwashed, the hoi polloi who, by the sweat of their brow and back, did all the work and paid all the taxes that kept the whole show on the road. The riff-raff, in other words.

Now 'riff-raff' is a term that's not heard much any more, which is a shame as it may lead to its demise and that of its colourful history. It has no connection to 'reffo' (refugee), though in early postwar Australia, in the eyes of some, all reffos were riff-raff (though, logically, not all riff-raff were reffos). Of course, there's a pattern here in the history of migration—those of the first wave are always considered riff-raff, they're reviled, even despised, before they eventually win respect for their hard work and their indomitable spirit. Then they, in their turn—now established and moving out to the suburbs—bring out the despise and revile verbs to pour over the next wave of human detritus from a more recent war zone. And so it goes on.

The story of 'riff-raff' starts in a set phrase of medieval French—*rifle et rafle*—where *rifle* meant to spoil or strip, and *rafle* to carry off. As a phrase, the words alluded graphically to the habit of plundering dead bodies left strewn on a battlefield and carrying off the booty. Apparently this is what would happen at the end of the day's battle. We're left watching the credits where, in real time, riff-raff marauders would creep back onto the field to plunder and pillage. Lovely image. I believe, in Mafia movies, this is called the 'wet work'—mopping up after the slaughter. I suppose someone has to do it. And the notion's not lost, if you think of pop culture's most famous wet worker, Harvey Keitel's character Mr Wolf from *Pulp Fiction*.

When the phrase first slipped into English as 'rif and raf', it meant 'every scrap'. You can see the link to the looting and plundering. Over the next few hundred years the meaning shifted towards 'everyone and anyone', that is, the common people, any ordinary person of no apparent rank. And it continued to leach downwards to its current status—the dregs of society, the lowest of the low. And they say you have to go to India for a true caste system.

That's where we are today. Of course, we can see the descendants of the medieval French—to 'rifle', to search hurriedly; and a 'raffle', a lottery where the winner carries off the prize. In the early 19th century, the adjective 'raffish' appeared, and was applied to people considered disreputable or common, in the sense of vulgar. Later, 'raffish' came to suggest a certain attractive Bohemian quality of the unconventional; perhaps dishevelled but not to the point of being challenged in the body hygiene department. (It's interesting how both 'snob' and 'raffish' have changed their connotations, both having begun in lowly positions before clawing their way to the top, but where 'raffish' draws on its origins for its hint of subversive allure, 'snob' has seemingly forgotten where it came from.) These days, 'raffish' accompanies the kind of charm that absolutely excludes any whiff of the unwashed, so the suffix –ish definitely exerts its mitigating influence. In any case, contemporary raffishness is a studied look; it eschews deprivation and hardship, even while, ironically, wooing waifdom. Today, we'd expect designer stubble at the very least, and maybe an aftershave called RAF, priced to exclude the very element that is the basis of the allusion. Quite mad, really.

PART VI

THE PAST IS DEAD, LONG LIVE THE FUTURE

～ 33 ～

Doing food

THEY SPEAK OF A POST-9/11 WORLD. They could just as easily speak of a post-fried world. In the before-world, food— as in fat and fried—connoted flavour, finger-licking, indulgence. Eating was time-out. Consuming involved some effort, albeit enjoyable effort: there was chewing, the teeth were involved, cud was not that far off. I can imagine a time, in the days before the war on fat, when lingering over a tasty, fatty morsel of meat was a wholly positive experience. Now we live in a new era— defined perhaps by the fact that the 'Fried' has gone from Kentucky Fried Chicken, a handy omission afforded so serendipitously by the abbreviation KFC.

In the after-world, food and especially fat, are mostly bad. We're into light and lean (consider those pre-packed, home-delivered services like 'Light 'n' Easy'). There are big demands on food these days—it needs to be everything: fast, economical, minimal, tasty, diverse.

Overall, it's less interactional and more transactional. It gets things done; it's not trying to improve the quality of one's relationships. It's also blurred its edges so that it bleeds into 'lifestyle'. When the doctor says, 'Let's talk about lifestyle factors that can impact on your condition', you have to be nuts not to read between the euphemisms. We've entered the Asian cup-o-soup world, a far cry from the crackling cosmos we came from. 'Gravy' is now a bad word—whether it goes with 'train' or just with the roast. I know this because of the number of gravy boats that have been appearing of late in St Vincent de Paul op-shops. If gravy is going out, the boat's not needed.

Related to the banishment of 'fried' is the accumulating knowledge and dissemination of information about nutrition. Most specifically, here, about fat. I mean surely we who are living today know more about fat than anyone who has ever lived on this planet. Hands up those who haven't been living on a desert island and don't know about bad fats, as in hot chips and Danish pastries, and good fats, as in nuts (some nuts, not all nuts) and avocado. Now, keep your hands up if you think your grandparents knew what you know. Mmm, I thought so. Back then, when they sat on verandahs and chewed the fat, you can bet it wasn't the Omega kind.

So, it's not a big assertion to state that food isn't what it used to be. I say this in a descriptive rather than an evaluative sense. I'm not about to nostalgically reminisce about the home, hearth and repasts of yore, but nor am I going to wax lyrical about contemporary cuisine. I'm simply noting the difference, neither grieving the loss, nor celebrating the gain. Very postmodern of me.

So let's see what this amounts to. Food has changed, both substantively, in terms of the 'what' of food and the 'how' of cooking; and representationally, in terms of how we talk about such matters. And, of course, it's the language that we're primarily interested in here, not the niceties of social history. The two phenomena are linked—a poke around in the language will usually yield some important insights into how we used to live compared with how we live now.

At the substantive level, there are new crops, new cuts and new taste combinations available that simply were not around years ago. The dinner table, or more correctly, that which appears on top of it, is qualitatively different. Gone are the stalwarts of a former cuisinary era—chicken Maryland, beef stroganoff, bombe alaska, flummery, lemon delicious, bread and butter pudding (which may be making a little come back). All that offal we now eschew—brains, lamb's fry, sweetbread, itself named as a euphemism—spurring on the sympathetic if etymythological notion that 'offal' and 'awful' are joined at the hip. The humble choko and squash are almost vanished, and pumpkin has to have ginger or coriander or crumbled Bulgarian fetta or a hint of Thai spices to render it acceptable. And despite the fact that sweet potato has an old, even prehistoric look, I don't ever remember it as a part of my childhood; nor do I recall more than two kinds of regular potatoes, unlike the seventy-one varieties now vying for our vegetable dollar.

In their place, a host of cuisinary arrivals. Take 'rocket', for instance, which launched itself onto the gourmet market a few years ago, its sexy piquant flavour forcing poor old lettuce into the nearest corner to limp out and cry. Then 'broccolini' arrived—lean, delicate, enticing—its very presence beginning to shame the mother plant, broccoli, which started to look comparatively shabby, much as cauliflower did when broccoli first appeared. Is this a kind of vegetative justice—what goes around, comes around? Or is it Realpolitik, writ small: out with the rogue state vegetable, in with the newly arrived (supposed) democratic replacement?

Then there's lamb 'backstrap'—delicious, expensive, versatile. And 'frenched' cutlets, which are nowhere near as lewd as they sound. And 'tenderloin' of chicken. I recall when I first heard it said, it almost made me blush, recalling my earliest encounter with 'loins', at least loins of the literary kind, in the D.H. Lawrence texts of English 101, where I wondered at length about the proximity of 'loin' to 'groin', both phonically and anatomically. Even 'lovely legs' caught me by surprise in a way that 'drumsticks' never would have, but then a lovely leg is not simply a drumstick by another name, is it?

And don't get me started on cheeses because, really, in my youth, cheese was cheddar and cheddar was cheese, and there you had it, in a nutshell. The only other place that cheese featured was in the instruction to smile. My European parents would bring home some smelly foul-looking thing they called cheese (I presumed they'd got the English wrong), and would then proceed to eat it while my brother and I would hold our noses, aghast. We called it 'stinky cheese' (sometimes pronounced 'shtinky'), and it wasn't affectionate.

As for taste combinations—what was mixed with what in the cooking and what was served with what on the plate—who'd have thought of adding pulp of passionfruit to a salad dressing or putting cloves in rice? It's a wonder that a generation reared on meat-and-two-veg can so nonchalantly combine an Asian-style entrée with a Moroccan main and an Italian dessert. How did the palate change, and did anyone notice it was happening?

All these changes—it's no wonder that the way we represent food has also changed. There's not a lot you can say about meat-and-two-veg to increase its power of seduction. By contrast, the menu in a classy restaurant can leave your heart aflutter. The flaked crab, lying back on a bed of pumpkin puree, yearning for the gentle touch of the avocado and coriander salsa, while the hand-fed calf emerges as a thin slip of an escalope, poached with a light squeeze of lemon and a hint of oregano, and served with tender baby carrots barely out of infancy. Sometimes you don't know where to look.

Food has changed because we look at it differently. And the new approach brought an extra something—a whole new dynamism. It's not just the shepherd's pie that's gone; even more important is the passing of stasis itself. Now, not only are our palates re-educated; they have ditched the very notion of restraint and now expect to continue to be challenged. So, not only do we look at matters of food differently from the way we once did, but we're continually re-constructing both ourselves and our eating styles. We've moved from a food-as-fuel society where food languished with 'shelter' right at the base of the Maslowian triangular hierarchy of needs. Now it's moved up, right to the apex, where it joins other elements of our self-actualising selves. It's part of our identity now. I am what I eat. I eat therefore I am. We define ourselves by our dietary predilections, our food intolerances, what we crave and what we eschew.

Food is now an aesthetic, a commodity, an accessory, a statement, a credential, a promise, a lifestyle, a philosophy. It sports an idiosyncratic and iconoclastic blend of the epicurean, the sensual and even the spiritual. As someone said to me recently in an email inviting me out to lunch and inquiring about any dietary restrictions or ideological orientations: 'You'll need to tell me if you're into a personal boycott of venues serving llama with jus de Anglican cumquat.' Indeed a whole etiquette has grown up about announcing and catering for your dietary peccadilloes. So much for being grateful for the plate that's served to you.

Perhaps it's best summed up as: whereas now we consume, before we ate. 'Eat' has always been fairly close to the ground. Like the German equivalent, *essen*—not as close as *fressen*, which is what pigs do, but along the lines thereof. 'Consume' is of an altogether different order. It implies something else; it suggests possibilities unknown to 'eat'. In terms of range, you eat foods, but you consume books, films, opera, paperclips, boyfriends. If 'eat' involves the highly mechanical, if naturalised, process of ingestion, digestion, absorption, elimination, helped along by the graciousness of the odd enzyme, and all of it pretty autonomous—then 'consumption' is all about volition, selection and indulgence. Of course, there are exceptions—there's little to get excited about in, say, 'electricity consumption'.

Yes, 'eat' is the low-grade Germanic cousin to the classy, passionate Romantic 'consume'. And at that nexus of sensuality and consumption, we find a new way of representing the world of food and cooking, a discourse that goes, tellingly, by the name of 'food porn'. Here an intermingling of sexuality and ingestion brings boundaries to the point where they simply don't matter. In the following advertisement for new-season oranges, the text becomes a romantic letter. The lover/consumer languishes forlorn and adrift in a dyad of unrequited love, addressing the food item as they would an object of carnal desire. As ever, the language sends its own meta-messages:

Dear Blood Orange,

You are the apple of my eye. Upon your return each winter season, my appetite gets aroused and dopamine starts to course through my body. The others—Valencia, the navel, for instance—lack your panache, your pure passion . . . It's not just your brilliant flesh that excites, but your tangy taste. Oh, how I love to pair you with a julienne of fennel and mint, covered with rich olive oil and Maldon salt. Raw fish desires your gentle acidity. Married to champagne, you make a mean mimosa. How fortunate am I that you now reside locally, [for] Sicily made our relationship tenuous. Still, you torture me with your transience and I fear this wintry romance is nearing its end. Please forgive me as I part you from your pith and pulse you in a blender . . . You've wound your way into my heart.

This is not the food that was once associated with home, hearth, mother and comfort. It's not food as fuel, gotta eat, gotta live. This food has ditched utility and adopted aesthetics. It's something you look at—whether that be gazing at amazing pictures of dishes that you know you'll never cook, watching Naked Chef Jamie Oliver doing his thing, or partaking in a classy foodies' do, where miracle dishes—requiring 'food stylists' as much as chefs—are created in front of you amid no pretense that anyone's going home to give it a whirl.

Food writer Molly O'Neill captures it well when she defines food porn as 'prose and recipes so removed from real life that they cannot be used except as vicarious experience'. It's in the removal from real life that food becomes objectified, making it, in the words of Anthony Bourdain—the *Kitchen Confidential* author who destroyed forever the innocent trust with which one once dined out—'a glorification of food as a substitute for sex.' But is there not something sadly Warholish about displays and descriptions of food preparation for an audience that has no intention of actual consumption?

In an article for *Columbia Journalism Review*, O'Neill found an inverse relationship between the amount of money people spend on kitchen appliances and the amount they cook. I know a woman who acquired a second rice cooker ('It had such lovely lines, I couldn't resist'), even though she already had one, which she'd used twice in as many years. It now sits alongside the first one, both of them waiting silently. Do they console one another? Or have they accepted their fate?

Cooking is now something to talk about, watch, read and generally know about, yet not something everyone can do. There are dozens of weekly TV shows to choose from. You can have your chef naked or in iron, or take bites of Nigella or Huey for breakfast, lunch, or anytime at all on the Lifestyle Channel. Watch them all if you like—order in, and keep watching—then, when it's all over, go out to eat. If you prefer to get your information from the internet, key in 'carbonara' or 'white bait', and sit back and choose. Read them and then go out to eat. If you prefer the print medium, there are magazines by the dozen, as well as cookbooks so glamorous, so seductive, they're inching, in both size and aesthetics, towards being coffee-table books. Then there are books—like *Chocolat*—that interweave an intimate narrative in and around personal recipes. Who beyond the locals and the globe-trotting jetseterati knew about Tuscany and Provence before the genre of olive-oil literature?

So food literacy is up. Seems everyone's a foodie now. They know all about what's new, what's on, what goes with what, what wine to drink and what not to drink with what dish. Monolingual foodies can navigate the hyper-self-conscious French or Italian of the menus with finesse and panache. Stolid, boring married men watch Jamie Oliver as entertainment. None of this implies they can cook. To be a foodie is to know *about*, not to know *how*. We really need two different verbs for the two different kinds of knowledge.

At home, foodies can have a secret cache of comfort food—baked beans or Nutella on white bread—that they'd die under torture rather than fess up about. Where once you might have checked out the contents of the bathroom cupboard, when invited over, now you might sneak a peek in the pantry to see what secrets lurk backstage in your host's life and psyche.

For, of course, the new urban apartments have no real kitchen. It's the stainless-steel galley look. It's not a kitchen; now it's a nook. Urban contemporary. Sharp clean lines. No clutter. No time to spend in kitchens. Cartoon yuppies— singles, marrieds, live-in companions—who can't boil water between them but can use the complicated espresso machine. Got to get your priorities in place. Some people don't associate 'home' with 'food'. They can't/won't cook. They only eat out— a bite on the run for breakfast, a mid-morning coffee somewhere close by, lunch from the little bistro down the way, grab a meal on the way home or come home, shower and change, and go out to dine. Stop off somewhere else later for dessert. There's that chocolate place that's to die for. Next day, it starts all over again. Your old family restaurant—à la Sizzler—is so déclassé. McDonald's doesn't get a look-in.

Molly O'Neill suggests that perhaps consumers of food writing/shows are lured by the seduction of another reality 'where cooking is slow and leisurely and imbued with a comforting glamour'—all the reassurance of the traditional home comfort without the messy sink or the dowdy oil-spattered apron. If urban-dwellers living in an increasingly violent world watch crime shows to feel safe, then perhaps food-watchers turn to objectified and glamorised food for reassurance of another kind.

An interesting development within the engourmisation of a nation is its strange bifurcation. At some point, it seems to have gone off in a sensual and aesthetic direction, dispensing, almost entirely in some cases, with the boring bits, the daily drudgery, the grind and grudge factors—purchase, preparation, serving and cleaning up. This is food that doesn't mess things up, not even a little. Like those off-white, minimalist *Belle*-style house interiors where you can't imagine yourself, or anyone else, actually living. No way would you have children there.

Is there a gender factor mixed in with the ingredients? The old-style approach to food and cooking was uber-gendered. Molly O'Neill tells us it distinguished between those who cook (traditionally, women) and those who savour but tend not to cook (traditionally, men). These boundaries have blurred somewhat. There's a story told, it may be apocryphal, about a former politician who wanted to marry a woman who happened to be a merchant banker. In response to his proposal, she said, 'I don't cook, I just don't cook.' A suitcase full of meaning is packed into that line: it has to do with expectations and assumptions, traditional roles, laying down your cards, setting conditions—'If you want a wife who cooks, look elsewhere.' I've been telling my daughter for years that it's a great line, one she should keep a note of and keep at the ready for use at the appropriate time. She just laughs, more at the idea of marriage itself than at my recommended strategies.

Of course, at the pointy end of the social triangle, things have always been done differently from the way they're done down among the great unwashed. The air up there is more rarified, I'm told. For instance, when the American *Gourmet* magazine was introduced in 1941, food was not its focal point. During its first ten years, its tenor was unashamedly elitist, with the target demographic indistinguishable from 'a pre-war London gentleman's club', according to food historian Anne Mendelson. We're talking in other words about 'a small social elite that could afford to hunt, fish, and travel, and that viewed fine dining much as it did art, theater (sic) and opera: as something one need only appreciate in order to possess.'

In a way, the much more common contemporary urban approach to food has borrowed its sensibility from the old *Gourmet*, but dispensed with the terribly passé social pretensions. They-with-the-shiny-galley-kitchen spend the time they've saved (by not tiresomely preserving traditional social graces) on earning the big bucks that enable them to live the throwaway lifestyle they want.

So it's a new world in the kitchen. Out has gone the all-purpose bay leaf, the baking soda, the chickory and the cochineal (is that related to the implant?). Out, too, has gone the mixmaster and the pressure cooker. Now you have to have a kitchen gadget that has multi-task dexterities. It's got to slice, dice, chop and grate, and also look good just sitting there, otherwise you won't consider it. But even within the new trends there are seeming contradictions: with all this relentless change, who would have guessed that the trendiest of us would take so much pride in making our own ice-cream and bread.

And anyway, pass the wasabe, will you?

~ 34 ~

Historical artifacts

DUTCH COURAGE, ENGLISH ROSE, Irish curtains, Spanish fly. What do you notice? Apart from a nationality adjective followed by a noun, what these phrases have in common is that their meanings are not readily retrievable from the words alone. We might know what 'Dutch courage' is meant to mean (bravery inspired by an alcoholic beverage), but we'd be hard-pressed to come up with an explanation. Perhaps after one or two drinks, an explanation might be more accessible. I wonder if the Dutch have the same expression, or if they substitute something else for 'Dutch', like the English and French so comically do with their condoms (the English used to say 'French letters'; the French used to say 'English hats'—*chapeaux anglais*).

The words themselves are peculiarly unforthcoming both in isolation and in combination, and of themselves, they do not guarantee comprehension. We can know what 'Dutch' and 'courage' mean and still be no closer to the combined Dutch plus courage. Of one thing we can be sure: there once was a context that propelled 'Dutch courage' into the language and into its particular meaning. And the stories that nested in that context must have been known.

Etymologist Michael Quinion attributes the pejorative pattern in English about the Dutch to the traditional imperial enmity between England and Holland, which reached its height in the 17th century, when wars were fought over maritime routes linking Europe to the East Indies. He writes: 'The Dutch were powerful, they were the enemy, they were the bad guys, and their name was taken in vain at every opportunity.' At one point, they even blockaded the Thames, and if there's one thing the English do not take lying down, it's anyone questioning Britannia's rule of the seas. From this ocean of festering resentment, we get a Dutch widow (a prostitute), Dutch metal (an alloy substitute for gold foil), a Dutch concert (distinct lack of harmony), a Dutch uncle (someone who is too familiar in their criticism); a Dutch treat (where you pay for yourself).

No one today would express these old grudges, which have all long since dropped off planet English. What remains is the expression. Today, finding the meaning requires a dictionary or a strongly inferential approach to context. The story qua story is, by and large, gone. And in any case, the zeitgeistian politically correct consciousness may well encourage the gradual removal of the qualifying 'Dutch' from expressions that retain a whiff of the pejorative. So too, with 'Irish curtains' and 'Spanish fly'.

Another example. The expression 'gets my goat' (to irritate, annoy) allegedly originated in early 20th-century America, referring to the practice of soothing a horse-in-training by placing a goat in its stall. If you wanted a horse to lose a race, you'd take the goat away. Why a horse should be calmed by the proximity of a goat is a whole different question and need not be addressed here. If you get my goat, or get on it, as some people prefer, you cause me to be unnerved and to lose my calm. Today we're not bothered by the rather peculiar goat. The context has so soaked into the expression that its meaning is unaffected by the literal disjunction.

Surprising really, that some savvy businessperson hasn't done to a goat product (fur? milk?) what has been done to eel skin and emu oil. That is, made it into middle-class commodities. Perhaps goat's cheese, currently very gourmet, is linked to the commercialisation of goat products but no one seems to be pushing the connection. You'd think at least the big pharmaceuticals would get on board. Woops, I speak too soon. Have just seen an advertisement for 'Horny Goatweed' (from good pharmacies and health food stores everywhere), which is pitched to both male and female (his is Goatweed PLUS), the male for stamina and endurance, the woman for stress and flopped libido. It's billed as 'hope for desperate housewives everywhere', with the caption: 'Don't get desperate! Get horny.' No doubt the nervousness once associated with the goat has been pushed aside to make room for the more contemporary association: horny (as in sexually enthusiastic) and horns as in male goats.

No need to ponder too deeply. Connections, after all, is what marketing is all about. We need go no further than Vegemite for evidence of this. For baby boomers, a 'happy little Vegemite' is inextricably linked to the breakfast spread itself. More specifically, it is linked to the trademark jingle that was once used to market the product, so successfully that it (the jar, not the jingle) is reputed to have a place in nine out of ten Australian pantries. Vegemite long ago achieved national icon status notwithstanding the fact that it has been wholly American-owned since 1935. 'A happy little Vegemite', the *Macquarie Dictionary* tells us, is a person—an actual child, or a grown person momentarily and benevolently childlike—who is wholly contented with their life, at least for the moment at which the phrase is uttered.

It is an amazing feat of salesmanship to succeed in establishing a link between, on the one hand, the qualities of deliciousness and contentedness and, on the other hand, the smell of rancid seaweed and a taste formed by such an amazingly high density of salt that the product seemingly never goes off. If you move into a derelict old house that has stood vacant for ages and find a jar of Vegemite in the pantry, along with dust, silverfish, and who knows what else, chances are the Vegemite will be quite edible. Thank you, salt.

In years to come, perhaps when the yeast product itself ceases to be—from the present standpoint, hard to imagine, I concede, but perhaps in the future some health scare may remove the current safe-as-houses status. I mean, once salt and butter were considered good for you, too. So, imagine a time, far far from now, when Vegemite is no more. What may continue to linger is the phrase 'a happy little Vegemite', and people may well wonder about the phrase's etymology, at which time the then high priests and priestesses of lexicology will tell the story of how Vegemite came to infiltrate a national mindset, or perhaps a folklore of apocryphal explanations will grow up and capture the popular imagination, as these are wont to do. Meanwhile, a few remaining jars of Vegemite may be used at breakfast at the hospice, where 'happy little Vegemite' may still be heard.

Today, there are many expressions which time has distanced from their original sources. And it is this very process—the unhinging of the term from its literal source or origin—that is the making of an idiom. It's helpful to consider the origin of the word 'idiom'. It comes from the Greek for peculiar or strange—consider our words 'idiosyncratic' and 'idiotic', for instance. And idiom is peculiar or strange precisely because it no longer has literal sense. Sometimes it is so very peculiar (e.g., 'raining cats and dogs') that it seems to self-eject, like a pilot in a crashing plane, and come down so far away from the smouldering metal that the two seem to have no chance of reuniting.

But that's putting it too dramatically. It ignores the gradual bleaching out of literal meaning over time. Mostly it's a slow, imperceptible process of distancing from the original source that does not affect the ongoing currency of the expression. The explicit link is gone, but we keep on 'getting on someone's goat' and referring to a 'social circle' or 'whetting your whistle'. Sometimes, with the loss of the link, the meaning also starts to shift, as though now detached and unstable, the idiom can grow legs and develop its own individuality. There's an oddity to the expression but, as few of us consciously think about the language we ordinarily use (unless we're speech writers to the prime minister or copy writers for an advertising agent), we're rarely struck by the oddity. Can't help but wonder where 'happy little Vegemite' will drift to in the future.

Nevertheless, it's rather unrefined to group all idiomatic language in one basket. I prefer to think of it as falling roughly into three categories, none of which is impermeable. The first and least useful in terms of currency, comprises idioms that are close to being archaic. They've lost their original meanings and have failed to take on related or new ones. For example 'to set the Thames on fire', a phrase that dates back to the late 18th century. Mostly used negatively and ironically, it describes someone who is lacking in energy, initiative or enterprise. One explanatory example has been given as, 'I hardly expect him to set the Thames on fire, but I hope his mother will never have reason to be ashamed of him.' Of interest is the fact that Latin has a similar saying, except, logically, featuring the River Tiber in place of the Thames: *Tiberim accendere nequaquam potest*. And there's also one in German, related to the Rhine: *Er hat den Rhein und das Meer angezündet*. A similar use has been reported, but less ironically and more affirmatively: 'You are looking good, girl. You're going to burn a river.' Note that the river in the last example is not named. Perhaps when things are going well, any river will suffice as fuel.

Another term that has completely lost its currency is 'to go for a Burton', which is a softened way of referring to the fact that someone has died. It was common in World War II among pilots when one of their own did not return from a mission, an example of black or coping humour. There are multiple explanations for its origins, none of them totally certain. Some argue that it relates to Burton Ale, a strong beer popular in the inter-war period. The implication—and herein lies the euphemism—was that the missing person had only popped out for a drink. A series of advertisements for Burton Ale showed a group of people with one obvious absence—a sports team with a gap in the line-up, an empty chair at the dinner table—the tag line implying that the missing person was out getting a beer. However, it's odd to reconcile this explanation with the fact that the phrase was recorded in the 15th century as a euphemism for 'to die'.

My second category for idioms comprises those that are still used, some perhaps infrequently, but whose original meanings are quite lost to us in the ordinary course of daily life. Often, a kind of folk etymological explanation grows up. A good example is 'dead ringer', which has nothing to do with dead as in dead and buried, and nothing to do with bells. A dead ringer means an exact duplicate. The 'dead' here means precise or spot-on, as in 'dead shot', 'dead centre', 'dead heat'. A 'ringer' is a substitute or exchange—for the purpose of defrauding—and the term 'dead ringer' arose in American horseracing slang at the end of the 19th century. Today we have 'car ringing', which means replacing the identification numbers of a stolen car with the real thing. However, dead ringer has since lost its underhand associations, and we can say, 'he grew up to be a dead ringer for his father', without any untoward implications. Unless, of course, the father was an unsavoury type.

My third category of idioms comprises those that have changed their meaning over time, moulding and adapting with Darwinian finesse. Sometimes they retain something of the original meaning, and often the process of amendment is the abandonment of the literal meaning, and the substitution of metaphorical meanings. Consider here 'spill the beans'. One meaning of spill, itself metaphorical, is to divulge or let out, and over the centuries many items have been spilled literally and metaphorically. You can, it seems, spill quite a lot of things—the works, the soup, everything, what you know, and your guts. You can also just spill, intransitively, in the sense of divulging what perhaps you shouldn't.

The beans of the idiomatic phrase 'spill the beans' has mysterious origins. One lexicographer cites a 19th-century agricultural expert, Henry Stephens, who wrote a two-volume exposition called *The Farmer's Guide to Scientific and Practical Agriculture* (1853). In a section called 'On Reaping Beans, and Pease, and Tares when Grown for Seed', he noted: 'It is of importance to keep bean sheaves always on end, as they then resist most rain; for if allowed to remain on their side, after being blown over by the wind, the least rain soaks them, and the succeeding drought causes the pods to burst and spill the beans upon the ground.' This very literal bean-spilling is quite clearly a no-no.

Sometimes, a mythology grows up—these days liberally spread by the bushfire that is the internet—about the supposed original literal meaning. Take the case of 'throwing baby out with the bathwater', where a folklore has arisen about life in England in centuries past as well as early colonial Australia. It dates from a time when families bathed once a week, if they were lucky, in one lot of bath water, in order from the oldest to the youngest. The water had to be hauled from outside to inside and then heated—no easy task, so no wonder sharing was the order of the day. By the time it was baby's turn, the water was so dirty that baby could slip under and drown, and then be thrown out with the bathwater. Part of the intuitive, perhaps gothic, appeal of this story is not simply our notion of the poor hygiene of earlier times. It's also that we imagine that, with about fifteen children in a family and no television to keep them occupied, it would be exceedingly easy to misplace one or two. It might even be some time until you noticed the absence.

Generally speaking, then, when it comes to idioms, we have the expression but we've lost the story. There are different ways to respond to this loss. We could deem it grievous, even tragic, and devote ourselves to discovering and publicising the original connections. But to what end? After all, we don't put goats in with horses in training any more, do we? (Did we ever, really?) Times move on and we make our own meanings.

This approach would have us seeing language as a cemetery of lost stories. We risk being labelled romantic or melancholic, and some might be nasty and put an adverb like 'hopelessly' before either or both of those adjectives. Of course, there are some contexts where forcing a connection between idiom and origin makes a lot of sense. I remember talking to a young, talented teacher about how he introduced the notion of idiom to his class of overseas English language learners. The expression in this case was 'the last straw that broke the camel's back'. He'd set up the context of his camel's travails, drawing a reasonable looking camel on the whiteboard (the two humps allow a great deal of licence to poor artistry). Graphically, and gradually, he established his camel's credentials, adding loads of various weights, one by one, to the back of his archetypal beast-of-burden. He was almost finished. The load was very heavy, but the camel, showing much fortitude, could cope nonetheless. Then one straw was added. And the camel collapsed. Diagnosis: broken back. Prognosis: shooting, in the 'they shoot horses, don't they?' tradition.

The philosophical implications alone are massive. What caused the back to break? Can we say it was the straw? Or should we more rightly blame the burden that preceded the straw? Its application to life is endless. How much can you take before you can take no more? When is the best moment for action? If you wait till the end, you're incapable of action. If you're pre-emptive, you risk being labelled aggressive.

Other languages and cultures have the same concept, albeit differently expressed. Sometimes it's a horse or a donkey, or the last drop that makes the cup run over. The stories vary, they're known to varying degrees of certitude or 'folkority'; and they're well on the way to being lost, and therefore to the state of being detached idioms.

An alternative to the cemetery view is a semiotic explanation. Reframed, we might see 'Dutch courage', 'Spanish fly' and such expressions as signs that have slipped their original moorings yet have somehow, miraculously, maintained their original signification, or something semantically connected. The same would apply to other opaque expressions, like a 'Dutch cap' (a diaphragm), 'to be in Dutch with' (be in trouble), or 'I'm a Dutchman' (a way of emphasising that the previous sentence is truthful).

In each case, think of the expression as having slipped its mooring and floated away. Perhaps these expressions are like rowboats. Despite the fact that they've been transported from the seaside, or marina, where they may have started out, to a faraway estuarine fate, they still float and they still function, apart from those that have drifted off into the great blue yonder and never been heard of again (with the crew succumbing to storms or pirates or, alternatively, surviving, forming relationships and living incognito in Brazil).

Maybe the rowboat is to the cemetery what the bagel is to the hole. Yes, you might want to retrieve the distilled wisdom of ages, motivating you to chase these expressions, like holy grails, and the journey will be the reward for your efforts. But equally, for many who use the boat, it's unimportant where it came from or what the coast or coastline was like back there. The boat floats. The weather's fine. Be happy.

~ 35 ~

Dog days

....

IT SEEMS UNCOMPLICATED. We call them our best friends. Without doubt, they're loyal, loving and life-enriching. For their particular qualities of devotion and loyalty, many of us prefer them to spouses. But a closer look at the language reveals a core disjunction between the way we think of our dogs today and the evident bias against them in the language we have inherited from the past. Granted this language about dogs is fading now, but even so, it's not yet been adequately replaced by terms that are more congruent with contemporary attitudes. So we're left with a dissonance, and that's always uncomfortable.

Dogs seem to have had an uncommonly unfair share of bad press. We use 'dog' to say and mean awful things such as, 'It'll look like a dog's breakfast.' To describe an existence defined by ill-treatment, we used to talk of 'a dog's life'. An extreme point on a continuum of negativity was, 'you wouldn't give it to a dog'. For the point beyond which we can't learn anything new, there's 'you can't teach an old dog new tricks'— quite fuddy-duddy today, but once very common. When there's less likelihood than Buckley's, it's 'a dog's chance'. To express the end point of decline and degradation, there's 'gone to the dogs'. When the end is nigh, it's 'every dog has its day'. For over-the-top attendance, we say 'every man and his dog'. For no one showed, there's 'two men and a dog'. For counting purposes, we like to say someone has more (whatevers) 'than a dog has fleas', notwithstanding the fact that contemporary urban dogs have multiple treatments, all of them expensive, to rid them of flea contamination. For manipulative dishonesty, we used to say 'a sly dog'. For total exhaustion, we were 'dog-tired'. For someone or something that follows you persistently and relentlessly, there's the verb 'to dog'. For meanness and spite, there's 'a dog in a manger' (thanks, Aesop). For depression, Winston Churchill gave us 'black dog'. For a total put-down retort, there's 'dog's bollocks'. For *Everyone Loves Raymond*-style disgrace, there's 'in the doghouse'. For a warning not to disturb or stir up past problems, there's 'let sleeping dogs lie'. For scrappily overused, we have 'dog-eared'. For a circuitous route, we have the 'dogleg'. For fighter planes doing what fighter planes do, we have 'dogfight'. And to get lower even than dog, there's the female form, 'bitch', that serves man very well as the uber-handy adjective for every annoying thing in his life.

Even when we're acknowledging canine qualities, we're shortchanging our dogs. My dictionary of clichés claims that 'dog eat dog' derives from an even older (16th century) saying, 'dog does not eat dog'. So, here's the thing: ordinarily, dogs don't eat dogs; so when they do, things must be really bad. I'm not sure if this is a backhanded compliment or a front-handed insult, but for dogs, at least, it's not good, and that's pretty typical of how dogs fare in the language.

And then there's the Americanism, 'dog days'. Many of us would have owed our comprehension of 'dog days' to television in the 1950s and 1960s, or perhaps to reading Carson McCullers or William Faulkner. I can see it now—the graphic (if blinkered and prejudiced) image of listless white folks, à la *To Kill a Mockingbird*, hanging about chewing

tobacco in hammocks on verandahs, giving their broad
Southern accents a bit of a rest, while passing time between
lynchings. Did the climate contribute to the racism? Is it the
listless heat that stirs the malevolent humours? Or, as Harper
Lee would be the first to contend, are the forces and factors
that contribute to such savagery beyond simplistic analysis?

There are no easy answers to the big questions. More
success lies with the small ones. The phrase 'dog days' comes
from *dies caniculares* and means the hottest days of summer, or
a period marked by inactivity, ostensibly because of the heat. A
time of evil, according to Brady's *Clavis Calendarium* (1813):
'. . . the sea boiled, wine turned sour, dogs grew mad, and all
creatures became languid, causing to man burning fevers,
hysterics, and phrensies.' The ancients believed that Sirius, the
dog star which rises at the same time as the sun at this time of
year, adds to the oppressive heat, making people listless and
sickly. (The increased thunder didn't help either.)

Then there's 'doggone', which also has a colourful history.
Way back when the Christian Church was powerful enough to
seek to deter people from doing what they didn't want them
to do, damning was an act in which only the privileged few
clerics could engage. But taboos don't really stop acts; they just
send them underground (think Prohibition), and what emerges
are euphemisms for achieving the same ends.

Thus developed the many hundreds of regional variants
of 'damned', a large number of which became euphemistic
exclamations, expletives or intensives. A lot began with 'dad',
itself a euphemism for 'god', generating expressives like
'dadblamed', 'dadblasted', 'dadburn' and 'dadgum'. Combine
any one of these with 'it' and you have a nicely explosive
expressive, offering great flexibility. It's a short leap to
'doggone', which began in the American South, but spread its

wings and today has morphed, like so much else, into a brand name. A quick internet search yields a host of business products—for everything from dog-walking services to graphic design and natural food products.

Apart from the expressions that explicitly mention dogs, and usually pejoratively (with some notable exceptions like 'top dog'), there are some dog expressions that allude to the animal without explicit mention. 'Don't bite the hand that feeds you' is an admonition against ingratitude. 'Chasing your tail' clearly points to frenetic energy destined to take you nowhere. Having 'a bark that's worse than a bite' means appearing more aggressive than in fact one is. 'Barking up the wrong tree' is not unlike chasing your tail, implying pointless activity.

Perhaps the bias against dogs can be accounted for at the point of origin—after all, notwithstanding the Royal obsession with corgis, the cat has always been the traditional upper-class English preference *qua* domestic animal. It's so easy to imagine the literati in their drawing rooms, stroking their much-indulged cats, pontificating about this or that sensibility, while imbibing port, or perhaps crustless cucumber sandwiches. Not for them the baser species, the dog, who howl on the moors at night and have a purpose only in the context of country estates, where as hounds they are an important element of the hunt. Even there, dogs are only midway on the hierarchy, the horses being the most prestigious, then the dogs, and finally at the bottom the poor creature (bird? rabbit? fox?) being hunted for sport.

When dogs occur in English literature—think of *Oliver Twist* or *The Hounds of the Baskervilles*—they are quite beastly, altogether wild and inexplicable, offering neither friendship nor comfort. Sykes had a dog in *Oliver Twist*, and we're in no doubt that the two low-lifes were well suited. If you want to see dogs as indoor companions, hop across the channel to France, where small fluffy canine varieties, more doglet than dog, are fetishised to the point of serving as handbags or accessories. Love me, love my dog.

It would seem that the notion of the dog as man's best friend is a relatively modern one, a positively connoted set of associations perhaps best summed up by the icon—patient, obedient, loving dog—that used to accompany the record label His Master's Voice. A dissenting voice here would be Jeremy Paxman's, a writer whose favourite hobby is watching the English with the scrutiny of an anthropologist. Paxman likes to blame much on loss of Empire, which he says, killed off a lot that was great about the English, including the bulldog breed—'fearless and philistine, safe in taxis and invaluable in shipwrecks.' A second dissenting voice is another English-watcher, Kate Fox, who reminds us that the RSPCA was formed long before the equivalent association that looks after the wellbeing of children. But then Fox also argues that pets—dogs and cats equally—serve the English as an outlet for their stuffy, bottled-up emotions, as an alter ego or a 'wild side', allowing their owners to break social rules, if only by proxy.

All very interesting but no explanation for my particular conundrum—why does the language we've inherited about dogs make it so hard to love our dogs? Put another way, the question looks like this: When we're known to be loving towards our best friends, why then is our language so replete with base allusions to dogs? Perhaps the language seems to be lagging behind because it hasn't had the time to catch up with the changed canine zeitgeist. Hence the discordance mentioned earlier between a modern indulgent stance on dogs and the fast-fading old expressions that have served us idiomatically and metaphorically, but that almost unanimously project dismissive, patronising and rejecting attitudes to dogs. Given what we've done to the dog's reputation, it's a final irony that we have the expression 'to give a dog a bad name'.

It would seem only a matter of time, then, before all our doggy expressions are relegated to the Hospice of Fading Words. Or at least its doghouse.

❧ 36 ❧

Retronyms

SOMETIMES, WHEN I'M in an aberrant mood, I think aberrant thoughts. One such is a sudden perception of dictionaries as the attempt by neat precise people to impose their taxonomic footprint on language. At such times, it seems to me that huge amounts of lexicographical effort are channelled towards one very focused end—to corral the beast that is language.

But as many have said, language is much more like a garden growing wild than it is a neatly completed brick wall. In other words, the beast resists corralling. It's all a lot messier than the dictionary suggests. Like teaching, dictionary-compiling strives to look neat, but in fact is un-neat by nature. At some point, one has to ask: how much effort is worth expending when the outcome goes against the grain? My thoughts turn to women with curly hair who straighten it, and women with straight hair who perm it.

Lexicography involves many tasks that give off a whiff of the definitive but, in fact, are far messier. Like, predicting which new words will make it into the new edition. Or which old ones will be newly flagged with a sad *obsolete* or *archaic*. And which words will—now, how shall I put this—be let go, be dropped, be axed. Someone said, at the root of all psychological problems is the fear of abandonment. Perhaps words suffer, too.

We can make guesses—some of them quite educated, others wildly haphazard—about why some words cease being used over a generation or two. Fortunately this withdrawal from centre-stage happens slowly enough so that the old and the young can still communicate—though it may at times not appear thus.

And sometimes, it's true, what passes as communication can completely break down. Picture this scene witnessed in a high school corridor: a senior teacher (in age and rank) leaning belligerently over a schoolboy, saying, in an exasperated voice and with a slight shaking of his head, the words enunciated as if clarity of diction might support the message: 'When—is—the—penny—gonna—drop, son? When—is—the—penny—gonna—drop?' And the boy, looking up at the face so uncomfortably close to his own, his expression blank, having absolutely no idea what to make of this talk of dropping pennies.

Words fade for many reasons. Of the various, sometimes complex, factors involved, the easiest, and most transparent conceptually, are the words whose referents no longer exist in the real world of the speakers. Words like 'heath' and 'moor' and 'woods' faded from the English of the descendants of the early settlers of Australia because the landscape didn't reinforce them. When was the last time you walked on a local heath or across a wild and windy moor?

In recent years we've no longer needed 'gramophone' or 'quill pen', have we? Beyond the needs of period pieces, on stage for instance, we have no use for them. Things for which we have no more use lose their currency and fade to the wings of the stage. I'm reminded of the sweet fifteen-year-old babysitter to whom one evening I was explaining my child's going-to-bed routine, including the information about lights off in room, on in corridor, door left ajar about four inches. 'What's an inch?', she asked curiously.

The list of such newly referentless obsolete words is long—as long as a piece of string, really. Consider these: telegram, pocket watch, icebox. I'm sure a moment's thought will allow you to expand the list.

Such words would no doubt fade right away to dust were it not for retronyms. A retronym is a word or phrase devised because the existing term now needs to be distinguished from a new term referring to a recent development, often driven by technology. A 'watch' needed to become a 'pocket watch' when 'wristwatches' started being worn. Pocket watches have faded in alignment with their fading from use as personal time-keepers. (A timekeeper today would be more likely to be thought of as a Filofax.) Now 'digital watch' has created the old-technology term 'analogue watch'.

There are plenty of examples of this process. When movies began to talk we needed to create 'silent movies'. 'Mail' was fine before we got 'email', so now we have 'snail mail' to avoid confusion. It's going this way, too, with address, as in 'email address' and 'dirt address' (for your residence or office). 'Television' was fine until colour came in, making it necessary to distinguish between 'black-and-white' and 'colour'. Soon 'DVD recorder' will do the same to 'video cassette recorder' (or has that already happened?) Cable has created the need for 'free-to-air', and I'm still sorting out the exact meaning of 'Pay TV'. Like, I only just managed to feel comfortable with floppy disks when my IT consultant dismissed my expertise as 'old technology'.

So what happens is the new technological development turns the old word into a new (adjective + noun) form. Think of 'birth mother' (made possible by 'surrogate mother' and 'adoptive mother'); 'acoustic guitar' (as distinct from an electric guitar); 'manual typewriter' (before they went electric); 'convection oven' (necessitated by microwave ovens); 'regular coffee' (thank you, decaf), 'landline phone' (only relevant since mobile phones). When we look back on how pocket watches were replaced with wristwatches, which then simply became 'watches', then the process is crystal clear. While we're still in the transitional period, some semantic fog may hover over the use of terms, making some people—especially the technically challenged—feel confused, if not rather dinosaurish.

Indeed the appearance of the retronym might be said to signal the passing of old technology. As such, it has the potential for built-in nostalgia. In theory, foul trenches notwithstanding, one might look back fondly to 'conventional warfare', rendered 'conventional' by developments in nuclear and biological weaponry. I said, theoretically.

And so, among our residents at the Hospice of Fading Words, we'll encounter many who found their way there because new developments in technology meant their active days were severely numbered. At least at the hospice, the pace is less cut-throat and they're among friends. All told, it's a far more congenial environment than the lexical scrap-metal yard.

Epilogue

IT WAS MARK TWAIN who suggested that death and taxes are the only certainties in life. I'd like to add one more, if I may; there always have been and always will be people who resist the currents of change they encounter in language through their lifetime.

Such evidence is amply available in letter-to-the-editor pages of daily newspapers where those who consider themselves custodians of 'the language' (considered singular) bemoan, decry, lament and castigate, in between rants. It is significant, though rarely pointed out, that these bemoanings concern changes in language in the present time, not changes in language in the past. In contradistinction, the past is venerated, even to the point of being laminated; past change isn't called 'change', it's called 'etymology'.

Inside my own head, I quietly think of these critics as the 'frowning educated lay', benevolently motivated if thoroughly deluded. I understand where their attitude comes from. It's born of a view of language as a collection of systems and subsystems governed, underpinned and held together by a network of iron-clad rules. While I appreciate their love of grammar, which I share, theirs is a blinkered, limited and ultimately fact-denying understanding of what language is.

If one immutable truth exists about language, it is that it is hard-wired for change. This is because, rather than being a set of rules and regulations, language is social. With it, because of it, we are social beings. It enables us to do what we do in a social world. And the social world is never still. Language is as fluid and still-defying as the river in that Chinese proverb which says you can't cross it twice; when you come back tomorrow to cross it again, it's no longer the same river.

Contemporary linguists describe, they don't prescribe. They note what happens. They don't deplore, abhor, tut-tut, lament, deprecate and censure. And they don't laud, admire, approve, respect and protest in favour of. So while occasionally a hint of a hue of a timbre of the nostalgic may have crept into my tone through this book, as I outline the evidence for the demise of fading words headed for the hospice, on the whole I am sanguine about the change process. I think of the changes as the ebb and flow of the tide, as the subtle, almost imperceptible shifts and movements in the coastline of a continent.

Cheerio Tom, Dick and Harry has focused on words in demise because that is its topic, but the emphasis may skew the overall picture. What is left out is the other myriad changes that are evident in language on a daily basis. Yes, we lose words because of new technology ('record-player'), because of changes in fashions ('top hat', 'petticoat'), because of medical advances ('consumption'), because of cultural shifts ('luncheon', 'bosoms', 'step-ins') or historical events ('League of Nations' , 'Common Market'), or because what once was new and whiz-bang is now ordinary ('mod cons'). But at the same time, even while technology wipes out actions like 'dialling' and 'hanging up', we continue to use many of the 'old' words. Just think: we kept our 'telegraph poles' long beyond the era of telegraph.

Other changes happen about us but we rarely note them. These may involve the reinvention of old (literal) words into their new (figurative) senses. A 'harbinger', for instance, in its original form, was the person who was sent ahead of a travelling party with the task of arranging lodgings for the night. An 'aftermath' once denoted the new grass that would grow after mowing or harvesting. A whole generation is already blind to the fact that Watergate was a building.

Cheerio Tom, Dick and Harry has focused on words in the process of retreat. But even as we recognise that some of these are headed for the hospice, this of itself is no cause for despair. Let's consider what might happen once the words find their place in their new abode. Some will experience increasingly restricted usage until they're eventually designated in dictionaries as archaic or obsolete, though we should take comfort in the fact that lexicographers do not flag a word as such without a great deal of thought, consultation and heavy-heartedness.

Death, however, is not the only trajectory that leads from the hospice. Some fading words will be awarded a new lease of life. This is what happens with words we later think of as retronyms, revived with a new signification, one that's in sync with the times. Some words seem invested with the putative nine lives of cats. I'm thinking of the famous 'gay' that has moved from 'happy' to 'homosexual' to 'fey' in my own lifetime. It's as if they find themselves headed for the hospice but suddenly, like an Entebbe rescue, they are seized and catapulted back into the land of the living.

Other words are buoyed artificially, rather like an externally applied method of resuscitation. This is what happened with 'recalcitrant' after Keating launched it into the public consciousness in 1993. In fact this fate could await virtually any low-currency and dated word that a given individual might choose to adopt into their idiolect and then nurture, like a pet rabbit, bringing it out every now and again to the bafflement of people who have no idea what they mean.

I used to know a man whose parting words typically include some sort or reference to 'Let's away/to part the glories of this happy day', and failing that, you'd be sure to get a mention of 'yonder tent'. A friend of a friend of mine has several low-mileage words that he clearly finds enjoyment in the opportunity to use. One of these is 'crepuscular' (meaning having to do with the indistinct quality of light at the end of the day), which drips with irony in being such a distinct word for an indistinct phenomenon, and not likely to be in the lexicon of his interlocutor. Now, I have nothing against people acting on their love of words, but at the same time I am reminded of Humpty Dumpty's delusion that meaning was an individual thing, not an agreed contract by members of the same discourse community.

And as a parting note, to any readers out there who may be inclined to be soppily nostalgic about words that are vanishing with little hope of re-morphing through bypass surgery or other means, there's some comfort to be had. It lies in the fact—think of it spiritually if you like, as an Afterlife—that such words in fact will ultimately cheat the cemetery. They will live on as long as there are dictionaries, for among their many functions, dictionaries are institutions committed to providing definitions even for words, like 'alas' or 'prithee', that are only heard occasionally, perhaps in the half-light of a medieval stage and in full costume. When you think about it, it may be as close to eternity as you get.

Notes

'The *Sun Herald*'s *Sunday* magazine . . .' (p. x) Wajnryb, 2005: 22–23.

'As in Thomas Mann . . .' (p. xiv) Mann, 1924; James, 1908.

'The Slow Food movement . . .' (p. 5) Parkins & Craig, 2006; Honore, 2004.

'There's even a suggestion that it is theatre slang . . .' (p. 18) According to Bret Hart: http://worldwidewords.org/articles/money.htm.

'If Al Gore (in his *An Inconvenient Truth* . . .' (p. 19) *An Inconvenient Truth*, 2006, directed by Davis Guggenheim.

'In the film *To Kill a Mockingbird* . . .' (p. 22) Lee, 1966.

'In these words of American journalist Ellen Goodman . . .' (p. 22) See http://www.quotationspage.com/quotes/Ellen_Goodman/.

'One word that's occasionally used about Generation Y is . . .' (p. 27) Sheahan, 2005.

'On the internet dating website, RSVP . . .' (p. 28) See http://www.rsvp.com.au/.

'The wound in my foot is now . . .' (p. 28) Personal communication, John McArthur.

'In the film *Man of Fire* (p. 30) *Man of Fire*, 2004, directed by Tony Scott.

'A steady hand on the till . . .' (p. 31) Personal communication, Mark Cherry.

'Perhaps one that can speak for the zeitgeist . . .' (p. 32) www.steady.org.uk.

'He tells his charges . . .' (pp. 36) Jim Gallagher quotes Allen Davenport in 'Buying a new car'; See http://www.highbeam.com/library/doc3.asp?DOCID=1P1:41938060&num=10&ctrlInfo=Round10%3AProd%3ASR%3AResult&ao=&FreePremium=BOTH.

'Here's an excerpt from a newspaper report . . .' (p. 36) 'Long-lost '55 Chevy heads home', in *The Columbian*, 10 March 1998, AP.

'In a consumer society everything revolves around . . .' (p. 37) http://www.trendwatching.com/trends/status-skills.htm.

'The earliest recorded use . . .' (p. 38) Jaloppi, in Hostetter & Beesley, 1929, cited in Ayto, 1990: 148.

'*gillopy* (from Steinbeck . . .)' (p. 38) Steinbeck, 1936.

'Versions of possible connections . . .' (p. 38) http://www.worldwide words.org/qa/qa-jal1.htm.

'A recent remark of Jane Fonda's . . .' (p. 39) Televised interview on Australian television, in conjunction with the publication of her autobiography, *My Life So Far*.

'To dispose of the offending phlegm in the Western way . . .' (p. 41) http://www.jref.com/culture/japanese_manners_etiquette.shtml.

'Men's Armbands . . .' (p. 42) http://www.eshopone.com/smx/lambournes/armbands/.

'Just open a Max Dupain collection . . .' (p. 45) White, 1999.

'Edward de Bono utilised this metaphor . . .' (p. 48) De Bono, 1985.

'An article about cricketer Shane Warne . . .' (p. 55) Stevenson, 2005.

'Writer Luke Slattery reminds us . . .' (p. 55) Slattery, 2002.

'As Sidney Baker wrote . . .' (p. 56–7) Baker, 1976: 135.

'Having the mickey taken out of you . . .' (p. 57–8) Milner Davis, 2006.

'In the words of Sue Hart-Byers . . .' (p. 58) Hart-Byers, 1999: 21.

'As Luke Slattery puts it . . .' (p. 59) Slattery, 2002.

'A cartoonist on the Melbourne *Herald* . . .' (p. 59) Cited in Baker, 1976: 135.

'According to the *Macquarie Word Map* . . .' (p. 60) Richards and the *Macquarie Dictionary*, 2005: 25.

'Gilbert and Sullivan operetta . . .' (p. 74) See http://www.lyricsdown load.com/album-00008BXGK.html.

'Pearls before swine . . .' (p. 82) See http://www.wordwizard.com/ch_forum/topic.asp?TOPIC_ID=17897&#44266.

'Everyone to their own taste . . .' (p. 82) Keesing, 1982: 26–27.

'A linguist who studied this . . .' (p. 84) Tannen, 1999.

'This applies to jokes, too . . .' (p. 85) This joke arrived anonymously by email so the source is unknown.

'There's many a slip . . .' (p. 90) 'There's many a slip twixt cup and lip'.

'Linguists who analyse workplace humour . . .' (p. 98) Holmes, 2006; Holmes & Schnurr, 2005.

'Coded insider-speech known as Cockney Rhyming Slang . . .' (p. 99) See http://www.businessballs.com/moneyslanghistory.htm#slang %20money%20meanings%20and%20origins.

'While there's no longer a functional basis . . .' (p. 101) See http:// www. whoohoo.co.uk/cockney-translator.asp and http://www.whoohoo. co.uk/redir.asp?http://www.phespirit.info/cockney/.

'The amazing morphological flexibility . . .' (p. 104) See further, Wajnryb, 2004.

'One person is Don Aitkin . . .' (p. 111) Aitkin, 2005.

'Referring to how they were introduced . . .' (p. 111–12) Aitkin, 2005: 126.

'One of the stories Aitkin tells . . .' (p. 112) Aitkin, 2005: 126.

'C.S. Lewis once commented . . .' (p. 112) Cited in Wajnryb, 2004.

'The subtext was always . . .' (p. 113) The line 'Nudge, nudge, wink, wink. Say no more!' was originally associated with the Monty Python comedy group in UK. See http://news.bbc.co.uk/1/hi/ special_report/1999/10/99/monty_python/458827.stm.

'The British music-hall comedian . . .' (p. 114) See http://www. phrases.org.uk/bulletin_board/20/messages/553.html.

'There was no shortage of synonyms . . .' (p. 114) See http://www. peevish.co.uk/slang/h.htm.

'Two for a kiss, four for a feel . . .' (p. 115–16) Aitkin, 2005: 127.

'There's a fashion label for a line of T-shirts . . .' (p. 116) Rocca, 2002.

'We might turn to the Bible . . .' (p. 121) See http://www.geocities. com/bible_translation/euphemisms.txt.

'The tradition of euphemising pregnancy . . . (p. 122) See 'Up the duff': http://www.phrases.org.uk/meanings/397300.html and http://www.topfive.com/arcs/t5110800.shtml.

'Here's one young woman . . .' (pp. 123–25) See http://www.sothe fishsaid.com/archives/000445.php.

'According to one authoritative source . . .' (p. 128) Allan & Burridge, 1991.

'Particularly for siblings . . .' (p. 129) Wajnryb, 2001, Chapter 8.

'The pièce de résistance . . .' (p. 132) Guiliano, 2005.

'The Grim Reaper is so passé now . . .' (p. 133) See http://www.eurekastreet.com.au/articles/0310sendziuk.html.

'And when Nicole Kidman's character' (p. 136) *Moulin Rouge*, 2001, directed by Baz Luhrmann.

'Consider Ralph . . .' (p. 137) James, 1908; Mann, 1924; Quiller-Couch, 1919.

'Let's look a little closer . . .' (p. 139) Knight, 2002.

'There it is called "cotillion" . . .' (p. 143) See www.thecotillion.com.

'You can click onto a calendar . . .' (p. 143) See www.californiajunior cotillion.com.

'Take, for instance, this blurb . . .' (p. 146) *Sydney Morning Herald*, TV Guide, SBS Friday 17 February 2006, *The International Madam*.

'Humour was also a way of coping . . .' (p. 147) Moran, 2002, 2005.

'Psychiatric nurses got a very harsh press . . .' (p. 148) Kesy, 2002.

'In films like . . .' (p. 148) *Rain Man*, 1988, directed by Barry Levinson; *As Good As It Gets* (1997), directed by James L. Brooks; *A Beautiful Mind* (2001), directed by Ron Howard.

'What we did have was the "rule of thumb" . . .' (p. 148–49) Michael Quinion disputes the allegation; see http://www.worldwide words.org/qa/qa-rul1.htm.

'Today it's "black dog" . . .' (p. 151) The Black Dog Institute; see http://www.blackdoginstitute.org.au/depression/explained/index.cfm.

'There used to be a whole grab bag . . .' (p. 155) Hughes, 1998.

'Nancy Keesing tells a lovely story . . .' (p. 156) Keesing, 1982: 26–27.

'This is an outcome of the so-called politically correct movement . . .' (p. 161) Beard & Cerf, 1992; Cameron, 1995.

'The early so-called PCers . . .' (p. 162) See Cameron, 1995.

'Once on a lovely mountainside . . .' (p. 163) Garner, 1994: 17.

'In another example, the story "Peter Pan" . . .' (p. 163) Held, 1995: 39.

'Art critic and cultural commentator . . .' (pp. 163–4) Hughes, 1993: 18–19; see also Kennedy, 2003.

'In her excellent book . . .' (p. 164) Cameron, 1995.

'Deborah Cameron also relates . . .' (p. 165) Cameron, 1995: 116–17.

'Lear himself, speaking of another . . .' (p. 168) *King Lear*, Act II, Scene iv.

'Think Russell Crowe's character . . . (p. 169) *A Beautiful Mind* (2001), directed by Ron Howard.

'Quite dated now is . . .' (p. 169) See http://www.worldwidewords.
  org/qa/qa-mad2.htm.

'Martin Gardner reports . . .' (p. 170) See http://keywords.oxus.net/
  archives/2005/03/08/mad-hatters/.

'Centuries before Lewis Carroll . . .' (p. 170) Carroll, 1978.

'The shower scene in . . .' (p. 171) *Psycho*, 1960, directed by Alfred
  Hitchcock.

'Two competing theories . . .' (p. 171) See http://www.snopes.
  com/language/phrases/hatter.htm and http://www.worldwide
  words.org/qa/qa-mad2.htm.

'Rather, it's a corruption of . . .' (p. 172) Ward, 1980; Edwards, 1968.

'Some advocates in particular . . .' (p. 173) See http://www.madnot
  bad.co.uk/index.htm and http://publicsphere.typepad.com/
  mediations/2005/11/i_went_along_to.html.

'If Sidney Baker is right . . .' (p. 174) Baker, 1976.

'The latter having first been used . . .' (p. 174) Ayto, 1999.

'Such as the name-changing . . .' (p. 175) Beard & Cerf, 1992: 5.

'Linguists Keith Allan and Kate Burridge . . .' (p. 175) Allan &
  Burridge, 1991. See also http://www.phrases.org.uk/meanings/
  minced-oath.html.

'But on this one day . . .' (p. 188) Rosenblatt, 1985. See also
  http://www.pbs.org/newshour/essays/rosenblatt_2-14.html.

'This emerged during the palimony trial . . .' (p. 188) See
  http://image.eonline.com/Features/Features/Valentine2002/
  Breakups/index5.html and http://www.highbeam.com/library/
  doc3.asp?DOCID=1G1:3646817&num=2&ctrlInfo=Round18%
  3AProd%3ASR%3AResult&ao=&FreePremium=BOTH.

'She sued him for palimony . . .' (p. 188) Ayto, 1999: 491.

'The Duke of Edinburgh had used . . .' (p. 189) *Sunday Times*, UK,
  20 August 2006.

'The French call their dear ones . . .' (p. 190) Rosenblatt, 1985.

'I rather prefer Rosenblatt's verdict . . .' (p. 190) Rosenblatt, 1985.

'Dr Julie Coleman . . .' (p. 191) Coleman, 2002.

'Coleman's study is called . . .' (p. 191) Coleman, 1999.

'A survey in the United Kingdom . . .' (pp. 193) See http://funny
  business.typepad.com/funnybusiness/2005/06/terms_of_endear.
  html.

'There's your celluloid fort . . .' (p. 198) *Dances With Wolves*, 1990, directed by Kevin Costner.

'The generation born before 1946 . . .' (p. 201–2) See http://www.in-business.com.au/magazine/issue-25/Managing+the+generation+mix.

'Smile though your heart is aching . . .' (p. 203) See http://www.lyrics domain.com/23/westlife/smile.html.

'Robert Hughes wrote an entire treatise . . .' (p. 203) Hughes, 1993.

'According to Sidney Baker . . .' (p. 205) Baker, 1976: 130.

'One claims that in 1920s America . . .' (p. 207) See http://www.worldwidewords.org/qa/qa-bee1.htm.

'The word itself has origins . . .' (p. 209) See http://www.worldwide words.org/qa/qa-sno1.htm.

'Within twenty years . . .' (p. 209) See http://www.etymonline.com/index.php?search=snob&searchmode=none.

'Sportsmen of independent means . . .' (p. 210) Personal communication: Val Bellamy, John McArthur.

'Now "riff-raff" is a term . . .' (p. 211) See http://www.worldwide words.org/qa/qa-rif1.htm.

'Pop culture's most famous wet worker . . .' (p. 212) *Pulp Fiction* (1994) directed by Quentin Tarantino.

'*Dear Blood Orange* . . .' (p. 222–3) See http://www.newsletterarchive. org/2006/03/14/23188-Globe-Style:-Taste:-Blood-Orange.

'Food-writer Molly O'Neill . . .' (p. 223) See http://www.cjr.org/issues/2003/5/foodporn-oneill.asp.

'In the words of Anthony Bourdain . . .' (p. 223) Bourdain, 2000.

'Then there are books . . .' (p. 224) Harris, 1999.

'Molly O'Neill suggests that . . .' (p. 225) See http://www.cjr.org/issues/2003/5/foodporn-oneill.asp.

'Molly O'Neill tells us . . .' (p. 226) See http://www.cjr.org/issues/2003/5/foodporn-oneill.asp.

'According to food historian . . . .' (p. 226) *Gourmet*, Sept 2001, cited in http://www.cjr.org/issues/2003/5/foodporn-oneill.asp.

'A small social elite . . .' (p. 226) See http://www.cjr.org/issues/2003/5/foodporn-oneill.asp.

'Etymologist Michael Quinion . . .' (p. 228–9) See http://www.world widewords.org/qa/qa-dut1.htm.

'So too, with "Irish curtains" . . .' (p. 229) 'Irish curtains' refers to dust hanging from the ceiling or bags around the eyes; 'Spanish fly' refers to an aphrodisiac made from a crushed beetle.

'Horny Goatweed . . .' (p. 230) See http://www.lewtress.co.uk/subprod/horny-goat-weed-0001304.aspx.

'We need go no further than Vegemite . . .' (p. 230) See http://whatscookingamerica.net/History/VegemiteHistory.htm.

'The origin of the word "idiom" . . .' (p. 231) Personal communication, Scot Hill, curator, at Vaucluse House, Sydney.

'For example, "to set the Thames on fire" . . .' (p. 232) See http://www.phrases.org.uk/bulletin_board/6/messages/596.html and http://www.phrases.org.uk/bulletin_board/6/messages/616.html.

'Another term that has completely lost its currency . . .' (p. 233) See http://www.phrases.org.uk/bulletin_board/20/messages/776.html and http://www.worldwidewords.org/qa/qa-gon1.htm; see also Quinion, 2004.

'A dead ringer means . . .' (p. 233) See http://www.phrases.org.uk/meanings/dead%20ringer.html.

'Consider here "spill the beans" . . .' (p. 234) See http://www.randomhouse.com/wotd/index.pperl?date=20010223.

'One lexicographer . . .' (p. 234) See http://www.randomhouse.com/wotd/index.pperl?date=20010223.

'Perhaps these expressions are like rowboats . . .' (p. 237) I'm grateful to Mark Cherry for this concept.

'My dictionary of clichés . . .' (p. 239) Rogers, 1985: 68; see also, Kirkpatrick, 1996: 143.

'à la *To Kill a Mocking bird*' (p. 239) Lee, 1966.

'According to Brady's . . .' (p. 240) See http://www.irving.lib.tx.us/insights2002.html.

'Damning was an act . . .' (p. 240) Montagu, 2001.

'A dissenting voice here would be . . .' (p. 242) See http://www.amazon.co.uk/English-Portrait-People-Jeremy-Paxman/dp/0140267239; see also: Paxman, 1998.

'A second dissenting voice is . . .' (p. 242) Fox, 2004: 234–35.

'But as many have said . . .' (p. 244) Burridge, 2002.

'It was Mark Twain who suggested . . .' (p. 249) Twain, 1883; see also http://www.twainquotes.com/Liberty.html.

'The river in that Chinese proverb . . .' (p. 250) Proverbs are notoriously difficult to authenticate as they're often passed down through oral traditions. One source attributed the following to the Greek philosopher, Heraclitus, 'No man ever steps in the same river twice, for it's not the same river and he's not the same man.' See http://www.usbr.gov/pmts/writing/doctech/quote.html.

'A "harbinger" . . .' (p. 251) Quinion, 2006: ix.

'An "aftermath" . . .' (p. 251) Quinion, 2006: ix.

'Like an Entebbe rescue . . .' (p. 251) This is an allusion to the rescue of airline passenger/hostages by the Israeli army in 1976.

'This is what happened with "recalcitrant" . . .' (p. 251) See, for example, http://www.abc.net.au/am/stories/s317154.htm.

'Some sort of reference . . .' (p. 252) 'Let's away / to part the glories of this happy day'?the final lines of *Julius Caesar*.

'I am reminded of Humpty Dumpty's delusion . . .' (p. 252) 'When I use a word,' Humpty Dumpty said, in a rather scornful tone, 'it means just what I choose it to mean—neither more nor less.' Lewis Carroll, *Alice's Adventures in Wonderland*, 1865; http://history.enotes.com/famous-quotes/when-i-use-a-word-humpty-dumpty-said-in-a-rather.

References

Aitkin, D. (2005). *What Was It All For? The reshaping of Australia.* Allen & Unwin: Sydney.

Allan, K. and Burridge, K. (1991). *Euphemism and Dysphemism: Language used as shield and weapon.* Oxford University Press: New York.

Arthur, J.M. (2003). *The Default Country: A lexical cartography of twentieth–century Australia.* UNSW Press: Sydney.

Ayto, J. (1999). *20th Century Words: The story of the new words in English over the last hundred years.* Oxford University Press: Oxford.

Baker, Sidney J. (1976). *The Australian Language: An examination of the English language and English speech as used in Australia, from convict days to the present, with special reference to the growth of indigenous idiom and its use by Australian writers.* Sun Books: Melbourne.

Beard, H. & Cerf, C. (1992). *The Official Politically Correct Dictionary and Handbook.* Grafton: London.

Bowden, T. (1989). *The Way My Father Tells It: The story of an Australian life.* ABC Books: Sydney.

Bourdain, A. (2000). *Kitchen Confidential.* Bloomsbury: London.

Burridge, K. (2002). *Blooming English: Observations on the roots, cultivation and hybrids of the English language.* ABC Books: Sydney.

Cameron, D. (1995). *Verbal Hygiene.* Routledge: London.

Carroll, L. (1978). *Alice in Wonderland.* Hodder & Stoughton: London.

Coleman, J. (1999). *Love, Sex and Marriage: A historical thesaurus.* Rodopi: Amsterdam.

Coleman, J. (2002). 'Sex and Semantics: The Language of Love'. *University of Leicester Bulletin,* Newsletter, February, p. 4.

Davis, J.M. (2007). '"Aussie" Humour and Laughter: Joking as an Acculturating Ritual' , in *A Serious Frolic: Essays on Australian humour.* Eds. F. de Groen and P. Kirkpatrick, University of Queensland Press: Brisbane.

De Bono E. (1985). *Six Thinking Hats: Your success in business depends on how well you think.* Little, Brown: Boston.

Delbridge, A. and the Macquarie Dictionary (1984). *Aussie Talk.* Macquarie University: Sydney.

Edwards, E. (1968). *Words, Facts, and Phrases. A dictionary of curious, quaint and out-of-the-way matters.* Gale Research Co.: Detroit.

Fox, K. (2004). *Watching the English: The hidden rules of English behaviour.* Hodder: London.

Guiliano, M. (2005). *French Women Don't Get Fat: The secret of eating for pleasure.* Chatto & Windus: London.

Garner, J.F. (1994). *Politically Correct Bedtime Stories.* Souvenir Press: London.

Harris, J. (1999). *Chocolat.* Transworld: London.

Hart-Byers, S. (1999). *Snobs, Nobs and Yobs: A classy guide to Australia.* Lothian Books: Melbourne.

Held, L. (1995). *Once a Jolly Swagperson*, Macmillan: Sydney.

Holmes, J. (2006). 'Sharing a laugh: Pragmatic Aspects of Humour and Gender in the Workplace'. *Journal of Pragmatics* 38, 1: 26–50.

Holmes, J. & Schnurr, S. (2005). 'Politeness, Humor and Gender in the Workplace: Negotiating Norms and Identifying Contestation'. *Journal of Politeness Research*, 1 (1): 121–49.

Honore, C. (2004). *In Praise of Slow: How a worldwide movement is challenging the cult of speed.* Orion: London.

Hughes, G. (1998). *Swearing: A social history of foul language.* Basil Blackwell: Oxford.

Hughes, R. (1993). *Culture of Complaint: The fraying of America.* Oxford University Press: New York.

James, H. (1908). *The Portrait of a Lady.* Arnold: London (1967).

Kacirk, J. (1997). *Forgotten English: Merry guide to antiquated words, packed with history, fun facts, literary excerpts, and charming drawings.* William Morrow & Company: New York.

Kacirk, J. (2000). *The Word Museum: The most remarkable English words ever forgotten.* Touchstone: New York.

Keesing, N. (1982). *Lily on the Dustbin: Slang of Australian women and families.* Penguin: Melbourne.

Kennedy, R. (2003). *Nigger: The strange career of a troublesome word.* Vintage Books: New York.

Kesey, K. (2002). *One Flew Over the Cuckoo's Nest.* Picador: London.

Kirkpatrick, B. (1996). *Clichés.* Bloomsbury: London.

Knight, K. (2002). 'A Precious Medicine: Tradition and Magic in Some Seventeenth-Century Household Remedies'. *Folklore*, vol. 113, no. 2.

Lee, Harper (1966). *To Kill a Mockingbird.* Heinemann: Oxford.

Mann, T. (1924). *The Magic Mountain.* Translated by H.T. Lowe-Porter, Secker & Warburg: London, 3rd ed. (1961).

Montagu, A. (2001). *The Anatomy of Swearing.* University of Pennsylvania Press: Philadelphia.

Moran, C. C. (2002). 'Humor as a Moderator of Compassion Fatigue', in *Treating Compassion Fatigue.* Ed. C. Figley. Routledge: New York, pp. 139–54.

Moran, C.C. (2005). 'Humour and Meaning after Trauma'. *Trauma: Responses Across the Lifespan.* Psychology, Psychiatry, and Mental Health Monographs. NSWIOP: Parramatta, pp. 2, 113–124.

Ostler, R. (2003). *Dewdroppers, Waldos and Slackers: A decade-by-decade guide to the vanishing vocabulary of the twentieth century.* Oxford University Press: New York.

Parkins, W. & Craig, G. (2006). *Slow Living.* UNSW Press: Sydney.

Paxman, J. (1998). *The English: A portrait of a people.* Michael Joseph: London.

Quiller-Couch, A. (Ed.) (1919). *The Oxford Book of English Verse: 1250–1900.* Clarendon: Oxford.

Quinion, M. (2006). *Gallimaufry: A hodgepodge of our vanishing vocabulary.*
Oxford University Press: Oxford.

Quinion, M. (2004). *Port Out, Starboard Home and Other Language Myths.* Penguin: London.

Rees, N. (1996). *The Cassell Dictionary of Catchphrases.* Orion: London.

Richards, K and The Macquarie Dictionary (2005). *Word Map: What words are used where in Australia*. ABC Books: Sydney.

Rocca, J. (2002). T-shirt—Hearts on our chests, in *The Age*, July 31 2002; http://www.theage.com.au/art

Rogers, J. (1985). *Dictionary of Clichés*. Angus & Robertson: Sydney.

Rosenblatt, R. (1985). 'Let me call you Volvo', *Time Magazine*, 18 February 1985; http://www.time.com/time/magazine/article/0,9171,960770-300.html

Sheahan, P. (2005). *Generation Y: Thriving (and surviving) with generation Y at work*. Hardie Grant Books: Melbourne.

Slattery, L. (2002). 'Cultural Binge'. *The Spectator*, 25 May 2002; http://www.looksmartindianapolis.com/p/articles/mi_qa3724/is_200205/ai_n9092744/pg_2?pi=locind

Steinbeck, J. (1936). *In Dubious Battle*. Penguin: New York.

Stevenson, A. (2005). 'The Spin Doctor'. *The Sydney Morning Herald*, 31 December 2005, p. 19.

Tannen, D. (1999). *Talking Voices: Repetition, dialogue, and imagery in conversational discourse*. New York: Cambridge University Press.

Wajnryb, R. (2001). *The Silence: How tragedy shapes talk*. Allen and Unwin: Sydney.

Wajnryb, R. (2004). *Language Most Foul*. Allen and Unwin: Sydney.

Wajnryb, R. (2005). 'Going Going Gone'. *Sunday Life*, 17 July 2005, pp. 22–23.

Ward, P. (1980). *A Dictionary of Common Fallacies*. Oleander Press: New York.

White, J. (1999). *Dupain's Sydney*. Chapter & Verse: Sydney.

Wilkes, G.A. (1980). *A Dictionary of Ausralian Colloquialisms*. Fontana Books: Sydney.

Webography

http://worldwidewords.org

http://www.firstfoot.com/index.htm (gaelic terms)

http://www.homehighlight.org/entertainment-and-recreation/humor/twits-twerps-twizzle-sticks.html

http://www.michaelkelly.fsnet.co.uk

http://www.phrases.org.uk

http://www.urbandictionary.com

ALSO BY RUTH WAJNRYB

....

Language Most Foul

Have we always sworn like troopers? Has creative cursing developed simply because we can't thump someone when they make us mad? And if verbal aggression is universal, why is it that some languages (Japanese for instance) supposedly have no offensive words?

Language once reserved for the footy field—or the labour ward—has broken through the tradesman's entrance, much to the horror of a few refined individuals, but seemingly not anyone much else. Ruth Wajnryb takes an entertaining look at how this came about, and at the origins of some of our more colourful words and phrases. Stepping outside the confines of English, Wajnryb explores whether 'bad' words are mirrored in other languages, and the cultural differences that exist when it comes to giving offence. Why is it that in some countries you can get away with intimating that a person and their camel are more than just good friends, while pouring scorn on their mother's morals guarantees you a seat on the next flight out?

An amusing and idiosyncratic look at the power of words to shock, offend, insult, amuse, exaggerate, let off steam, and communicate deep-felt emotions, *Language Most Foul* is a must-read for anyone who loves language—or has ever stubbed their toe.

'Ruth Wajnryb has gone where almost no linguist before her has dared to go . . . This well-researched study of foul language is simply fascinating. Written with great humour, it is full of interesting history and funny anecdotes. Giving examples here is not possible without using four-letter words, so just buy the f . . . ing book.' *The Age*

ISBN 978 1 74114 776 6 (pb)